STAGING THE WORLD
Theatre In The Space Age

Adventures in Site-Specific Performance

Paul Michael Davies

Some articles in this book were first published in
Australasian Drama Studies and *Popular Entertainment Studies*.
Papers were delivered at conferences held at Ludwig Maximillians Universitat, Munich, The University of Queensland, the University of Melbourne, Queensland University of Technology, and Monash University.

Cover Design by Tabitha Davies

First Edition
Gondwana Press
October 2020
Suffolk Park NSW 2481

Bringing the World
Back Together

Duke Senior: This wide and universal theatre
Presents more woeful pageants than the scene
Wherein we play.

Jacques: All the world's a stage,
And all the men and women merely players;
They have their exits and their entrances;
And one man in his time plays many parts.

(*As You Like It* - Act II Scene VII)

Classic "Proscenium Arch" Theatre – Teatro Colon, Buenos Aires

However, this is not a book about Proscenium Arch Theatre – quite the opposite. It brings together a collection of essays about plays that have been staged anywhere *but* in a dedicated theatre. Inspired by political street performances, independent filmmaking, and a desire to take theatre away from centralized main stages, these were shows on trams and boats, in pubs and cinemas, parks and gardens, tents and houses. They took Shakespeare's idea of "all the world" being "a stage" quite literally and were part of a revolution in theatre practice that occurred in Melbourne during the 1980s. The early success of TheatreWorks' *Storming Mont Albert By Tram* encouraged the production of plays in all kinds of locations. What took place here was a extension of the theatrical experience in which audiences became "fellow travellers" with the actors and complicit with them in the occupation of "created" or "bespoke" performance spaces. This also allowed for an engagement between characters and witnesses that involved not only the senses of sight and hearing (sight-specific theatre) but touch, taste, smell and balance. Here you could literally "feel" the actors. This type of production is now more generally called "site-specific theatre" and is discussed in more detail in *Really Moving Drama – Taking Theatre for a Ride* (Gondwana Press 2016) available at:

https://www.amazon.com.au/Really-Moving-Drama-Taking-Theatre/dp/1534866752

CONTENTS

"A SHORT HISTORY OF THE TRAM SHOW"

Paper for the International Federation of Theatre Research
Ludwig Maximillians Universitat, Munich Germany
June 2010

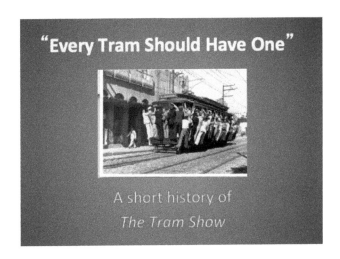

Thanks for the opportunity to talk at the IFTR conference in Munich.

And for chance to articulate out loud some issues I've been trying to wrangle on paper for about a year now, and in my mind for last 28 years:

- What made *The Tram Show* so immediately popular ?
- What was the key to its success? Not just in/of itself but in giving licence to, unleashing a decade long engagement with site-specific performance in Melbourne in 1980s
- And therefore what lessons does *The Tram Show* hold for theatre practice going forward...
-

An original season timed to coincide with the Moomba Festival in 1982 booked out in a couple of days. This first season ran for several months
The play was reproduced five more times s over the next dozen years
(equating to roughly 400 performances),

This made for a total audience of some 20,000 paying customers
(if more than 50 people per trip could have been included in the audience TheatreWorks would have solved most of its funding problems.

So the key to its success (small, immersive audience) is also its financial limitation.

What started as *Storming Mont Albert By Tram* in 1982
Was revised to become *Storming St.Kilda By Tram* in 1988 and 1991,
then *Storming Melbourne By Tram* in 1992
and finally *Storming Glenelg By Tram* in 1992 and 1994 - since Adelaide was the only other Australian city with a functioning tram system

The Idea caught on and Melbourne soon saw plays on boats, in gardens, pubs, grand mansions, private houses, boarding houses, gaols, cinemas etc

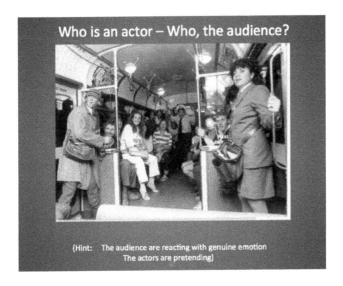

In all these site specific plays there is a simple answer as to why they worked:

The Appeal arises from two deliberate confusions:

i) Normal barriers between, ACTORS /AUDIENCE are blurred

ii) Rigid demarcation of Theatre/Stage space collapses. TRAM = Theatre, Stage, *and* Auditorium

Then there's a third element:

iii) The heterotopia of the street: The intercalation of the play with another layer of spectatorship outside the tram…

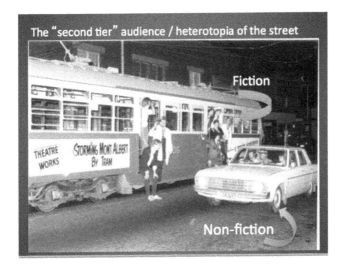

All of which amounts to a new kind of immersive experience in the theatre, in which you, as an audience member, are also part of the show. Which happens in amongst and all around you...

Its all about relationships, the relation of spaces, and people.

I am mindful here of Lefebvre's warning about the "hypercomplexity" of social space and that the *"places* of social space are very different from those of natural space in that they are not simply juxtaposed: they may be intercalated, combined, superimposed – they may even sometimes *collide"* (1991: 88 emphasis added).

One way of understanding this is to look at the collision of spaces that occurred on Tram Show's opening night.

At around 9.20 pm on the 26th of February 1982, in Victoria Parade, Collingwood, two buses heading north towards Fitzroy deliberately blocked the tracks of a tram heading east to Mont Albert.

The buses were part of this production:

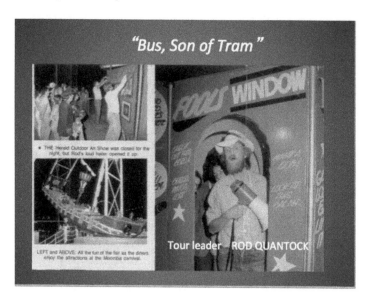

The peripatetic wanderings of Quantock's bus show varied in its itinerary from night to night.

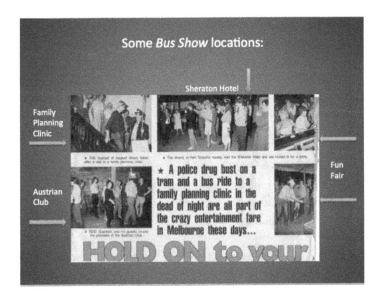

It started with dinner and singing rehearsals at the Comedy Café then he and colleague Geoff Brooks (dressed in Salvation Army uniform and holding the koala) took their accomplices (the audience), appropriately "masked" and thereby sharing a collective identity, to restaurants and family planning clinics, clubs, discos, fun fairs, the College of Surgeons (Rod had a joke about them "but it got cut out"), and once even to Russell Street police headquarters - where the group sang pre-rehearsed songs and caused mutual embarrassment all round (See Figure 1). In the case of the 'raid' on police headquarters the reception was described as "decidedly chilly" (Landray 1982:2).

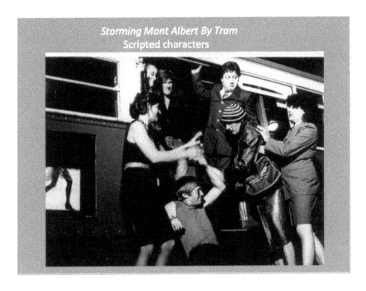

In contrast the narrative events of *The Tram Show* were largely contained within the vehicle itself as it trundled along its predetermined course and involved these characters above. Naturally, the action also flowed with certain characters as they left the tram and headed off into the streets outside. But essentially it was a scripted play, whereas the bus show was improvised. Nevertheless they used the spatial potential of their productions in similar ways.

The collision of these two shows on opening night was recorded by Suzanne Spunner in the *National Times* a week later where she noted that as a result of this near accident "(p)assengers in all vehicles were stunned but sustained no injuries except for a debilitating contortion of the facial muscles." She identified the "ancestry" of what took place in the "happenings and events of the late 1960s", and went on to note that here "the usual division between audience and performance is challenged, which gives rise to ambiguities that are confronting and often hilariously funny" (1982: 24).

So I'm proposing in this paper that much of the appeal of TheatreWorks' site-specific productions lay in disturbing this 'usual division'. By re-negotiating the contract with its audiences the company set in train a new kind of actor/spectator (and a theatre/space) relationship that only becomes fully possible when plays are produced in real locations.

Plot Summary (Narrative/Diegetic Space)

What is the heterotopia - the diegetic space - of the TRAM SHOW

Like *The Bus Show*, and despite the obvious structural difference of improvised vs scripted, the events in *Storming Mont Albert by Tram* largely revolve around one character, the novice conductress Alice Katranski.

Brimming with good will, but anxiously facing her first real night on the job, Alice's desire to see things run smoothly, to be personable and charming to all her customers all the time, is constantly undermined by circumstances beyond her control.

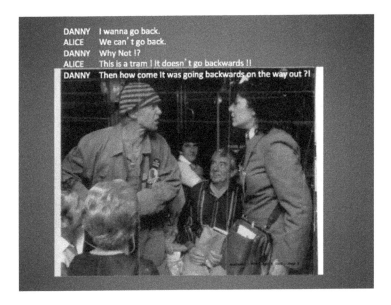

These are largely set in train by Daniel O'Rourke, an inebriated former politics lecturer from Monash University.

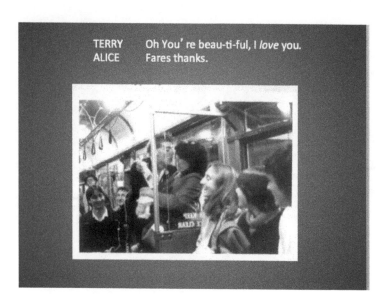

TERRY   Oh You're beau-ti-ful, I *love* you.
ALICE   Fares thanks.

Another problem for her is Terry Meagher, a larrikin punkster who scrambles on board carrying a large plastic dog normally used for collecting money for the Blind Society.

TERRY
Wanna feed
my puppy ?

Fellow Travelers

The images are jumping around a bit this is the St. Kilda Terry, the previous was one was the Mont Albert Terry. – Jeremy Stanford- who you see here also the direct connection between performer /spectator. Not that we picked on people as such. They could react or not. It was entirely up to them.

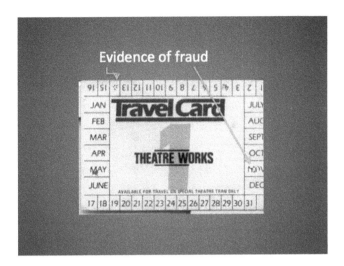

Except that Morris, the ticket inspector, used the theatre/tram ticket to accuse people (random audience members) of tampering with their tickets. Everyone had the same ticket and therefore everyone was guilty. MMTB issued fraud alert when they saw we had copied a real ticket. Until it was pointed out it was obviously four times larger and had the programme on the back.

So that even at level of the props there's a certain collision of fiction and reality going on...

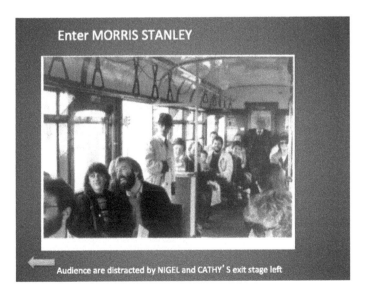

This is Morris entering the tram (in disguise). He's a hybrid of Basil Fawlty and Inspector Clouseau, his chief prop an enormous magnifying glass used to get guilty ticket tamperers. He also gives Alice a hard time, and when he discovers Terry hasn't been sold a ticket he sacks Alice on the spot. Much to the verbal disapproval of the passengers. Devastated Alice stays on for the ride home but Morris gets his come-uppance and Alice gets her job back. (gotta have a happy ending.

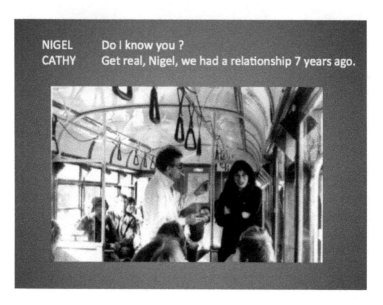

Into this mix are thrown Cathy Waterman, an "escort girl", and Nigel Davidson a pretentious Sydney film maker who, by sheer coincidence, happens to have had a rocky relationship with Cathy some years earlier.

Matters are further complicated by the arrival of a Balwyn housewife, running late for a production at the Melbourne Theatre Company and herself in the throes of a marital breakdown. Samantha Hart-Byrne's nervous apprehensions are exacerbated by the fact that she's never actually had to use public transport before, but having been evicted from the family Mercedes by an irate husband, she arrives on Alice's tram, totally out of her element and looking for the "first class" seats.

We built in a certain clash of social status into the character mix. Theory being that Melbourne trams were melting pots. Menzies used to catch # 42 to Kew from office in town. But also class conflict – all conflict is good for drama. The script workshops were built around the characters through improvisation. We designed the conflict into the character mix.

The stories of these various commuters unfold and coalesce as they arrive, interact and leave the tram, sometimes involuntarily.

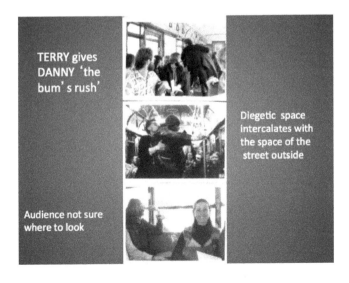

For example, when Danny tries to pay for his fare with an obsolete pound note Terry summarily evicts him- trying to help Alice. Of course she's appalled. Danny gets left behind but comes roaring back for vengeance on return journey- about where he got chucked off. So when that happens there's a resonance for the audience that directly connects the space of the play with the geography its passing through.

Witness the amazed audience reactions here.

Relationships form and fall apart, fares are evaded, confrontations erupt

All part of the commedia del arte style.

Even a threatened hijacking takes place using a retractable plastic knife which is only partly resolved by the arrival of the 'police'. Who soon discover drugs in Nigel's briefcase.

NIGEL   I only said I'd *like* to kill her.

In the confusion that follows the wrong people are arrested, a reconciliation of sorts takes place between Cathy and Nigel (even as he's carted off to gaol facing a potential drug conviction), while Alice and Terry begin what appears to be an unlikely but possibly enduring and mutually beneficial relationship.

Final duet

Or have these two always been an item? And has the whole interaction between them therefore been a playful pretence, a ploy to have some fun with a bunch of strangers on a tram? As Alice and Terry, after a final song together, walk off hand in hand into the night, it all remains somewhat ambiguous…

Site-Specific Theatre (Performance Space)

Michael Shanks and Mike Pearson in *Theatre/Archaeology* in talking about the democracy of the circle that forms when a fight breaks out in public, argue that "events create spaces". This occurs when Danny returns on board during the trip home a fight breaks out:

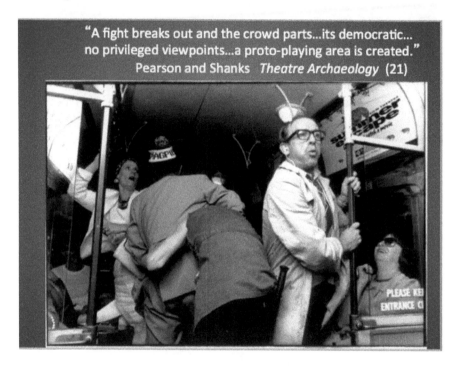

Events create spaces. As a fight breaks out the crowd parts, steps back, withdraws to give the action space. Instantly they take up the best position for watching, a circle. It's democratic, everyone is equidistant from the centre, no privileged viewpoints…A proto-playing area is created, with an inside and an outside, constantly redefined by the activity of the combatants, who remain three dimensional (21).

A circularity of spectatorship was built in to the 'stage space' of the Tram Show by virtue of the layout of the vehicle

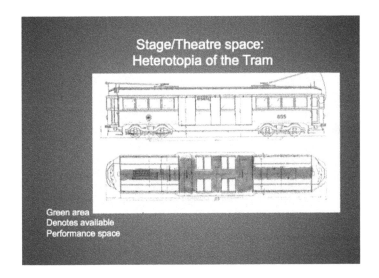

For the Mont Albert and St. Kilda seasons TheatreWorks was able to secure a unique version of the W class model (the No 938, sometimes the 983) where all the seats at both ends of these trams faced the centre. Some were seats recycled from an old bus that had been fitted during the shortages and austerity measures dictated by the Second World War.

Because there's not a lot of space left after the passengers are seated the
Action happened in the aisles and around the doorways

But the space of the narrative related to the space of the street in other more direct ways. Because of its reliance on entrances and exits to further the narrative, *Storming Mont Albert By Tram* was also critically dependent on an itinerary linked to the streetscape through which it moved. Scenes were structured around and determined by the arrival and departure of characters.

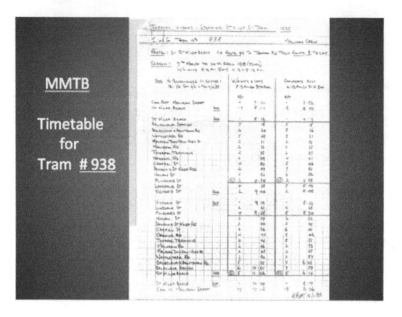

This inter-dependence of space and text also meant that during the opening night encounter described by Spunner, *The Bus Show,* in blocking *The Tram Show's* progress, caused the latter's unfolding narrative to come to a complete halt. In effect, the story of *Storming Mont Albert By Tram* was unable to continue until the vehicle itself did. To this extent the text was totally dependent on the tram's predictable movement through the streets of the city.

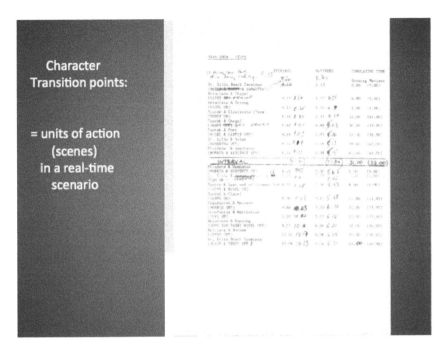

The text intercalated with the streetscape in other, more explicit ways. Towards the end of Act 1 (Outward Journey), Samantha Hart Byrne finally reaches the Melbourne Theatre Company just as some late comers from the audience she's intending to join are finally going in. At which point Morris Stanley reveals he is in fact the author of *Storming Mont Albert By Tram* and becomes quite angry that she is walking out on 'his' show.

Thus the script was located in the "real" space of the tram but inevitably tied to the streetscape through which it moved - not only in the logistical (temporal) sense as indicated, but also in a socio-political one as well.

For example, the socialite character, Samantha Hart-Byrne, gets on in Balwyn (an upper-middle class suburb) whereas Cathy, the escort girl, catches the tram from her commission flat in a more down market part of town. Either way, the random element of the street also came back *into* the tram in the form of confused members of the public or indeed members of the public authorities who felt they had detected some problem on the tram requiring their intervention.

The search for new performance spaces grew initially from the company's stated aim, as defined in its early mission statements, "to dramatise the stories of the suburb" and create "relevant and vital cultural work pertinent to contemporary Australian life", work which "reflects the energies of urban society"

(TheatreWorks Archive, "Artistic Policy" folder Box 16. Fryer Library. Brisbane. TS).

The idea was to take drama out of conventional theatre buildings and mount original plays in innovative ways. TheatreWorks set out to locate its area of operations in the social demographic of Melbourne's Eastern suburbs. The tram, an item of public transport servicing its suburban heartland, seemed a perfect vehicle (literally) with which to meet the company's stated objectives. And although there has been some debate over whether productions like *Storming Mont Albert By Tram* are 'legitimate' examples of the 'Community Theatre' model, certainly what TheatreWorks discovered in the implementation of their site-specific works, was the *community of the audience within the play*.

O'Toole accounts for this synchronicity of text and space as "a further layering of metaxis" which he defines as "a tension caused by the gap between the real and the fiction, *and* a recognition of that gap" (emphasis added):

At this point...the 'tram inspector' revealed that he was a fringe theatre worker (true), and only working on a tram because he was 'resting' (fiction but likely). He then hung out of the tram shouting humorous insults at the Melbourne Theatre Company and its real patrons until the tram had passed the building...This gentle metaxis of real and dramatic contexts was layered further by a Brechtian ambush of the whole convention, bringing the **medium** into the metaxis. Maintaining his 'officious tram inspector' persona, this actor simultaneously overlaid it with the real role of the TheatreWorks stage manager explaining the interval procedure for the audience, including prearranged drinks at a city hotel bar. (1992:181)

The MMTB timetable above shows a working master plan of character entrances and exits adapted for the *Storming St. Kilda* season (1988). Since the normal St. Kilda route was not sufficiently long enough, a hybrid tram route was put together for this second season in order to flesh out the forty minutes of travel time required for each Act (Outward and Return Journeys). As the street map in Figure 2 indicates this itinerary detoured the story into a wide eastern arc through the upmarket suburbs of Toorak and Malvern. In this version of the script, Samantha Hart-Byrne boards the tram in St. Kilda, at the beginning of the play, having been dumped en route to the Melbourne Theatre Company from her residence in equally upper class Brighton. Whereas, Cathy Waterman now gets on at the 'red light' end of Chapel Street, as befitting her 'escort girl' status. Figure 3 offers a wider view of the St. Kilda route used in 1988 and 1991. A note from Ken Kimber (the liaison officer from the Melbourne Metropolitan Tramways Board) indicates that the total distance covered, "depot to depot", was 41 kilometres- a factor in calculating both script length and the tram hire costs.

The character transition points shown above uses the working timetable supplied by the Melbourne Metropolitan Tramways Board on which the script plan (for *Storming St. Kilda*) was based- a time map on which to imbricate the spatial (physical) journey. Units of action in the text between character entrances and exits (effectively 'scenes' in a real time scenario) were calculated to run for as long as it took the tram to reach the relevant stops - given normal traffic flows. In most cases the text came first, in other cases the text was stretched or elided to facilitate major plot points. It was important for example, that Terry throw Danny off well before Morris gets on, so that the ticket inspector remains ignorant of the chaos that has preceded him, and Terry's role in it. (All of which, of course, the audience knew about and was already a party to). This document (Figure 4) was then provided to the various tram drivers employed on the show as an ideal chronology for them to follow. In practice, as traffic congestion in the inner city worsened and other unforeseen events interrupted the tram's progress (such as the opening night encounter with *The Bus Show*, not to mention several interventions by actual police officers), this timetable became increasingly optimistic and was rarely accurate. Figure 5 shows that what began as roughly a two hour production (with interval) soon started much later and grew a lot longer.

The Audience Contract (Spectators and Space)

In an Artistic Policy statement dated December 1983, in which TheatreWorks wrote of its intention to "dramatise the stories of the suburb", to create plays which "reflect the energies of urban life and build a symbolic vocabulary which serves and sustains people in their search for meaning and identity," the document went on to argue for a body of work that is

…both celebratory and disturbing. 'Celebratory', in that a sense of wonder and curiosity about the everyday functioning of the community is embraced and reflected in all aspects of our work. 'Disturbing' in that we do not see our role as passively reflecting the status quo, but as intervening against certain spurious images disseminated in the mass culture, thereby opening up new channels of perception. (And t)o *explore the processes which maximize the possibilities of the audience/participants both identifying* (placing themselves in the work) *and evaluating* (looking at the wider implications or broader issues at stake). (TheatreWorks Archive, box #16 "Company Files" folder. Fryer Library. Brisbane. TS. emphasis added)

In a redraft of this policy a year later the sentence, "We aim to engage the audience in more meaningful ways than is normally possible in the conventional theatre," was added.

In *The Tram Show* the audience were, to all intents and purposes, fellow commuters on a number 42 tram, making its way from Mont Albert to the City and back. They were not pestered by the actors to be part of anything, or more crudely, to get up and perform. Yes, there were "in your face" moments especially as a result of Terry's challenging nature (see Figure 11), but unlike Rod Quantock and Geoff Brooke's audience, *The Tram Show's* commuters didn't need a funny mask to hide behind or to unite them as a group. They could, as fellow passengers, merely sit there and observe the goings on all around them - much like the pigeonholed, numbered and regulated passengers in the grid of de Certeau's railway car, or the more passive audience members of a darkened, 'conventional theatre' - albeit without the directed gaze demanded by dramatic action taking place exclusively behind a proscenium arch.

Moreover, the "audience space" of *The Tram Show*, to borrow from Gay McAuley's taxonomy - the "auditorium" part of this "theatre space" (or *lieu théatral*), (1999 :19) - was not darkened, and the audience view in *The Tram Show* was not directed towards a singular stage; because the action of the play was designed to happen in every available part of the tram - in amongst and all around its spectators. Thus the audience space, the theatre space and the scenic space of *The Tram Show* were, in a further demonstration of Lefebvre's spatial hypercomplexity, essentially the same thing. There was no escape

As Suzanne Spunner went on to point out there is always another layer of spectatorship going on in the street outside: in the space of de Certeau's "ordinary practitioners of the city 'down below,' below the threshold at which visibility begins" (1988: 93).

Both shows (*Bus* and *Tram*) begin with a paying intentional audience and an intentional performance by actors, and acquire a second audience and a second layer of performance which is neither intentional nor paying. The interaction between the performers, the bus and tram passengers, and the natives met along the way constantly raises the question: "Who is the audience and who the show?" (*National Times* 14, April 1982)

I argue that this ambiguity underpins the appeal of much site-specific theatre, especially when it takes place, like *The Tram Show*, in proximity to a 'real world'.

Henri Lefebvre in *The Production of Space,* argues, in concert with Shanks and Pearson, that "human space" (or "social space") like physical space was the product of the "energy deployed within it" (13). This is the energy which might be produced by an improvised fight or the collaboration of performers and audience members around a chook on a pole, or via the authority that an actor playing a tram conductress arrogates to herself simply by virtue of the uniform (her costume) and adherence to an unfolding narrative. De Certeau makes a similar point about the potential for the interplay of spaces where he proposes that "stories carry out a labour that constantly transforms places into spaces or spaces into places" (93). Peter Brook in *The Empty Space* throws the way open for this energy to be deployed in theatre practice with his assertion that: "I can take an empty space and call it a bare stage. A man walks across this empty space whilst someone else is watching him, and this is all that is needed for an act of theatre to be engaged" (1).

Accordingly, the energy generated by the text known as *Storming Mont Albert by Tram* with its prescribed incidents and invented characters, bringing their own fictional back stories to bear on a pre-determined set of circumstances, essentially creates the 'space of the play' within the space of the familiar public transport vehicle. In a similar way the pole impaled chicken and koala of *The Bus Show,* held by its two principal "characters", may be seen as effective nodal points for the energetic production of their fictional space. the representational space, the metaphori of *The Bus Show* event.

Another way of understanding how these productions used space relates to Foucault's notion of the heterotopia as defined in his lecture *Of Other Spaces* (*Diacritics,* Spring 1986) where the concept of the heterotopia is defined as "a kind of effectively enacted utopia" (24). Foucault then outlined a number of principles that applied to heterotopias, the third of which applies here:

The heterotopia is capable of juxtaposing in a single real place several spaces, several sites that are in themselves incompatible. Thus it is that the theatre brings onto the rectangle of the stage, one after the other, a whole series of places that are foreign to one another... (1986 : 25)

There are echoes here of Lefebvre's 'hypercomplexity' of social space when it is 'intercalated, combined or superimposed'. The key is not so much that these collisions happen, but that the *relationship* between spaces that is thereby uncovered. In other words, the ways in which the performance of a site-specific play *engages* with its space is the key to understanding its popularity. Because it is in this dynamic (the constant, often unpredictable oscillation between fiction and reality, and the alternating suspension/application of disbelief that flows therefrom), that the site-specific play finds its fullest expression. Of course

Foucault, in talking about 'theatre' here is referring to the stage of a traditional, purpose built building with its dedicated performance area. But the same principle applies (even more so) to something produced 'on location' where both 'stage' and 'auditorium' are contained by the 'theatre' of the tram or bus itself, the no-longer-pretending site of the narrative with its complement of fictional characters (pretending to be real passengers).

Foucault's train, "an extraordinary bundle of relations", also moves *through* a landscape and therein lies the third heterotopia (in addition to tram space and narrative space): the physical and social space of the street, with its compliment of potential spectators moving randomly past outside, what Spunner calls the "second audience" and the "second layer of performance".

Figure 6 shows an example of this second tier audience in the form of passengers in a car temporarily halted beside the tram. Traffic rules in Melbourne dictate that people exiting trams have right of way over passing cars who must stop to allow them to safely cross to the adjacent footpath. The occupants of this car seem somewhat distracted and perhaps uncertain about the intentions of *The Tram Show* cast in this regard as they pose for a group shot in the tram's doorways after an evening's performance.

There was also, occasionally a 'third tier' audience if one includes the radio audience listening to the broadcast station 3AW made (in real time), or various people at taxi call centres, or police stations along the way, receiving accounts of strange things occurring on a passing tram. And even though police stations were notified in advance of performance times and intended route, real police officers continued to turn up anticipating some sort of trouble. Matters reached a point after one "high speed chase" in which there were calls to close *The Tram Show* down.

Foucault's idea of the train as being something one 'moves through' translates in *The Tram Show* to an interior space measuring approximately 14 metres long to less than 3 metres wide, which, with 50 seated passengers, did not leave a huge amount of free space to move around. Architecturally, the available common performing space reduced down to two narrow aisles at either end of the tram, with slightly wider areas around the four sliding doors (see Figure 7 for side plan of a W class tram showing front and back cabins partitioned by the two sliding doors) (floor plan pending).

Figure 8 shows the scene, late in the Second Act where the police mistakenly suspect Nigel's briefcase may now contain a bomb. It illustrates how the cast maximized the available aisle space to stretch the action. In this case the police are drawing back as far as they can, fearing an imminent explosion. This was one of those 'robust', 'broad brush stroke' moments O'Toole referred to that were dictated by sound constraints and the "distractions of the passing landscape". In this particular instance audience members at the back (the worse seats in the house), have had to stand up to get a better view. Others have taken to literally sitting on top of each other in order to maintain a 360 degree point of view. In either case, one confidant way of separating actors from spectators in this image is to ask the question: who is pretending and who is reacting with genuine emotion?

Figure 9 shows 'the cut', in filmic terms, to the other end of the tram, the opposite, narrow performance area, where Nigel, mistaken for some kind of terrorist, panics and spills the contents of his briefcase, effectively revealing a film can soon found to contain suspicious herbal material- enough to see him removed from the tram in handcuffs.

At points in the narrative conversations would occur simultaneously in these front and back cabin areas. As in any tram journey no one audience member could overhear every conversation. It was important however, in both the design of the script, as well as the direction and performance delivery of the lines, that certain key plot points (such as the bomb scare scene) were clear to as many people on board as possible.

Thus, in spatial terms, the dramatic potential of a play on a moving vehicle arrives as a result of two deliberate confusions: the blurring of the performer/spectator relationship and the melding of scenic and theatrical territories. Lefebvre shows how these 'social spaces' can be produced and Foucault demonstrates that several can be imbricated onto each other and coexist in the one place at the same time. Finally de Certeau links all of this to the business of "ordinary practitioners" experiencing their city by moving through it (as *Wandersmanner*) whose bodies "follow the thicks and thins of an urban 'text'…The networks of these moving intersecting writings compose a manifold story that has neither author nor spectator, shaped out of fragments of trajectories and alterations of spaces…" (1988: 93).

All these performance and staging strategies, arriving as a direct result of the site-specific nature of *The Tram Show*, allows the audience to become, not just passengers, but *accomplices* with the cast in a fictional journey that is largely scripted but partly at the mercy of random events. Following Artaud's prescription, and in a direct application of TheatreWorks community intentions, the barriers were removed, and a direct communication between performance and real world, actors and audience, (who were certainly placed in the middle of the action) was thereby established. What TheatreWorks demonstrated with its *Tram Show* was that in bringing together these various arenas of performance and spectatorship with their divergent expectations, involvements and understandings, a new form of theatre practice opens up and its potential for entertainment amply demonstrated.

Concept and Development (Time and Space)

Theatre practice is no stranger to the idea of a stage on wheels. From the medieval period to early modern times, pious representations of scenes from the bible, 'mysteries' and 'miracle plays', were organised by the civic corporations, funded by local guilds, and recreated by actors on the backs of wagons which travelled through the European countryside and parked for performances in the squares of small towns and villages. In a strange etymological twist, the two shafts on which such carts rode would have been called a "tram" (OED: 1993).

Storming Mont Albert By Tram grew from a short story of the same name which was written in late 1981 and published in the *Springvale Journal* in January 1982 (Vol 121 No 5 28/01/1982) where it won 3rd prize ($150) in the paper's *Age/Journal* Australia Day short story competition. The events of the story were in turn based on an incident witnessed by myself and TheatreWorks founding member Caz Howard on a late night Mont Albert tram in 1980. On that eventful ride home we found a young man having an altercation with an older, clearly inebriated, fellow passenger. Also implicated in their confrontation was a tram conductress and the driver. It was both an amusing and slightly threatening experience, carrying a sense of being trapped aboard a vehicle against our will - with an unexpected and humorous denouement. (see Davies, Paul *Storming Mont Albert By Tram,* a short story. TheatreWorks Archive. Fryer Library. Brisbane. TS.)

The incident reinforced for Caz and myself the idea that trams were places where drama happened all the time. The company had only just positioned itself in Melbourne's eastern region as a professional community theatre company. It seemed a natural step to marry this outreach ethos with the idea of a play on public transport. The tram provided an ideal means of containing an audience (in order to extract money and attention from them) and required merely the design of a narrative that could encompass the two 'acts' of a tram journey (from its suburban terminus to the city and back).

For workshop purposes the text was broken down into units of action, ('Ejection' 'Going Back' 'The Hard Sell' 'Scream Therapy' 'Fatherhood' 'The Bum's Rush'

'Arrest' etc.). In effect these were short, discrete scenes (capsules of action) played sequentially, sometimes simultaneously, within the larger Act structures of the Outward and Return journeys. Script development included the application of certain VCA techniques applied to the 'discovery' of character - principles learnt by TheatreWorks founding members as students there.

Indeed, as the average time span of the journey became longer, certain 'reserve scenes' were written to fill these potential (and recurring) gaps in the action.

Official suspicion was aroused in the MMTB however, when TheatreWorks issued its tickets for the show - just prior to opening night. Several times larger than a normal travel card, this mock ticket was however based (necessarily – in the interest of preserving the reality of a tram journey) on an actual tram ticket (see attached Fig 10). In fact, the template was based on a used card, so that the blocked up punch hole in this master copy (November 14), is repeated on every theatre/tram ticket issued. In Figure 10 this particular ticket has been punched at 'May 4' by Alice as well). However, the evidence of tampering (November 14 covered up) was then used by Morris Stanley to confront some unlucky member of the audience with criminal fraud. The discomfort this spreads through an audience on realising that all their tickets are similarly 'modified', and that they are all potentially guilty, again implicates them in the story. They could all be picked on by Morris ! Nevertheless, despite the unmistakable exaggerated size difference between a real travel card and the TheatreWorks *Tram Show* ticket (not to mention the TheatreWorks logo), the MMTB issued an immediate fraud alert across the entire Melbourne Tramways system. So that even at the level of its props, there is, in any site-specific production such as this, a frisson between the invented and the real. And from this disruption of found realities with constructed ones, comes much of the enjoyment of participation – O'Toole's 'Brechtian ambush'.

A further suite of senses is available to the authors of site-specific plays - beyond those of sight and hearing. When Morris Stanley accidentally stabs Danny (with the retractable plastic knife brought on by Terry), he emerges from the altercation with his hands covered in a red viscous substance, and immediately assumes that this is Danny's blood. Leaping to the (incorrect) conclusion that he has seriously wounded, if not actually killed the man, Morris wallows in a Macbeth-style shock/horror exit, staring incredulously at the 'blood' on his hands, displaying them to startled motorists waiting for him to cross the road in front of them. However, the substance is in fact, merely tomato sauce from Danny's concealed pie, put under his shirt to keep it warm. But the fact that the audience can already *smell* the sauce amplifies their enjoyment of Morris's discomfiture. They know he knows they know he's acting, they know the blood is fake, but they also accept that his character is *not* pretending. It is altogether another order of the notion of suspension of disbelief. And another example of O'Toole's *metaxsis*: the juxtaposing of the real and the fictional, *including* a tacit acknowledgment that such a manipulation is what is going on. In this way the comedic potential of the ticket inspector's delusion is enhanced and extended, and eventually explained by Danny himself, angry that his 'lunch' (the squashed pie) is ruined. But Morris is no longer there to blame ,having sailed off into the night at Kew Junction, startling other members of the public with his incoherent mumbling, feeling guilty of manslaughter, never to be seen again.

There is another moment where smell became a key component, again involving Danny. After Samantha Hart-Byrne loses her balance on the unfamiliar moving platform of the tram, she accidently plants a stiletto into Danny's foot. Naturally, he reels back yelping in pain and immediately pulls his shoe off to reveal a rubber glove for a sock (because there's holes in his shoes and he wants to keep his feet dry). In most cases, in the Melbourne summer, when and the rubber 'sock' gets snapped off, it was invariably glistening with the actor's sweat. Whether it smelt or not was more a matter of a spectator's individual imagination. Certainly Danny's costume indicated a catastrophic failure of personal hygiene. Extending the olfactory dimension, Danny in moments of action where he wasn't directly involved, tended to go to sleep on an adjacent audience member's shoulder. In the confined space of a tram body odour can be also be major signifier of character.

Critical Reception (Newspaper Space)

Also writing in *The Age* a few months later, Jack Hibberd described *The Tram Show* along with Rod Quantok's *Bus, Son of Tram* as "one of the most original and surreal events ever to animate Melbourne theatre"

According to Phillipa Hawker in her review for *The Age* ("Stormtroupers hit Mont Albert Track" 4th March 1982: 9) the off-duty policeman referred to by Leonard Radic, who intervened to arrest Danny, decided to stay on board and watch the rest of the show. Although this is disputed in Simon Kinch's account in the *Nunawading Gazette* (17th March 1982) where he claims the "embarrassed off-duty policeman apologised and got off at the next stop." 'Peg' in the *Progress Press* also claimed the policeman "joined in the laughter on finding he had bumped into a travelling show (3rd March 1982: 17). Clearly this incident of Danny's fare evasion became an iconic part of the mythology surrounding *The Tram Show* and is probably one of the best examples of the intercalation of all the social and physical spaces in the production.

for *Theatre Australia* Spunner found the play had "created a complete event that is more than just being on a tram with a group of actors. The event they have created, like real-life, has a multiplicity of focus and the script is only a part of it: what is really at issue and of interest is *the subversion of the boundaries between theatre and life* (May 1982 emphasis added).

Ed Southern writing for *The Camberwell Free Press* described the show as "the world's first-ever play on a tram" (arguably still). In a subsequent article Southern confidently dubbed it "one of the most popular shows playing anywhere in Australia." He found it to be an "inspired piece of lunacy" and felt it should become a "future must" on the Mont Albert social calendar. "The play
IS the people on the tram…where the funniest things happen…
The Box Hills *Eastern Standard* in an article called "Rolling Theatre" found the production "unique" and "intriguing" (20th April 1982) while the *Nunawading Gazette* headlined its review "Dastardly Doings on the 42 Tram", noting the show's 'riotous debut'

Ken Healey in *The Canberra Times* spoke of the "remarkably different" *Bus* (an extraordinary piece of theatre) and *Tram Shows* as part of a "theatrical upheaval". In particular he found the latter to be "unique and precious and must be preserved." He also recognised the difficult nature of the relationship between text and space and put his finger on the spatial intricacies involved:

Technically, it is fascinating to watch the cast trim its ad libbing to the actual time between stops…(d)ebriefing in a café at the Mont Albert terminus is an enjoyable, almost integral part of the night's experience…There is something very special about this project, which Melbourne must not let slip out of its communal life. Not only are trams virtually unique to Melbourne, but the possibility of stylising some of the events that all tram travellers have seen has been realised triumphantly. Television brings a form of drama to where we live; this play brings live theatre into the public space we share, not like street theatre, at which we are passing spectators, but to a defined space of which we have elected to become part for a specified time…This is not however, risk-taking theatre in the way that Rod Quantok's virtually unscripted invasion of Melbourne street life is risk-taking…Actors from TheatreWorks… are simply revolutionising theatre space by performing a play as though it were life, in the safety of a moving tram." ("Re-enactment of real-life fiascos" 25th April 1982: 8.1982).

Like San Francisco's cable cars, Healey referred to the tourism potential of the piece and went on to imagine four different tram shows running simultaneously, with different stories in different parts of the city- the "flavour" of each show influenced by local character and characteristics. His dream embodies a wonderful vision that so far remains to be fulfilled.

MELBOURNE'S PLAYS ON PUBLIC TRANSPORT
(1982 -1994)
Paper for English, Media Studies, and Art History Conference,
University of Queensland
September 15, 2010

Collisions in Space

At around 9.20 pm on the 26th of February 1982, in Victoria Parade Melbourne, a collision of physical and social spaces occurred which, I would argue, was unique in the world at that time. Physically speaking, two buses heading north towards Fitzroy, deliberately blocked the tracks of a tram heading east to Mont Albert. The event was recorded by Suzanne Spunner in the *National Times* a week later where she noted that as a result of this near accident "(p)assengers in all vehicles were stunned but sustained no injuries except for a debilitating contortion of the facial muscles." She identified the "ancestry" of what took place in the "happenings and events of the late 1960s," and went on to note that here "the usual division between audience and performance is challenged, which gives rise to ambiguities that are confronting and often hilariously funny" (1982: 24).

Much of the appeal of TheatreWorks' site-specific productions lay precisely in disturbing this 'usual division'. By mounting works in found spaces the company set in train a dynamic actor/audience relationship that proved immediately popular. Starting as *Storming Mont Albert By Tram* in 1982 and then moving to the St. Kilda line and later the Glenelg route in Adelaide, what became known generically as *The Tram Show* notched up 300 performances during six seasons spread over a dozen years, travelling a distance equivalent to halfway round the world and attracting roughly 15,000 paying customers. These were less the passive witnesses of a traditional 'proscenium arch' theatre and more *accomplices* with the performers in an act of public misbehaviour.

In its simplest form, *The Tram Show* is an account of an 'ordinary' suburban journey enacted by characters who get on and off a tram as it proceeds along its quotidian route from a suburban terminus to the city and back. In tandem with a certain blurring of the relationship between performer and spectator therefore there was an equivalent collapsing of the normally separate domains of scenic and theatre spaces (as defined by Anne Ubersfeld, and later codified by Gay McAuley in her thesis *Space in Performance*). That is to say, both the 'theatre building' itself (the tram) and the locus of the action – the 'scenic space' – (a tram) were one and the same thing. Out of these performative 'collisions' (actor/audience, theatre/stage, insiders/outsiders) a genuinely three dimensional form of theatre practice opens up as the production itself affects and is effected by the city it takes place in.

Another way of investigating the social forces at play here is to consider the spatial collisions taking place as an intercalation of Foucauldian heterotopia. Something Foucault defines as a real space "a kind of effectively enacted utopia" which can "juxtapose... in a single real place several spaces, several sites that are in themselves incompatible" (24). His idea of the train (23-24) embodies the three main arenas of contention here: 1) **the narrative space** of the play which carries its audience "from one point to another" both figuratively and geographically, 2) the interior **theatrical/stage space** of a tram ("through which one goes") with its familiar public transport rituals and protocols, and 3) the **external streetscape** which "goes by", a random, urban reality in which the fictional events of the play take place. Again I argue that it is in the resonance/confusion/juxtaposition of these separate worlds for audiences, that the pioneering importance of *The Tram Show* lies.

Why a tram ?

The search for new performance spaces grew initially from TheatreWorks' stated aim, as a community theatre company, "to dramatise the stories of the suburb" and create "relevant and vital cultural work pertinent to contemporary Australian life," work which "reflects the energies of urban society" (TheatreWorks Archive. Fryer Library. Brisbane. TS). The company set out to locate its area of operations in the social demographic of Melbourne's Eastern suburbs. Although this shifted to the inner South East with the move to St. Kilda in 1985 (where three decades later the company still operates). Along with other small professional companies active in Melbourne in the 1980s, TheatreWorks was part of what came to be described as the "Next Wave" of Australian Drama (see Milne, Radic)

The tram, an item of public transport servicing its suburban heartland, seemed a perfect vehicle (literally) with which to carry forward the company's objectives. And although there has been some debate over whether plays like *Storming Mont Albert By Tram* are 'legitimate' examples of the 'Community Theatre' model, certainly what TheatreWorks discovered in the implementation of their site-specific works, was the *community of the audience within the play*. Dwight Steward in his study of American street theatre and 'happenings' made a similar point at the beginning of the 1970s:

> Part of theater's [sic] power lies in the sense of participation that it gives. The audience shares in an experience, feels a sense of community that they could never get from a novel, poem, or speech. (*Stage Left*: 57)

To which one might now add: could never get from a film, television programme, digital reproduction, game theory, cos play, or an item of social networking. Yet scholarly discourse, including many published accounts of Australian theatre history, has paid little attention to TheatreWorks' or equivalent companies of the Next Wave, let alone the outbreak of site-specific theatre that flourished in Melbourne throughout the 1980s.

This oversight has allowed certain historical blind spots to emerge, an example of which can be found in Laura Levin's recent description of *Nights In This City* (a bus show by British theatre group Forced Entertainment in 1995) as "the *celebrated prototype* for urban site-specific work" (*Performance And The City*: 241 emphasis added). Yet more than a decade earlier, Melbourne's celebrated *Bus Show* carried passengers wearing Groucho masks, who were being lead to improvised performances at random sites around the city by two 'tour guides', one (Rod Quantock) holding a chicken on a pole as a rallying point for his fellow travellers, the other, a koala. See Figure 1:

Whereas, the tram it "collided" with in February 1982 contained an audience attending the world premiere of *Storming Mont Albert by Tram.* See Figure 2:

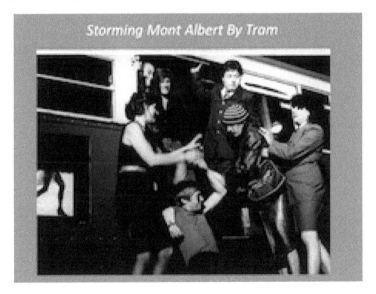

Both *Bus, Son of Tram* and *The Tram Show* were classic but quite different examples of the types of site-specific theatre that became commonplace in Melbourne – well before oddly similar "prototypes" in the northern hemisphere.

Diegetic Space (the heterotopia of the narrative)

Like *The Bus Show*, the events in *Storming Mont Albert by Tram* largely revolve around one character, the novice conductress Alice Katranski. Brimming with good will, but anxiously facing her first real night on the job, Alice's desire to see things run smoothly, to be personable and charming to all her customers all the time, is constantly undermined by circumstances beyond her control. These are largely set in train by Daniel O'Rourke, an obnoxious and difficult drunk. Another problem is Terry Meagher, a larrikin punkster who scrambles on board carrying a large plastic dog normally used for collecting money for the Blind Society. Into this mix are thrown Cathy Waterman, an "escort girl", and Nigel Davidson a pretentious Sydney film maker who, by sheer coincidence, happens to have had a rocky relationship with Cathy some years earlier. Matters are further complicated by the arrival of a Balwyn housewife, running late for a production at the Melbourne Theatre Company and herself in the throes of a marital breakdown. Samantha Hart-Byrne's nervous apprehensions are exacerbated by the fact that she's never actually had to use public transport before, but having been evicted from the family Mercedes by an irate husband, she arrives on Alice's tram, totally out of her element and looking for the "first class" seats. The stories of these various commuters unfold and coalesce as they arrive, interact and leave the tram, sometimes involuntarily. Relationships form and fall apart, fares are evaded, confrontations erupt and a threatened hijacking takes place using a retractable plastic knife which is only partly resolved by the arrival of the 'police'. In the confusion that follows the wrong people are arrested, a reconciliation of sorts takes place between Cathy and Nigel (even as he's carted off to gaol facing a potential drug conviction), while Alice and Terry begin what appears to be an unlikely but possibly enduring and mutually beneficial relationship. Or have these two always been an item? And has the whole interaction between them therefore been a playful pretence, a ploy to have some fun with a bunch of strangers on a tram? As Alice and Terry, after a final song together, walk off hand in hand into the night, it all remains somewhat ambiguous... See Figure 3:

Final duet

Not surprisingly, Geoffrey Milne, in his sweeping survey, *Theatre Australia (Un)limited* found the plot of *The Tram Show* "surprisingly ordinary" (2004: 294). But as John O'Toole recognised, a quality of ordinariness ('painted in broad brush strokes', 'stereotypic characters') was part of the intention (*The Process of Drama, Negotiating Art and Meaning* 1992:178). He refers to the way in which the script developed through improvisational workshops involving writer, director, cast and a lot of tram travelling. O'Toole understood that the connection being aimed for in the text was between recognisable incidents on a tram *and* the need for humour and dramatic tension:

> The team decided that a number of pieces of action should occur among these characters, which should be recognisably within the aegis of a tram journey, *but only just.* In that gap between the expected and the unexpected would lie both the dramatic tension and the humour. All the main connecting incidents of the plot are of this ilk: a coincidental meeting between embittered ex-lovers is both unlikely and believable, until they reveal their true natures, and the audience is immediately in the comic soap opera tension of their bizarre lives and quarrel. A modern audience is familiar with the grandiose concept of a political hijack of a public conveyance, but a tram being hijacked by a derelict with a trick knife deflates it into gentle burlesque. (1992: 179)

Laurie Landray, in his review, also observed that "(n)one of it was real, but all of it was the sort of thing that could happen" ("Hold Onto Your Seat..!" *Australasian Post* April 8, 1982: 4).

It follows that *The Tram Show*, because of the need to embed itself credibly within the 'social space' of its chosen location, required and implemented a certain colloquial inflection both in text and performance.

Text and the City

Because of its reliance on entrances and exits to further the narrative, *Storming Mont Albert By Tram* was also dependent on an itinerary linked to the streetscape through which it moved. Scenes were structured around and determined by the arrival and departure of characters. As O'Toole pointed out these have a "finality about them quite unlike a normal theatre; (the characters) can only re-enter where they exited" (1992: 176).

Figure 4, the working master plan used to 'stage manage' *Storming St. Kilda by Tram* (Davies 1988), shows a direct imbrication of diegetic space onto cartographic space:

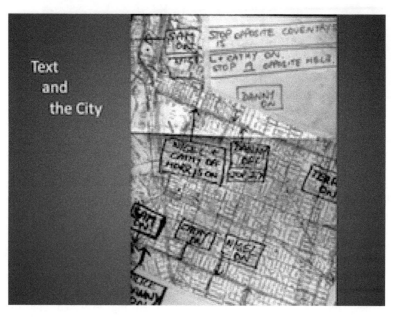

Recognition of the synchronicity of these entry/exit points carried a certain resonance for the audience, given that such transitions had a geographical logic. On a tram, as in the journey of life itself, what goes around comes around. The inflexibility of the track system and the fact that a tram only ever goes either forwards or backwards was the source of much of the humour in *The Tram Show*. Danny comes roaring back on full of high dudgeon at the same stop where Terry had thrown him off on the way in. Similarly, Cathy and Nigel reboard the tram at the point where they originally got off to have a coffee and chew over old times.

This total inter-dependence of space and text also meant that during the opening night encounter described by Spunner, *The Bus Show,* in blocking *The Tram Show's* progress, caused the latter's unfolding narrative to come to a complete halt. In effect, the story of *Storming Mont Albert By Tram* was unable to continue until the vehicle itself did.

The peripatetic wanderings of Quantock's production, on the other hand, varied its itinerary from night to night. He and colleague Geoff Brooks (dressed in Salvation Army uniform and holding the koala) took their accomplices (the audience), appropriately "masked" and thereby sharing a collective identity, to restaurants and family planning clinics, clubs, discos, fun fairs, the College of Surgeons (Rod had a joke about them "but it got cut out"), and once even to Russell Street police headquarters - where the group sang pre-rehearsed songs and caused mutual embarrassment all round. In the case of the 'raid' on police headquarters the reception was described as "decidedly chilly" (Landray 1982:2) See Figure 5:

The narrative events of *The Tram Show* were largely contained within the vehicle itself as it trundled along its predetermined course. Naturally, the action also flowed with certain characters as they left the tram and headed off into the streets outside. Conversations kept going and the reactions of ordinary passers-by were noted as the narrative space of the play intersected with the exterior reality of the street. Thus the script was located in the "real" space of the tram but inevitably tied to the city through which it moved - not only in the logistical (temporal) sense as indicated, but also in a socio-political one as well. For example, the socialite character, Samantha Hart-Byrne, gets on in St. Kilda having been dumped en route to the city from Brighton (an upper-middle class suburb), whereas Cathy, the escort girl, catches the tram from the 'red light' end of Chapel Street. The random element of the street also came back *into* the tram in the form of confused members of the public, or indeed members of the public authorities who felt they had detected some problem on the tram requiring their intervention.

In his summary of Australian Theatre at the end of the 1980s, critic Leonard Radic agreed that part of the "fun" of *Storming Mont Albert By Tram* "lay in working out who were actual passengers and who were the actors in disguise" (1991:176). He refers to one "memorable occasion" in which an off duty policeman forced his way aboard the tram just as Danny is insisting on paying for his fare with an obsolete pound note. The policeman promptly demanded to know how many times Danny had tried to "pull this one on", and deferring to Alice (as the other authority figure present), offered to "take him into custody" for her - an offer immediately declined by the 'conductress', determined as ever to avoid conflict and keep things on her first night running smoothly. Of course Mary Sitarenos, playing the connie, (quite apart from not wanting to see a fellow cast member end up in gaol) knew instinctively that Danny's character was needed on board for most of the Second Act- the 'Return Journey'. Radic mentions that the audience "never did discover whether the off duty policeman was real or not, or simply an inventive addition to an already inventive and lively script" (1991: 176). Thus, although a random element was inherent in the location of *The Tram Show* in its real setting, the performance was largely occupied with predetermined dialogues and interactions, some of which occurred simultaneously in different parts of the tram.

John O'Toole found that this split focus was in part made necessary by the acoustical limitations of the vehicle but was also the outcome of a directorial decision to make the play somewhat "larger than life" in *commedia del arte* fashion (while still maintaining a certain continuity with the mundane, diurnal realities of public transport).

> The action also needed to be robust enough, engaging enough and painted in broad enough brush strokes for the audience to follow in spite of the distractions of the passing landscape and the noise of the moving tram... important plot points and character revelations had to be heard right down the car: this predicted very clear, simple and brief dialogue, with a lot of it spaced out so the characters needed within the dramatic logic, to shout at each other. In movement terms, it necessitated a lot of linear movement, with characters needing motivation to move regularly from one end of the car to the other – walking off in pique, moving over threateningly, etc. (*The Process Of Drama*, 1992: 178, 180)

The text intercalated with the streetscape in other, more explicit ways. Towards the end of Act 1 (Outward Journey), Samantha Hart Byrne finally reaches the Melbourne Theatre Company just as some late comers from the audience she's intending to join are finally going in. At which point Morris Stanley reveals he is in fact the author of *Storming Mont Albert By Tram* and becomes quite angry that she is walking out on 'his' show.

SAM.	Oh- they've all gone in!
MORRIS.	(PERPLEXED) What?
SAM.	Stop! Stop the tram.

(ALICE PULLS THE CORD FOR HER)

MORRIS.	What? (PAINED) Oh- you're *leaving* are you? (THREATENING)
SAM.	This is the most upsetting public journey I've ever been on!
MORRIS.	And where is madam going may I ask?

SAM.	(PROUDLY) To the Melbourne Theatre Company.
MORRIS.	(HORRIFIED, REVOLTED) MELBOURNE THEATRE COMPANY!
SAM.	Yes you pathetic little cockroach, I'm going to see *Cuckold In The Nest* (WHATEVER'S ON)
MORRIS.	"CUCKOLD IN THE NEST"? What's wrong with my little show- Hmmm?

(THE TRAM STOPS AND SHE SWEEPS TRIUMPHANTLY OFF)

SAM.	(CONTEMPTUOUSLY) It speaks for itself.

MORRIS MOVES OVER TO THE DOOR, YELLING BACK AT HER OUT ON THE STREET.

MORRIS.	Not good enough for you eh? Oh yes (AS SHE CROSSES TO THE ATHENAEUM). Oh yes, go on, go off to your boring proscenium arch melodrama. See if I care (ALMOST CHOKES ON IT) Don't you realise what an adventure in realism this is? (TURNS TO THE PASSENGERS) What's wrong with exciting, innovative, documentary theatre, huh? (BACK AT SAM, YELLING OUT INTO THE STREET) You're bypassed lady! Bypassed! I hope you drop your jaffas! If you'd brought a broom you could've flown there! ...(TURNS BACK TO THE PASSENGERS INSIDE THE TRAM, EXHAUSTED, CLUTCHING HIS CHEST, MOPPING HIS BROW) Excuse me if I seem a little distant from time to time ladies and gentlemen. (WEEPS IT) *Cuckold In The Nest* !

(From *Storming Mont Albert By Tram* 1982 at:
https://www.amazon.com.au/Storming-Mont-Albert-Tram-Attempt/dp/0648599868
)

Cuckold In The Nest was, of course, the title of the play on at the Athenaeum Theatre at that time (February 1982), its posters visible to *The Tram Show* audience across the street. If the tram was stuck at the lights long enough they could watch SAM join the latecomers and move into the theatre, in effect, projecting the diegetic space of *The Tram Show* into the theatre space (foyer) of the Athenaeum. Such transitional elements could be adapted into the script and adjusted from season to season or route to route. For example, the production of *Storming Glenelg By Tram* in Adelaide required adjusting a whole suite of local and geographic references, although of course, the same basic template of a trip from the suburban outlands into the city and back remained paramount.

O'Toole accounts for this synchronicity of text and space as "a further layering of metaxis" which he defines as "a tension caused by the gap between the real and the fiction, *and* a recognition of that gap" (1992: 166 emphasis added):

At this point...the 'tram inspector' revealed that he was a fringe theatre worker (true), and only working on a tram because he was 'resting' (fiction but likely). He then hung out of the tram shouting humorous insults at the Melbourne Theatre Company and its real patrons until the tram had passed the building...This gentle metaxis of real and dramatic contexts was layered further by a Brechtian ambush of the whole convention, bringing the **medium** into the metaxis. Maintaining his 'officious tram inspector' persona, this actor simultaneously overlaid it with the real role of the TheatreWorks stage manager explaining the interval procedure for the audience, including prearranged drinks at a city hotel bar. (1992:181)

With the story so directly linked to its route, worsening traffic flows caused a certain
inconsistency of scenic duration. This necessitated the casting of actors who were able to improvise *within character* in order to fill in the time (and space) needed to reach the next transition point (exit or entrance). Fortunately, improvisation as a technique was much in vogue within the Drama School of the Victorian College of the Arts, from whose alumni many of *The Tram Show* cast were drawn as the director, Mark Shirrefs explains:

There were a couple of instances where the tram did stop for various reasons but the play didn't stop ...that's why we did so much improvisation... the actors really developed the characters themselves rather than being given them, and my feeling is that worked really well. They were good enough improvisers to carry the thing off when the tram stopped for some reason... The *Tram* and the *Boat Shows* (*Breaking Up in Balwyn* Davies, 1983) were quite unique I think in the sense that you were throwing yourself upon the vagaries of whatever was happening on that particular night. And no night was ever really the same. (Shirrefs, Mark. Personal Interview. St. Kilda. 26 February 2010)

The Audience Contract (Spectators and Space)

In *The Tram Show* the audience were, to all intents and purposes, fellow commuters on a number 42 tram, making its way from Mont Albert to the City and back. They were not pestered by the actors to be part of anything, or more crudely, to get up and perform. Although there were some "in your face" moments - especially as a result of Terry's challenging nature.

"Wanna pat my doggie?"

Unlike Rod Quantock and Geoff Brooke's audience, *The Tram Show's* commuters didn't need a funny mask to hide behind or to unite them as a group. They could, as fellow passengers, merely sit there and observe the goings on all around them - much like the pigeonholed, numbered and regulated passengers in the grid of de Certeau's railway car (111), or the more passive audience members of a darkened, 'conventional theatre' - albeit without the unidirectional gaze demanded by the dramatic action taking place exclusively behind a proscenium arch.

Moreover, the "audience space" of *The Tram Show*, to borrow again from Gay McAuley's taxonomy - the "auditorium" part of this "theatre space" (or *lieu théatral*), (1999 :19) - was not darkened, and the audience view in *The Tram Show* was not directed towards a singular stage; because the action of the play was designed to happen in every available part of the tram - in amongst and all around its spectators. Thus the audience space, the theatre space and the scenic space of *The Tram Show* shared essentially the same architecture.

But as Suzanne Spunner went on to point out there is another layer of spectatorship going on in the street outside:

> Both shows (*Bus* and *Tram*) begin with a paying intentional audience and an intentional performance by actors, and acquire a second audience and a second layer of performance which is neither intentional nor paying. The interaction between the performers, the bus and tram passengers, and the natives met along the way constantly raises the question: "Who is the audience and who the show?" (*National Times* 14, April 1982)

Who is an actor – Who, the audience?

Hint: The audience are reacting with genuine emotion
The actors are pretending

I argue that this ambiguity/confusion underpins the appeal of much site-specific theatre, especially when it takes place, like *The Tram Show*, in proximity to a 'real world'. In TheatreWorks' other plays in found locations such as *Living Rooms* and *The Pub Show,* and to a lesser extent, *Breaking Up In Balwyn* (*The Boat Show*) this outside reality, the real world of the street going past, is held at bay (or indeed invisible to an interior audience in a house or hotel).

Performance Space (the heterotopia of the tram)

Michael Shanks and Mike Pearson in *Theatre/Archaeology* in talking about the democracy of the circle that forms when a fight breaks out in public, argue that "events create spaces" :

> As a fight breaks out the crowd parts, steps back, withdraws to give the action space. Instantly they take up the best position for watching, a circle. It's democratic, everyone is equidistant from the centre, no privileged viewpoints…A proto-playing area is created, with an inside and an outside, constantly redefined by the activity of the combatants, who remain three dimensional (21).

Certainly there were a number of fights, both physical and verbal in the play. Conflict was inherent in the way the narrative grew from the divergent types of characters chosen, and further enhanced by the larger than life *commedia del arte* style. Figure 7 also shows how a circularity of spectatorship was built in to the 'stage space' of the Tram Show by virtue of the layout of the vehicle as the cast draw back during the bomb scare scene to maximise the available aisle space.

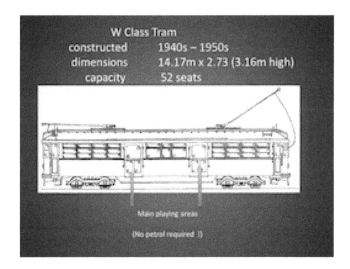

Figure 8 above shows how the open space of the four sliding doorways also offered free space to perform in. Seats in the 'cabins' at either end of the vehicle faced towards these central doorways, only the block of sixteen seats situated in the centre of the tram (between the doors) looked both ways (floor plan pending). In either case, no matter where one sat, the audience view was inherently multi-focal.

Henri Lefebvre in *The Production of Space,* argues, in concert with Shanks and Pearson, that "human space" (or "social space") like physical space, was the product of the "energy deployed within it" (13). This is the energy which might be produced by an improvised fight or the collaboration of performers and audience members around a chook on a pole, say, or via the authority that an actor impersonating a tram conductress arrogates to herself simply by virtue of the uniform (her costume) and her adherence to an unfolding story arc. De Certeau makes a similar point about the potential for the interplay of spaces where he proposes that "stories carry out a labour that constantly transforms places into spaces or spaces into places" (93). Peter Brook in *The Empty Space* throws the way open for this energy to be deployed in theatre practice with his assertion that: "I can take an empty space and call it a bare stage. A man walks across this empty space whilst someone else is watching him, and this is all that is needed for an act of theatre to be engaged" (1).

As I've tried to demonstrate, the energy generated by the text known as *Storming Mont Albert by Tram* with its prescribed incidents and invented characters, bringing their own fictional back stories to bear on a pre-determined set of actions and circumstances, essentially creates the 'space of the play' (the diegetic heterotopia) within the space of the familiar public transport vehicle (the heterotopia of the tram) with its own set of behavioural codes and odd traditions and rituals. In a similar way the pole impaled chicken and koala of *The Bus Show,* held by its two principal "characters", may be seen as effective nodal points for the energetic production of *The Bus Show's* fictional/play space.

The point is not so much that these spatial collisions happen, but that a *relationship* between social spaces is thereby unmasked. In other words, the manner in which a site-specific play *engages* with its location holds the key to its effectiveness as a dramatic artefact. Because it is in this performative dynamic (the constant, often unpredictable oscillation between fiction and reality, and the alternating suspension/application of disbelief that flows there from), that the site-specific play finds its full expression. Of course Foucault, in talking about heterotopically dense stage space of the 'theatre' (25) is referring to the stage of a traditional, purpose built building with its dedicated often rectangular performance area. But the same principle applies (even more so) to something produced 'on location' where both 'stage' and 'auditorium' are contained by the 'theatre' of the vehicle itself.

Urban Space (heterotopia of the street)

Foucault's train, "an extraordinary bundle of relations" (22), as well as being something one can move through and something that takes one from point A to B (physically as well as metaphorically) also moves *through* a landscape and therein lies a third heterotopia with its own compliment of potential spectators, what Spunner calls the "second audience" and the "second layer of performance".

Figure 9 shows an example of this second tier audience in the form of passengers in a car temporarily halted beside the tram.

Traffic rules in Melbourne dictate that people exiting trams have right of way over passing cars who must stop to allow them to safely cross to the adjacent footpath. The occupants of this car seem somewhat distracted and perhaps uncertain about the intentions of *The Tram Show* cast in this regard as they pose for a group shot after one performance.

There was also occasionally a 'third tier' audience, if one includes the radio listeners to the broadcast from station 3AW made in real time by an on board reporter, or various people at taxi call centres, or police stations along the way, receiving accounts of strange things occurring on a passing tram. And even though police stations were notified in advance of performance times and intended route, real police officers continued to turn up on *The Tram Show* anticipating some sort of trouble. Matters reached a crisis point after one "high speed chase" when there were calls from the police to close the whole thing down.

Some of the chaotic nature of the play is recalled by Mary Sitarenos (Alice Katranski in the original production):

> "There was an hysteria...I remember the tram driver going fast. Really fast. And I remember bashing on his door ...tap tap tap three times meant 'slow down'. So I'm bashing his door down. His English was very limited...I'm saying 'slow down'. I remember faces, faces up close, and faces outside. It was like you were in some kind of tardus. We were just going through time and space, at such a dynamic pace. And it was a very suburban audience. People who had never been to theatre before...whole families hysterically laughing. People with tears streaming down their faces. It was hilarious.
>
> (Mary Sitarenos. Personal Interview)

Her recollection echoes Antonin Artaud's earlier call for a more immediate relationship between performer and spectator:

> We abolish the stage and the auditorium and replace them by a single site, without partition or barrier of any kind, which will become the theatre of the action. A direct communication will be re-established between the spectator and the spectacle, between the actor and the spectator, from the fact that the spectator, placed in the middle of the action, is engulfed and physically affected by it. (1958: 96)

Thus, in spatial terms, the dramatic potential of plays on a moving vehicles arrives as a result of two deliberate confusions: the blurring of the performer/spectator relationship and the melding of scenic and theatrical territories. Lefebvre shows how these 'social spaces' can be produced and Foucault demonstrates that several can be imbricated onto one another and coexist in the same place at the same time. Finally de Certeau links all of this to the business of "ordinary practitioners" experiencing their city by moving through it (as *Wandersmanner*) whose bodies "follow the thicks and thins of an urban 'text'...The networks of these moving intersecting writings compose a manifold story that has neither author nor spectator, shaped out of fragments of trajectories and alterations of spaces..." (1988: 93).

In addition to this "urban text" a play produced on location, in and around its audience, offers playwrights a spectrum of sensual expression beyond the usual ones of sight and hearing. When Morris Stanley accidentally stabs Danny (with a retractable plastic knife brought on by Terry), he emerges from the altercation with his hands covered in a red viscous substance, and immediately assumes that this is Danny's blood. Leaping to the (incorrect) conclusion that he has seriously wounded, if not actually killed the man, Morris wallows in a Macbeth-style shock/horror exit, staring incredulously at the 'blood' on his hands, displaying them to the audience and to startled motorists as he crosses the road. See figure 10:

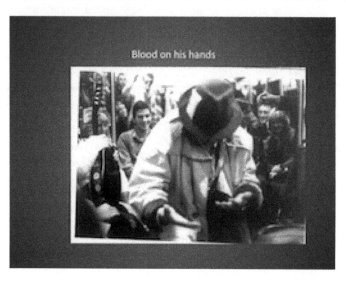

However, the red substance is in fact, merely tomato sauce (ketchup) from Danny's concealed pie, tucked under his shirt to keep it warm. The fact that the audience can already *smell* the sauce amplifies their enjoyment of Morris's discomfiture. They know he knows they know he's acting, they know the blood is fake, but they accept that his character is *not* pretending. It is altogether another order of suspended disbelief. And another example of O'Toole's Brechtian ambush- the *metaxsis* of the real and the fictional, *including* a tacit acknowledgment that such a manipulation is what is going on. In manipulating the olfactory senses, the comedic potential of Morris's delusion is enhanced and extended.

There is another moment where smell became a key component, again involving Danny. After Samantha Hart-Byrne loses her balance on the unfamiliar moving platform of the tram, she accidently plants a stiletto hard into Danny's foot. Naturally, he reels back yelping in pain and immediately pulls his shoe off to reveal a rubber glove for a sock (because there's holes in his shoes and he wants to keep his feet dry). In most cases, in the Melbourne summer, when and the rubber 'sock' gets snapped off, it was invariably glistening with the actor's sweat. See Figure 11:

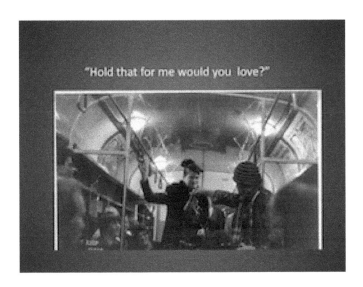

"Hold that for me would you love?"

Whether it 'reeked' or not was perhaps a matter of each spectator's individual perception. Certainly Danny's costume indicated a catastrophic failure of personal hygiene. Extending the olfactory dimension, Danny, in moments of action where he wasn't directly involved, tended to go to sleep on an adjacent audience member's shoulder. In the confined space of a tram body odour can be also be great signifier of character.

All of these performance and staging strategies arrived as a direct result of the site-specific nature of *The Tram* and *Bus Shows*. In these plays the barriers were removed and a direct communication between actor and audience, fiction and reality, performance and candid behaviour established and explored. As a result, a new form of theatre practice opens up and its potential for popular entertainment demonstrated.

As playwright Jack Hibberd noted in his review, *Storming Mont Albert* and *Bus, Son of Tram* were two of "the most original and surreal events ever to animate Melbourne theatre" (*The Age* 18th June 1982, Weekender Magazine). Ken Healey in *The Canberra Times* also spoke of the "remarkably different" *Bus* and *Tram Shows* as part of a "theatrical upheaval". He recognised the difficulty of the relationship between text and space:

> Technically, it is fascinating to watch the cast trim its ad-libbing to the actual time between stops…but the possibility of stylising some of the events that all tram travellers have seen has been realised triumphantly. Television brings a form of drama to where we live; this play brings live theatre into the public space we share, not like street theatre, at which we are passing spectators, but to a defined space of which we have elected to become part for a specified time…This is not however, risk-taking theatre in the way that Rod Quantock's virtually unscripted invasion of Melbourne street life is risk-taking…Actors from TheatreWorks… are

simply revolutionising theatre space by performing a play as though it were real life, in the safety of a moving tram." ("Re-enactment of real-life fiascos" 25th April 1982: 8.1982).

Quoting San Francisco's cable cars, Healey referred to the tourism potential of *The Tram Show* and went on to imagine four different versions running simultaneously with different stories in different parts of the city- the "flavour" of each show influenced by local character and characteristics. Although the success of *The Tram* and *Bus Shows* spawned a decade long engagement with site-specific performance in Melbourne theatre practice generally (a movement that has so far been largely overlooked), the ambitious dream of having four different *Tram Shows* running simultaneously remains to be realised.

FULL HOUSES
Staging Drama in an Historic Mansion

Popular Entertainment Studies Vol 2 No 1 (2011)
School of Drama Fine Art and Music University of Newcastle. Pp 79-95.
Web. 14 Aug. 2012

Keywords: Site-specific Performance, Community Theatre, Australian Next Wave, TheatreWorks, House Plays.

Abstract

One popular form of site-specific theatre as it developed through the 1980s involved the production of plays inside existing houses. This article examines *Living Rooms* which was first produced in 1986 by TheatreWorks – one of a number of small, alternative companies described as Australia's Next Wave movement. The play divided its audiences into three groups and rotated them through several rooms in a 'fictional' colonial mansion where discrete scenes, each depicting an episode in the building's history, were enacted simultaneously. Like many of Theatreworks' 'location plays', *Living Rooms* enjoyed full houses through a number of extended seasons and this success derives largely, I would argue, from the interplay of diegetic and real spaces inherent in
the production design.

Background

TheatreWorks was formed in 1980 by a group of students graduating from the Victorian College of the Arts' Drama School and in its first iteration as a 'Next Wave' company (1980-1990),[1] operated as a ensemble of actors, writers and directors concerned with producing work that both 'celebrated and disturbed' their suburban audiences.[2] The idea was to take live performance out of dedicated theatre buildings and produce it closer to the places where people lived and worked. Like its contemporaries (West, Murray River Performing Group, The Mill, Crosswinds) TheatreWorks was one of a number of small, professional theatre

---

[1] For a definition of the various 'waves' of Australian theatre practice I refer to GeoffreyMilne's *Theatre Australia (Un)limited: Australian theatre since the 1950s*. Edited by Veronica Kelly. (New York: Rodopi B.V., 2004), see especially pages 5-6 "Australian Theatre Chronology".

[2] TheatreWorks Archive (Fryer Library, University of Queensland, Brisbane: Company Papers Box, Artistic Policy Folder)

companies active in Australia in the wake of the 'New Wave': an earlier movement generally associated with the Pram Factory (in Melbourne) and the Nimrod (in Sydney). Throughout the 1970s these two ground breaking companies had provided a platform for the plays of David Williamson, Jack Hibberd, John Romeril, Alex Buzo and Stephen Sewell. Lacking a theatre of its own, TheatreWorks sought to continue this tradition of new Australian work by staging plays 'on location' as early as 1981,[3] and despite their experimental nature, these site-specific works soon found an immediate and popular response among the target audience.

Prior to *Living Rooms* (which I authored), [4] TheatreWorks had successfully produced plays on trams and riverboats. *Storming Mont Albert By Tram* for example, was staged on a Melbourne tram where the narrative unfolded as characters arrived, interacted, and exited the vehicle at various stops.[5] Posing as an ordinary public transport journey, the scripted events on board the tram soon became bound up with the random reality of the streetscape going past (including ordinary commuters who would attempt to board the tram not realizing a play was taking place). This synergy between the spaces of the story, the tram, and its location in the real world, resulted in a collision of real and fictional elements, constructed and unconstructed moments, that took theatre practice into literally new 'territory'. The *'Tram Show'* as it became known, was reproduced half a dozen times on a number of routes in both Melbourne and Adelaide, extending to around 300 performances, carrying approximately 15,000 passengers, and travelling a cumulative distance that would have taken the show almost half way round the world.

---

[3] The term 'location theatre' derives from TheatreWorks' members experience in low budget film production - a practice where screen actors frequently performed both exterior and interior scenes 'on location'. The term 'site-specific' is now more commonly used in scholarly discourse to describe such plays. See Fiona Wilkie's *Out of Place. The Negotiation of Space In Site-specific Performance.* (Ph.D. Thesis, University of Surrey, School of Arts, 2004) and Gay McAuley, *Space in Performance* (Michigan: University of Michigan, 1999).

[4] Paul Davies, *Living Rooms* (TS. TheatreWorks Archive. Brisbane: Fryer Library, 1986) was produced by TheatreWorks in 'Linden' at 26 Acland Street St. Kilda. It was directed by Andrea Lemon, Caz Howard, Peter Sommerfeld and Paul Davies and developed with the original cast of Cliff Ellen, Rosie Tonkin, Kevin Cotter, Leonie Hurry, Caz Howard, Peter Sommerfeld and Paul Davies.

[5] The play was published on its second outing six years later. Paul Davies, *Storming St. Kilda by Tram.* (Paddington, NSW: Currency Press, 1988).

On the back of this success, *Breaking Up In Balwyn* was staged the following year (1983) as a 'divorce celebration' (a kind of inverted wedding ceremony) on board a Melbourne riverboat, using the same strategy of a play set and performed on a moving vehicle whose characters interacted with an outside reality as it goes past.[6] This imbrication of the diegetic space of a play with the real place in which it was staged, became the trademark style of TheatreWorks and helped spark a wave of site-specific theatre in Melbourne that flourished throughout the 1980s. The result was a series plays and entertainments produced on buses (Rod Quantok's *Bus, Son of Tram*, 1982), in jails (West's *Hard Labour, Mate*, 1983), private homes (Home Cooking Company's *Looking In/Looking Out*, 1987), pubs (TheatreWorks' *Pub Show*, 1985), courthouses (Melbourne Comedy Festival's *A Royal Commission...*, 1986), and botanical gardens (Glen Elston's, *Wind In The Willows, A Midsummer Night's Dream*, 1984-2011).

Real Space: The world of 'Linden', 1900 – 1988.

In 1985 TheatreWorks shifted its base of operations from Melbourne's eastern suburbs to the bayside precinct of St. Kilda, a far less genteel part of the city. However, St. Kilda had a fascinating past and like the suburb itself, 'Linden' at 26 Acland Street, had gone through a number of dramatic changes. What had started 'life' as a family mansion, became a down-market boarding house in the 1960s, and at the time of making *Living Rooms* was being extensively renovated and restored to its former glory in the form of a stylish art gallery.

Moritz Michaelis, who built Linden in the 1880s was a prosperous German/Jewish leather goods merchant who had made his fortune in the wake of the great Victorian gold rush. Because of an upper class British faith in the efficaciousness of sea air, St. Kilda in the late Nineteenth Century had become the wealthiest suburb in Melbourne and home to a burgeoning 'squattocracy' – a colonial elite whose wealth derived principally from the occupation of prime agricultural land, often with questionable legitimacy.

---

[6] Paul Davies, *Breaking Up In Balwyn* (TS. TheatreWorks Archive. Brisbane: Fryer Library, 1983). Also available at: https://www.booktopia.com.au/breaking-up-in-balwyn-paul-michael-davies/book/9780648599807.html

Figure 1. Members of the Michaelis family, pose for a photograph
outside the building circa 1900. (Photographer unknown.)

This emerging upper class built the splendid hotels, coffee palaces, and grand
mansions (like 'Linden') that came to line the wide boulevards of St. Kilda – streets
that were themselves designed by the Italian architect Carlo Catani in imitation of
the grand public thoroughfares of Paris and Nice. The impression sought was of
elegance and spaciousness. However, with the coming of the Melbourne-St Kilda
railway line, Australia's first passenger train, people from the working class suburbs
of Fitzroy, Collingwood and Richmond suddenly had easy access to St. Kilda's
seaside distractions including its pubs, visiting circuses and foreshore
entertainments such as the iconic Luna Park. Eventually, the gentry abandoned St.
Kilda and escaped east to Toorak hill and the exclusive suburbs of South Yarra,
Hawthorn and Kew, leaving behind a seedy, red-light district that became home to a
criminal under class sustained by a world of prostitution, illegal gambling and drug
dealing. This new, increasingly itinerant and downwardly mobile population, now
usurped the once grand mansions and saw them turned into cheap, multi-room
boarding houses.

In 1985 'Linden', by then a dilapidated boarding house, was purchased by St. Kilda
Council with the intention of restoring it to its former architectural glory as a gallery
and arts centre. Having just arrived in the area, TheatreWorks saw an opportunity to
extend their 'location' theatre project from items of public transport to an actual
building. The 'community theatre' agenda of *Living Rooms* therefore, was to
portray a sense of the building's demographic roller coaster ride by situating the
three major acts of a drama at these key moments of change: aristocratic seaside
suburb, red light district, and up-market gallery. In contrast to the plays on public

transport, the *Living Rooms'* 'stage' remained static while here it was the spectators that moved.

Entering the world of the play.

As audience members came through the front door into Linden's wide central hallway, they were handed a coloured floor plan of the building (one of three) which indicated the rooms where each scene would take place. These different coloured plans effectively divided them into three separate groups.

Figure 2. *Living Rooms.*
Viewing orders for the three audience groups.

This division enabled each thirty minute scene to be staged simultaneously (and repeated three times) until everyone had witnessed the complete story, albeit in different running orders. If only by virtue of remaining silent witnesses, the audience thus became essentially voyeurs listening in on otherwise private conversations from a position of some intimacy.[7] Finally, a short, concluding scene

---

[7] *Living Rooms*, however, was not the first example of this tactic. The Women's Theatre Group at the Victorian College of the Arts, which included two founding members of TheatreWorks, Caz Howard and Hannie Rayson, staged *Fefu and Her Friends* (Marie Irene Fornés, 1977) in a two-storey art deco mansion in Elwood, Melbourne. Directed by Ros Horin, the audience met the cast in an initial, combined scene where they shared drinks and were then divided into four sub-groups to witness scenes produced simultaneously in four different rooms; so that again the story was accessed by each group in a unique order. Other plays have used a similar formula. John Krizanc's *Tamara* (1981) premiered in Toronto and subsequently ran for nine years in a Hollywood mansion. The play is the story of a

was staged in the Hallway which drew together all characters from the different time periods and all audience groups in a chronologically neutral space.

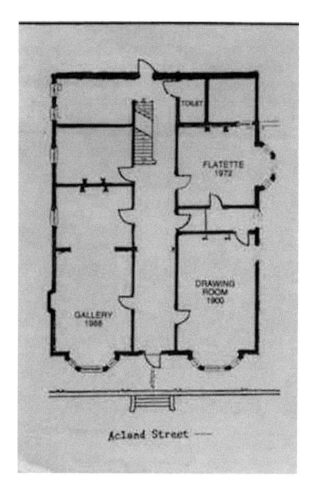

Figure 3. Linden floor plan showing the three main sites of performance.

visit by the artist Tamara de Lempicka to the country home of the Italian poet d'Annunzio in order to paint his portrait. It was staged in a large mansion (allegedly d'Annunzio's) and members of the audience were invited to either follow the progress of a favorite character from room to room or alternatively, stay in the one room and witness the scenes of the play that occur there as those fragments of the narrative flow through it. Later, the Welsh group Brith Gof, applying a different formula, staged *Tri Bywyd* (*Three Lives*, 1995) in a purpose-built, scaffolding structure inspired by the designs of Bernard Tschumi – essentially a 'house' where the walls and furniture were transparent.

Meeting the characters

Figure 4. TheatreWorks actors prepare for a cultural
re-occupation of the building in 1986.

In the Drawing Room scene set in 1900, a large seascape by the salon painter
Rupert Bunny (naked bacchanalian figures riding streaming white horses)
dominates the room and signifies considerable personal wealth.[8] As this room
'comes to life' the story unfolds of a triangular relationship between the building's
owner, Cuthbert Beaumgardiner, his mistress Estelle Lawson and Lt. Michael
Deegan, a young artillery officer about to depart for the Boer War with the
Victorian contingent.[9] Initially Deegan regards the war as a morally necessary
project in order to liberate the native South Africans from virtual serfdom to their

---

[8] Rupert Bunny was a Melbourne artist, born in St. Kilda in 1864 who became
famous for his 'salon paintings' especially among the belle époque elite of Paris at
the end of the Nineteenth century . The painting used in *Living Rooms* was owned
by St. Kilda Council and showed a mythologized beach scene.

[9] Prior to federation, the Australian colonies all had their separate armies and
navies. Deegan is a shearer whose ideals of mateship and social equality were
forged in the great strikes of the 1890s in Queensland, and he obviously migrated
to Victoria after that. These strikes in turn gave birth to the Australian Labour
Party which eventually saw the first socialist government in the world come to
power in Queensland in 1899 (albeit only for a week).

Boer masters. Only later, through the discovery of a letter from the battlefield in another room and another time (by Paul Bugden in the Flatette scene), do we discover the full extent of Deegan's eventual disillusionment with the war. Through this letter he reminds us that just as Boer tactics led to the creation of asymmetric 'guerilla warfare', so too did British counter measures lead to the creation of 'concentration camps' – both terms carrying a heightened sense of anxiety as the new century progressed.

Figure 5. *Living Rooms* – The Drawing Room, 1900.
Cuthbert toasts Michael's embarkation for the Boer War.
Photo © Ruth Maddison

Figure 4 shows the spatial arrangement of the audience in the Drawing Room scene where the spectators are silent, but 'semi-present' witnesses seated around the walls. They could be guests at Lt. Michael Deegan's farewell party, or they might be intruders from another century – present, but curiously 'absent' at the same time, pretending to be not there. The characters in this scene acknowledge that a party is going on throughout the house, but do not refer to the audience directly, whose 'role' thus remains uncertain, ambiguous. Nevertheless, the proximity of performers and spectators is so intimate that other senses beyond those of sight and hearing can now be engaged. A form of olfactory space arrives with the smell of Estelle's or Monika's perfumes (old and modern) as they enter or exit their respective rooms and time zones. Similarly, there is the stench of the dog food ("wallaby bolognaise") that Paul Bugden tries to heat up on the frypan in his Flatette (to save money)[10].

As Figure 5 indicates, the characters in the Gallery scene are already present within the audience. 'Monika' and 'Leon', are a well dressed, culturally articulate couple who carry on as if they are 'real' people who have come to see (according to their program) an 'exhibition of location theatre' – which, in their particular room, doesn't seem to be happening. They dutifully press their buzzer, as instructed, but no actors turn up – because of course, Monika and Leon *are* the play in this room. And so a 'location theatre piece' is happening, although as 'characters' the couple seem not to recognize this.

Figure 6. *Living Rooms* – The Gallery, 1988.
Monika and Leon seated within the audience,
waiting impatiently for something to happen.
Photo © Ruth Maddison

In a third scene, set in a 'Flatette' during Linden's boarding house era, the audience are positioned behind a light scrim and thus rendered invisible to the actors. In this way their view of the action is impeded. So again, they are present as witnesses, but now in an even more distanced manner – as if looking in on some form of social experiment, like trainee medicos observing an operation, or a team of detectives scrutinizing an interrogation.

---

[10] *Living Rooms*, 60-61.

Figure 7. *Living Rooms* – the Flatette, 1972.
A traveler frozen in time, Paul Bugden waits for the buzzer
that will summon him to life. Here the audience are 'hidden' out of sight.
Photo © Ruth Maddison

Here we meet a draft dodger Paul Bugden, and the night of 26th November 1972 on which the Flatette scene is set, is one of great hope for him. A few blocks away, a large political rally is about to be held in the St. Kilda town hall. Bugden plans to risk arrest and cheer on the dawning of a new era in local politics, one in which his current illegal status will shortly be overturned by a new government promising to end Australia's involvement in the Vietnam war. In a sense, like Deegan, Bugden is a 'moral soldier', a hippie outcast fighting to reclaim his legitimate place in society. For young men of Bugden's age, in a century that started with the Boer War and included two horrific global conflicts, the outcome of the federal election in a week's time could not have higher stakes. Similarly, Lt. Deegan believes he is bringing an enlightened society, characterized by principles of Westminster democracy and British ideals of freedom to an oppressed, indigenous black majority on a continent half a world away. Both of course, will be cruelly disillusioned by such high hopes and their current (contemporary 1986) audience, will know this, allowing for a sense of historical irony to enter the equation.

The audience contract

These different modes of witnessing (voyeurs, fellow travelers, scrutineers) allowed the *Living Rooms'* audience to become conscious of itself as an audience (albeit one composed of three sub-sets). They were engaging with and being engaged by the play in different ways. Their 'occupation' of Linden (a real and imagined place) therefore comes with a sense of trespass, of intruding upon the histories and living spaces of others; of being in a private place where the legitimacy of their presence is at best questionable. On one level they are all ghosts, spirits 'inhabiting' a troubled site. Despite being made complicit through their voyeurism, the audience are thus offered a shared experience, a sense of moving around as a group, of accessing the narrative sequence with distinct and separate plans – something which helped engender the idea of a community of the audience *within* the play. They are on a journey together, through time and through a set of re-enactments. These reconfigurations of the theatre-going experience engender a heightened sense of three-dimensionality that, despite its apparent experimental nature, found an immediate rapport with audiences.

In this way, and by theses means, TheatreWorks was able to experiment with increasingly subtle and complex actor-audience relationships. In the Gallery scene, for example, Monika and Leon's argument sees them eventually hire an audio guide for a 'tour' of the room: a "pleasant stroll through the city's years from the Boer War to the Bicentennial"[11] - a time span that matches the historical investigation of the play itself. This voice over explanation of the art works in the room, ends with Monika and Leon occupying a site-specific 'installation' at the far end called "St. Kilda Breakfast": basically a messy kitchen table covered in food, plates, cups etc. This is an 'artwork' that is part of the exhibition they have allegedly come to see. In this 'kitchen', which itself has been 'assembled' by a fictional, off-stage artist, two characters in a scripted play enact a typical breakfast scene in contemporary (1988) St. Kilda, surveying along the way their deteriorating relationship. Again the audience, by virtue of remaining proximate but passive, are complicit in Monika and Leon's invasion of 'St. Kilda Breakfast'. In this sense, the Gallery scene plays with 'layers' of social and cultural space within the same room and I argue that it is through this manipulation of theatrical space, the collision of found and invented

---

[11] Ibid., 80

spaces (and the experiences they offer and embody), that the chief attraction of this kind of 'embedded' site-specific theatre lies.

Spatial Interplay[12]

One way of understanding the generation of spatial energies involved here is to read the play's basic production strategy as a collision of heterotopia in the Foucauldian sense.[13]

Henri Lefebvre, applying the physical theories of Fred Hoyle (who "looked on space as the product of energy"), argued in 1974 that social space, in its various forms, could be produced by the energy deployed within it.[14] This is an idea that echoes in part, Peter Brook's 1967 claim that an act of theatre in its simplest form was an indissoluble triad of actor, witness and stage.[15] In the same year Michel Foucault adopted the term 'heterotopia', which he defined as "a kind of effectively enacted utopia in which…all the other real sites that can be found within a culture, are simultaneously represented, contested, and inverted."[16] As Foucault expressed it, the twentieth century was above all "the epoch of space" of "simultaneity" and "juxtaposition".[17] And with notions of space, as so often in the human story, come the anxieties of occupation, of moving in on someone else's patch. The key here therefore, is to interrogate how *Living Rooms* was able to deploy the space of its story inside the space of a real building and to do it in a number of different ways (for each particular scene). Not only is the 'fourth wall' put solidly back in place

---

[12] In the wake of the various occupations of public spaces that took place in the 1960s – what have been called "les evenéments du Mai 1968" – ('events' that resemble what is still occurring in the middle east today), public spaces and public buildings, parks, squares and monuments came to be regarded as not only accessible and available to all, but iconically useful. Out of this turmoil and experiment, the idea of a social space that could be 'produced' was born. And once it was 'produced' it was available to be deployed both culturally and politically. Foucault's idea of the 'heterotopia' offers one way of reading this.

[13] Michel Foucault, "Of Other Spaces," *Diacritics* 16 (Spring 1986): 22-27.

[14] Henri Lefebvre, *La Production de l'Espace*. Translated by D. Nicholson-Smith. (Oxford: Blackwell, 1991), 13.

[15] Peter Brook, *The Empty Space*. (Ringwood, Victoria: Pelican,1968), 11.

[16] Foucault, 24.

[17] Ibid, 22.

around the audience, but they become, to a certain extent, 'engulfed' in the performance in ways that Artaud called for in *The Theatre And It's Double*.

We abolish the stage and the auditorium and replace them by a single site, without partition or barrier of any kind, which will become the theatre of the action. A direct communication will be re-established between the spectator and the spectacle, between the actor and the spectator, from the fact that the spectator, placed in the middle of the action, is engulfed and physically affected by it. This envelopment results, in part, *from the very configuration of the room itself* (emphasis added).[18]

It remains to look at how each room was configured within the overarching narrative of the play itself.

Diegetic Space: heterotopia of the narrative.

The action in each room is set on one of three significant 'eves' in Australian history. Events in the Drawing Room take place on the eve of Federation in 1901, the Flatette scene occurs on the eve of a swing to the left in the federal election of 1972, and the Gallery scene takes place on the eve of the Bicentennial in 1988 – a national celebration of two centuries of European occupation. Consequently, all three scenes unfold in their separate slices of time, what Foucault would call their 'heterochronies'.

Heterotopias are most often linked to slices in time – which is to say that they open onto what might be termed, for the sake of symmetry, heterochronies...From a general standpoint, in a society like ours heterotopias and heterochronies are structured and distributed in a relatively complex fashion. First of all there are heterotopias of indefinitely accumulating time, for example museums and libraries.[19]

To which one might add: the accumulating time of historic houses – especially ones that have gone through such 'dramatic' demographic changes. However, as the heterochronies instituted by the different sub-narratives in *Living Rooms* play out, their strict separation in time and space starts to break down; and thus the rooms, operating as historical and dramatic containers, become unstable. Sounds, objects, narrative co-incidences, and even characters, bleed from one room to another. For example, a blackout caused by Paul Bugden's failure to pay his electricity bill in the Flatette scene in 1972 allows Cuthbert Beaumgardiner to wander from his Drawing

---

[18] Antonin Artaud, *Le Theatre Et Son Double* Trans. by Mary Caroline Richards. (New York: Grove Press, 1958), 96.

[19] Foucault, 26.

Room scene in 1900 into a suddenly darkened Gallery in 1988, where he mistakes Monika for his mistress, Estelle. After Beaumgardiner has left and the lights come on again, Leon (instituting another actor-spectator confusion and unaware of what has actually happened), blames a member of the audience for taking advantage of Monika. Hence, in an intercalation of heterochronies that results from these spatial and temporal instabilities, one room's past effectively becomes another's future and vice versa. The prosperity looked for at the turn of the century by the likes of capitalist entrepreneurs such as Beaumgardiner, is realized in the vacuous personalities of St. Kilda's new possessors: the rising inner-urban professional class of Monika and Leon. They exemplify the cultural re-appropriation of the former red-like district that St. Kilda had become in the wake of Beaumgardiner's well heeled cohort. This new, contemporary 're-invasion' followed on from, and in a sense was made possible by, the cultural and political tumult of the late 1960s and 70s: the era of draft dodgers like Paul Bugden. Such demographic changes and contestations, and their interplay would not be unfamiliar in the inner-urban histories of many western cities.

The Drawing Room Scene: heterotopia of a late Victorian mansion, heterochrony of 1900.

In the 'present' of 1900, on the eve of his departure for Capetown, Lt. Deegan struggles to declare his real feelings for Estelle, an equally idealistic and politically savvy young woman who survives as the kept mistress of Beaumgardiner. Estelle maintains what was euphemistically referred to as a 'Bachelor's Hall' for Beaumgardiner who epitomizes the nouveau riche, 'greed-is-good' attitude of the 1880s Australian 'squattocracy'. In fact, with Boer farms burning across the South African veld, Beaumgardiner's sheep station in Bacchus Marsh is now rocketing up in value. He connects back to a time when it wasn't safe to ride a pony from central Melbourne to St. Kilda (5 miles south of the city) for fear of being attacked by rogue convicts or parties of dispossessed aborigines. But the anxiety that substrates Michael and Estelle's relationship relates to larger concerns in the Australian imaginary that Joanne Tompkins identifies in *Unsettling Space* as an 'uncanny' – something which "is experienced when the repressed threatens to return":

Freud connects anxiety with the return of a dreaded commodity thought to have been safely absent …In Australia, the repressed usually signals knowledge of what was done to places and the people in them; a key theatrical response to this knowledge is the staging of issues of presence and absence particularly locating Aboriginal people in Australian history... But the anxiety that is expressed in terms of spatiality on Australian stages extends well beyond this absence (significant though it might be), reinforcing a fundamental discomfort with the process of settlement and the establishment of nationhood.[20]

An embryonic suffragette, Estelle can't fathom why an avowed republican and socialist like Deegan could participate in a colonial mis-adventure in a foreign country thousands of miles away (an enterprise obviously designed to ensure that the sun never sets on the British Empire). Deegan retorts that "[i]n Johannesburg the native people aren't even allowed to walk on the footpath. The president of Transvaal himself has said they have no more soul than a monkey."[21] However, Estelle maintains her pacifist position, and in the end Deegan comes to realize her anti-imperial take on the war is valid.

Throughout *Living Rooms* there is a sense of unease derived largely from the questionable legitimacy with which the characters occupy their individual rooms (and by implication, their audiences with them). Deegan clearly has a hidden agenda in relation to Estelle, desperate to drag her away from this 'Bachelor's Hall' which Beaumgardiner has acquired through a process of ruthless property speculation, and whose possession of it thereby remains contested in itself. In the Flatette scene, Paul Bugden's unease relates to his outlaw/refugee status. He arrives in Linden during its boarding house era, on the run from the Commonwealth Police as a conscientious objector – one of many hundreds who chose to go 'underground' rather than be conscripted for service in Vietnam. Leon, in the Gallery, is a town planner and architect, one of a cohort responsible for designing the new (re-gentrified) St. Kilda, plans that his wife Monika also has grave doubts about. Like Estelle, Monika constantly questions Leon's vision of the future and finds it wanting. Her unease relates to the lack of heart or the sense of any real community in his plans.

The Flatette Scene: heterotopia of a tiny flat in a boarding house, heterochrony of 1972.

Lt. Michael Deegan will be comprehensively brought back to reality by his experience on the battlefields of southern Africa (something we discover in the Flatette Scene) where, 72 years later, Paul Bugden lives in constant fear of arrest, his predicament an outcome of the slow erosion of principles Deegan thinks he is . fighting for, in his room, 72 years earlier. As the separate heterochronies start to overlap for the audience, they discover that Deegan's misplaced idealism has

---

[20] Joanne Tompkins, *Unsettling Space: Contestations in Contemporary Australian Theatre* (New York: Palgrave McMillan, 2006), 8.

[21] *Living Rooms*, 6-7.

morphed into Bugden's equally misplaced faith in an imminent Labour victory – itself another disillusionment-in-waiting. And yet, the occupations, disruptions, anxieties and contestations of this exterior political space (contemporary and historical) proceeds on one level in the world outside Linden, just as the occupations, movements and disruptions of the play itself unfold internally within the building's own chronology and its own separate spaces. And as Foucault predicted, it is in the *relationship* between heterotopia that their real power and usefulness lies, the inversion/subversion factor.

In an example of heterochronic permeability, Bugden hears the barely audible argument going on in the Drawing Room next door (between Estelle, Deegan and Beaumgardiner), as if he is party to it in his own time. Similarly, the raised voices of Monika and Leon in the Gallery across the hallway can also be occasionally heard from the Flatette, however indistinctly. If an audience group has already been in the Gallery (or the Drawing Room) they will know roughly what the shouting is all about and can now view the current scene before them from a position of narrative privilege, becoming more aware of the relationships, overlaps and ironies in play. Again they become engulfed in the story to the extent of becoming aware of it as 'meta-event', something happening both in front of them (in that room at that moment), as well as 'proceeding' all around them in the house generally.

For Bugden these noisy distractions are just more evidence of how low his circumstances have sunk: to be in lodgings this unsavory, full of shouting losers. Eventually, in attempting to kick-start an electric heater into life, he discovers a letter hidden behind the Flatette's fire place – effectively a post-script to the Drawing Room scene, a letter in which Deegan reveals to Estelle the extent of his disillusionment with what is going on in South Africa. Captivated by the discovery of this letter, Bugden imagines a story that connects his image of the writer of the letter (Deegan) with its addressee (Estelle). When Bugden finally meets these characters in the hallway in the climactic fourth scene, the different time zones in the play effectively collapse into the one space.

The Gallery Scene 1988: heterotopia of an 'historical exhibition', heterochrony of 1988.

As audience members enter the Gallery, the largest of Linden's downstairs rooms (originally the ballroom), they undergo another heterochronic shift, and now find themselves a couple of years into the future, at an 'historical exhibition' of artifacts, artworks, banners, photographs and posters, that trace a history of St. Kilda from the Boer War to the Bi-centennial, the same time line as the play. Indeed, some of the photographs contain images of characters that the audience might (or might not) have seen in other rooms: Beaumgardiner, Deegan and Estelle in formal studio portraits, and Paul Bugden at the tram stop in front of Luna Park. Yet here, in the Gallery space, there are no frozen characters waiting to be brought to life, only a well dressed couple (Monika and Leon) unselfconsciously involved in an argument about what is actually going on in their room and what they are meant to expect from this 'exhibition'. Monika is a social worker and her partner Leon a town planner and architect, someone who works with 'representations of space' in the Lefebvrian sense: the plans, drawings, and various projects with which he hopes to do his bit to shape St. Kilda through its third demographic transition: the era of an educated, urban middle class who were currently finding the suburb's quaint old buildings with their proximity to jobs in the city, all win-win situations.

The war at issue in this scene is the Cold War in its penultimate phase (a year before the fall of the Berlin wall) – almost over, yet still capable of bringing about global Armageddon. Leon, in fact, wants to build a nuclear fallout shelter under their new apartment which Monika vehemently opposes, just as she objects to all of Leon's plans to transform St. Kilda into some kind of sanitized yuppie paradise. Irritated and waiting for something to happen, Monika and Leon decide to pass the time by hiring an audio guide to take them (and fellow audience members) through a walking tour of the 'exhibition', and thereby a potted cultural history of the last century in St. Kilda.

This includes the installation "St Kilda Breakfast": a laminex table at one end of the room covered in the detritus of a very messy meal. Monika and Leon's painful argument about the artistic merit of this piece becomes a metaphor for their disintegrating relationship. As they try to make sense of the exhibition (and increasingly fail to do so), other characters from other rooms intrude into their space. Beaumgardiner does so in the blackout, and 'Martha', the maid from the Drawing Room, enters to change into her costume for her role as 'Miriam' in the Flatette. While Leon feels it almost demeaning to be parked in what appears to be the dressing room of some play going on elsewhere, Monica takes the opportunity to confront 'Martha' about their room not working, but 'Miriam/Martha' assures Monika that she will understand it all eventually. "It will come to you – or you'll come to it".[22]

Unfortunately, this doesn't seem to happen so, as Monika and Leon's bickering continues, the audio guide (another ghost in the machine) becomes annoyed by their argument and starts talking back – which doesn't seem quite right! At which point Monika discovers that the roses Leon gave her upon arrival (to celebrate their 10th anniversary as a couple) are in fact plastic – much like the props one would expect

---

[22] Ibid, 81.

to find on a stage. As it slowly sinks in that they themselves might be the victims of some kind of hoax, Monika and Leon come to occupy the breakfast 'installation' at the far end of the room with a practiced familiarity, as if it was now the kitchen of their own St. Kilda apartment: a sub-heterotopia within the heterotopia of the Gallery itself – effectively now a 'set' within a room proposing to represent a particular place at a particular time – or, in this case (because the Gallery encapsulates an historical exhibition), the one place over many times.

The anxieties and instabilities that now suffuse an increasingly chaotic set of spaces and times begins to reach a point of crisis. The Gallery scene ends with Leon believing that there are illegal drugs on their 'kitchen table' and, in an era before mobile phones, exits the room to find a public one, something that might summon the police and hopefully restore some semblance of normality to the proceedings…

The Hallway Scene: mixed heterotopia of three spaces in collision, heterochronies of 1900, 1972 and 1988.

Figure 8 Monika rips into Leon in the Hallway as
all three audience groups coalesce around her.
Photo © Ruth Maddison

Throughout *Living Rooms* the space of Linden's grand Hallway with its impressive front door and commanding staircase, operates as a very permeable portal through which the audience sub-groups and the characters from different rooms and periods merge, cross over, have interval and swap notes. The climactic Hallway scene begins where the scene in each room ended, as if the heterochronic clock of the narrative has been wound back and reset. This allows the characters from all three periods to formally and finally come together in the same space.

Deegan and Estelle are initially frozen (again) in the act of exiting the Drawing Room with a frozen Cuthbert in hot pursuit. Observing this tableau, Monika and Leon think they've finally found the play they've been expecting to see, enough for Leon to postpone his phone call. Monika presses a buzzer and is thrilled to see the three characters come 'to life'. The combined audience now hear that Cuthbert is still reeling from the discovery that Estelle is fact pregnant to Deegan – who in turn assumes she will have the child, stay with his cousin, and await his return from the war. However, Estelle, the 'new woman', the Nora of this particular *Doll's House*, has other ideas and is determined to make her own way, separate from dependence on any man. Into this tableau stumbles Paul Bugden, beating a hasty retreat from the boarding house, concerned that the police have been alerted by the landlord and are about to arrest him. Bugden is being pursued down the steps by Miriam, eager to collect his rent before he disappears. In his rush to escape however, Bugden accidently hits another buzzer and the 1900 scene continues. In this moment, Paul Bugden finally confronts in Cuthbert, Deegan and Estelle, what he assumes to be the figures of his own creation, all inspired by the 'real' characters glimpsed in the letter he found. Dazzled by Estelle's beauty, Bugden naturally falls in love with her. But confronted by an ending he didn't expect and can't accept, he 'intervenes' in the 1900 *ménage a trois*, and 'gives' Cuthbert a heart attack – which now starts to occur, on the steps, in real time – whenever that may be. At which point, the ghost of the house itself, Linden's own 'uncanny', intervenes in the action once more via the Gallery's audio guide, and institutes itself as an effective über-author, thus bringing on the play's final denouement.

As a slide of the house in 1900 (Figure 1) is projected on the back wall halfway up the staircase, the 'voice' of Linden, the uncanny at the heart of the play, reflects on the folly of all its prior inhabitants, indulging in a gentle but sharply focused put-down of humanity generally. Leon, always the architect/developer, threatens to end this nonsense by tearing the house down and replacing it with a block of Bauhaus-style apartments. However, as he goes to switch off the audio guide (and despite being warned), he and Monika become instantly frozen on the steps.[23] With the other characters all gone out the front door (trailed by Cuthbert, clutching his failing heart), Monika and Leon are returned to the state they were meant to have started from…had their room been 'working'. By which point all the heterochronies and

---

[23] Ibid. 118

heterotopias of *Living Rooms* have met and melded, and the ghost of the house enjoys a last laugh, as the lights slowly fade to black...

Conclusion

Placing dramatic stories inside real buildings (which those stories purport to be notionally about) creates a 'poly-dimensional' experience of live performance. This is something more than a simply a 'three-dimensional' or 'multi-dimensional' engagement – in the sense that the action of the drama takes place both in front of and all around an audience. It can also engage senses available in such proximate relationships (smell, touch, taste). By harnessing the energy of an enacted narrative, it can effectively occupy and manipulate found spaces, revealing a new resonance between text and stage. These levels of engagement effectively immerse an audience in the action of a play to an extent not possible in the more formal arrangements of purpose-built theatres. Site-specific plays in houses, despite their risky nature can, with reasonably effective scripts, direction and acting, prove to be very popular undertakings indeed.

Living Rooms enjoyed extended seasons, playing to full 'houses' for several months; and with twice the capacity of a tram (90 seats as against 50), proved a profitable exercise for TheatreWorks. Unlike the more widely produced *Tram Show*, however, *Living Rooms'* historically focused subject matter made it less readily 'transportable' than its more ubiquitous trambulating predecessor. Although in a later play, *Full House/No Vacancies* [24], the company used the same building and the same staging strategies to tell another story set entirely in Linden's boarding house era.

The critical reception for *Living Rooms* was generally positive. Clark Forbes writing in *The Herald* (July 24, 1986) felt that "What could so easily end in mayhem works surprisingly smoothly. The result is a hugely enjoyable ramble round an inventive mind and a delightful extension of the normal theatrical boundaries". Helen Thomson in *The Australian* (July 22, 1986) found that the play was "inventive and intriguing," "ingeniously constructed" and "community theatre at its best, socially relevant, artistically challenging, thought provoking in the contemporary issues it raises," something that "breaks down the normal constraints of place and time in the theatre." Finally, Leonard Radic, who noted in *The Age* (22 July, 1986) that TheatreWorks had "made something of a specialty of environmental or location theatre," found that *Living Rooms* "consciously sets out to extend the boundaries of

---

[24] Paul Davies, *Full House/No Vacancies* available at: https://www.bookdepository.com/Full-House-No-Vacancies-Paul-Michael-Davies/9780648599852

theatre to give audiences a new and interesting experience. At that level it succeeds admirably. Who knows? It may even inspire one or two theatergoers to think about the environmental issues which the play raises."

Two and a half decades later it also inspires us to think, perhaps, about the potential for such work to engage audiences in ways that are all encompassing as well as popular. Such stagings permitted spectators to be moved (literally) and implicated in the dramas they were witnessing in ways that were challenging and adventurous and effectively helped encourage theatre practice to regard all the world as a (potential) stage.

ON SHIFTING SANDSHOES
Comic farce or Postmodern Morality Play?
Paper for WIP (Works in Progress) Conference on
"The Seven Deadly Sins: Critical and Creative Contexts"
University of Queensland.
September 2011

Paul Davies

The English Morality Play

Figure 1. Everyman and Death
Wood cut from the title page of the Skot print of *Everyman*
(Henry E. Huntington Library copy)

First performed in later part of the 15th Century Everyman is probably the best known of the English morality plays and tells the story of Everyman as he is summoned by Death to his day of judgment and seeks desperately around for help from various characters designated as Fellowship, Kindred Goods the five Witts, Knowledge, Strength but they all desert him. Only Good Deeds takes him by the hand into eternal life. Clearly this was a kind of sermon presented dramatically just as the earlier medieval Miracle and Mystery plays had been enactments of scenes from the New and Old Testaments. In a play like everyman however we see the beginnings of a rudimentary human characters becoming more central to the drama, however embryonic

My focus in this paper is more with the construction of 'character' than 'space' and I argue that, just the idea of the fully rounded, psychologically coherent human being in drama emerges from the medieval morality play where ethical and physical attributes were first embodied in individual players (designated as Kindness, Good Deeds, Beauty, Wit, Strength etc.). So too, plays like *On Shifting Sandshoes,* half a millennium later, harbour within their dramatis personae, a certain tendency to prescriptive stereotyping (mono-typing?), or at best a form of personality constraint. [25]

This arises in *On Shifting Sandshoes* also because of the collaborative way it was written: by means of script workshops where character intentions and wants (their 'motives') could be reduced to simple workshop-able descriptors. Appropriately for this conference, the dominant personality traits that seem to have emerged for the characters of *On Shifting Sandshoes* can be read not as virtues, but as mortal sins, a list of spiritually fatal transgressions as first defined by Pope Gregory in the 6th Century.

In his introduction to *Everyman*, A.C. Cawley points out that

The earliest moralities…show a change from the biblical history to the contemporary world, from biblical characters to human types and personified human qualities; the struggle between good and evil is staged in the soul of the individual representative Christian, and his salvation is brought by the Christ-given sacraments of the Church. Man now becomes the leading personage in a play which is complete in itself and distinct from the cyclic pageant in that it is no longer part of a larger whole. [26]

J.L. Styan in his history of the English stage goes on to say that, as it shook off the influence of the Church, the morality play became increasingly secular and political, while it still "pursued its purpose by working with *abstract* characters that conveyed an

---

[25] Character stereotyping in *On Shifting Sandshoes* also derives from the commedia dell'arte tradition (emerging concurrently with the moralities in the 14th Century) a style of acting that was applied to TheatreWorks' other site-specific plays, where a certain exaggerated, or over-the-top acting manner became logistically necessary (in order to be seen and heard). This model for working up a script with the available actors and director had been used by the TheatreWorks ensemble since the original *Go Anywhere Show* in 1981

[26] *Everyman*. Old and Middle English Texts. Ed. Cawley, A. C. Manchester: Manchester University Press, 1961. Print. xiv.

allegorical story," and that the "struggle of good and evil automatically built a bold, confrontational dramatic structure." [27] This process still happens in drama today in a post-modern 'morality' play like *On Shifting Sandshoes* where the dramatic conflict also arises from a confrontation of stereotypes.

On Shifting Sandshoes

In 1988 I was commissioned by the Bicentennial Authority to write a play which would be part of a celebration of two centuries of European settlement in Australia. This was a rare opportunity to create a piece of theatre, in the Christmas pantomime tradition, but updated and in close collaboration with a director and cast. The basic dramaturgical strategy was to work up the shape and personalities of the characters drawing on the skills base and (comic) abilities of the people who would be performing them. In this way, the actors, to a certain extent, not only 'own' the story, but the plot emerges from the characters and the friction between them, rather than from some predetermined narrative architecture imposed from above. The methodology was to bring a potential outline of events to the table, a treatment effectively, which was divided into 'beats' or embryonic scenes such as "Arrival," "The Storm," "Men On Women," "Women on Men," "Night Games," "Xmas Day" etc. So that the final dialogue, and the order of events, grew out of improvisations based on the over arching intentions and drives of each person.[28] These 'wants' were driven in turn by a series of 'needs' and 'desires' – providing the conflicts of interest from which 'drama' flows. Sandy wants Diane, Bruce wants Paula, Margot once wanted Raoul, but of course he's gay and Bruce has all the money, so Raoul in turn pretends to want Sandy.

At the time, TheatreWorks' artistic agenda was to marry the idea of 'celebration' with that of 'disturbance' because of an ambiguous attitude to its suburban community.

Although *On Shifting Sandshoes* was not 'site-specific' it was born out of an intention to be potentially so, and in fact arrived on the back of two earlier TheatreWorks' tent shows which were site-specific.

The first of these was *The Go Anywhere (within reason) Show* in 1981.

---

[27] Styan, J.L. *The English Stage: A History of Drama and Performance.* Cambridge: Cambridge University Press, 1996. Print. 41.

[28] The TheatreWorks archive contains 14 hours of audio tapes from these script workshops and includes this author's notebooks from these discussions.

Figure 2. TheatreWorks' *Go Anywhere (within reason)Show*, March-December,1981
Back: Peter Finlay (Dick Dickens) Caz Howard (Dolly Dickens),
Susie Fraser, (Desdemona Dickens)
Front: Tony Kishawi (Darryl Dickens) Robin Laurie (director)
Hannie Rayson (Daphne Dickens)

This play revolved around the adventures of a lower middle class family forced to wander Melbourne's eastern suburbs because they were unemployed and therefore actually homeless. But cheerfully pretending that they were just on holiday and moving around (staying in a tent). It was performed as if the camping ground, shopping centre, street, school or community hall in which they pitched their tent was going to have to be the Dickens' residence for that night. The script was reworked three years later as *The Dick And Dolly Dickens' Show* and performed in similar locations.

Figure 4. Cast of *The Dick And Dolly Dickens Show*, 1984
Front: Phil Ceberano, (Darryl Dickens) John Wood Ingram (Dick Dickens)
Kate Kantor (Daphne Dickens),
Back: Debbie Helloran (Dolly Dickens), Helen King (Desdemona Dickens)

Lack of space prohibits further contextualizing these plays within the conventions of the castaway genre as it extends say, from Defoe's *Robinson Crusoe* to William Golding's *Lord of the Flies*; or even the venerable tradition of tent shows and other forms of travelling theatre reaching as far back as the pageants, strolling players and miracle/mystery plays of the early middle ages – a tradition of mobile entertainment that continued through to the great tent-located circuses of the late 19th and early 20th Centuries.

We chose as our starting point five apparently well-adjusted Brisbanites and one Melbournian who collectively participate in that great, annual Australian ritual of the Christmas camping holiday by the beach: specifically, Flinders Beach on North Stradbroke Island (Mingerriba). Loosely based on real events, this was also going to be one of those years when the Sunshine State morphs into the Cyclone State and in an odd premonition of the current fixation with climate change, our unhappy campers soon find their site wrecked, their food gone, their SUVs inoperable, their nerves frayed, the 'Fourex' running low, and little prospect of 'rescue' any time soon. By the time help arrives, all constraints have been lost and their lives, despite protestations to the contrary, will never be quite the same again. It seems improbable of course, that people could be effectively isolated and starving on a beach barely 20 kilometres from civilized Brisbane. But this is farce not fact, allegory rather than documentary and is Brisbane civilization anyway, or are there primitive, primeval urges festering away beneath the modern façade? Such was the broad narrative canvas onto which the detailed characters could then be sketched through the script workshop process. Above all, the theme of *On Shifting Sandshoes*, something with which to 'disturb' the Bicentennial moment, was the fraught nature of the Australian engagement with its continent, a point that Joanne

Tompkins underlines in *Unsettling Space* where she argues that "Representational space performed in Australian theatre not only contests a conventional Australian history and culture; it also stages alternative means of managing the production of space in a spatially unstable nation" [29]

As I wrote in the 1988 programme for *On Shifting Sandshoes*:

The human experience in Australia has been sited overwhelmingly in some kind of temporary camp. From the gunyahs of the aborigines to the tents of the First Fleet and the goldfields, Australians have housed themselves impermanently. Despite our weatherboards and brick veneers we still answer, every Christmas, some national primitive urge to escape from 'civilization' and camp under the stars.[30]

But in this dystopian, bicentennial year, as things go from bad to worse for our unhappy campers, Bruce becomes increasingly greedy, Margot vain, Diane angry, Sandy lustful, Raoul lazy, and Paula jealous. In addition, they collectively exhibit a ruinous gluttony as their growing hunger, excited by an accidental dose of hallucinogenic mushrooms, soon carries grave danger for the already endangered local wildlife.

Characters and their Sins:

Figure 6. Bruce McKenzie
(Greed)

---

[29] Tompkins, Joanne. *Unsettling Space Contestations in Contemporary Australian Theatre*. Studies in International Performance. General Editors Janelle Reinhelt and Brian Singleton. New York: Palgrave McMillan, 2006 Print. 5.
[30] TheatreWorks Archive. Fryer Library, University of Queensland, Brisbane. *On Shifting Sandshoes*. Box 3

Bruce is a property developer and tax avoider whose personality is driven by a relentless selfishness. He unapologetically sees himself (and without a hint of irony) as the sort of visionary builder who "made the Gold Coast what it is today."[31] Bruce will sell you anything you want, even if he doesn't technically own it yet and in fact he secretly plans to construct a toll bridge to Stradbroke from the mainland carrying a pipeline that will effectively drain the island's lakes of their pristine fresh water in order to profit from a drought-prone Brisbane's growing thirst.[32] In this one act he effectively bridges, literally, Pope Gregory's traditional sin of 'Greed' over to the modern sin of 'Environmental Destruction' as outlined in the list recently announced by Monsignor Gianfranco Girotti, head of the Vatican's Apostolic Penitentiary Committee.[33] Bruce is so locked into personal wealth creation that when his wife Margot's credit card is stolen in the Vatican during a tax deductible trip to Europe, he refuses to report it because as he soon discovers, the thief is spending less than Margot did.

Figure 7. Margot McKenzie
(Vanity)

---

[31] *On Shifting Sandshoes,* Paul Davies 2009 TS. TheatreWorks Archive. Fryer Library, University of Queensland, Brisbane. 7.

[32] Such a plan was proposed by Hon. Russell Hinze, Minister for Transport, Development and Gambling in the Bjelke-Petersen government at the time. In a cruel piece of political caricature Minister Hinze was himself parodied by cartoonists as the 'colossus of Roads'.

[33] Swartz,, Barney, "Seven deadly sins get a modern day makeover." *The Age* 11 March 2008, Print. Other new sins in the Vatican's canon of updated transgressions, include 'conducting immoral scientific experiments' and 'genetic manipulation'.

Bruce's wife Margot is a self-anointed 'Beauty Consultant' and former kindergarten teacher with pretentions to much higher things. Her 'day job' consists of running one of those temples of modern narcissism: a hairdressing salon called "Curl Up and Dye". This loss-making place of mirrors is funded by Bruce (primarily as a tax deduction), but mainly because it keeps Margott occupied with her talent for gossip even if it involves mainly talking about herself. Margott brings a huge collection of beach clothes to try out on holiday (and help hide any tiny little imperfections). The size of the wardrobe every year is something Bruce simply cannot fathom because, as he correctly points out, all that Margott does when she gets to the island is take it all off again!

Figure 8. Diane Stewart
(Anger)

Diane is a physical education teacher at an unnamed Brisbane high school. Bossy and almost permanently single, she carries a fairly large and apparently immutable chip on her shoulder, especially in relation to ex-boyfriends. Diane is annoyed with Bruce because he's such a 'boof-head', and deep down is intelligent enough to know that Margott is pretty shallow also. At work Diane is irritated by her students, other staff, parents generally and is quietly stewing over the increasingly audible ticking of her biological clock. Her last 'ex', Craig somebody, who we never see, had been playing a lot of night tennis and Diane only belatedly discovered that it was all 'mixed doubles.' Even though they had triathlons common, and he once took her to Port Douglas, infidelity on the tennis court, caught on court as it were, was more than enough to see Diane picking up her racket and walking. As she reveals to her closest girlfriends, Craig had "zero concept of what it was like to live on a planet that is slowly breaking down."[34] Finally, Diane becomes really annoyed when she cuts her well-conditioned foot on the toilet shovel and overnight succumbs to some dreadful tropical infection that soon sees her reduced to virtual immobility on Margot's banana lounge. The dramaturgical strategy here was to take a character's salient, empowering qualities and render her inoperable, to cripple her as it were, in Diane's case literally. The active person thus becomes inactive, the lazy, busy, the vain, humble, the ugly, lustful and so on.

---

[34]. Ibid 56.

Figure 9. Sandy Mills
(Lust)

An unfit, self-declared poet, Sandy runs a bookshop in Melbourne, wears a lot of black and rarely comes in contact with the sun, let alone tents or unpatrolled beaches. In an inversion of the usual stereotype (again for exaggerated comic effect) Sandy, by far the least attractive of the campers, becomes the unlikely Lothario. Just as opposites attract, he soon finds himself shamelessly ignoring Paula and lusting after both Diane's athletic body and her razor sharp mind. A hopeless hippie romantic at heart, Sandy soon engages in playful intellectual banter with Diane, much to Paula's growing unease. He even foolishly reveals his true feelings in a private diary (notes for a potential novel) that is soon discovered by Raoul and used to effectively expose Sandy's duplicity, destroy his relationship with Paula, and pretty comprehensively humiliate him in front of everybody – all at a point when he's also technically starving. As Sandy laments soon after: "This is the worst good time I've ever had."[35]

---

[35] Ibid. 83

Figure 10. Paula Edwards.
(Envy)

Sandy's partner, Paula, another former teacher and now an aspiring singer is the one character to have escaped her Brisbane nest, hoping to establish a musical career with an all women's band in artistically supportive Melbourne – only to find public disinterest and financial disappointment. Along the way she also finds Sandy, only to be disappointed by him too given his flirtations with Diane. Paula always plays low status and has little to offer. She quietly envies Margot's carefree lifestyle, Diane's strength and courage, Bruce's bonhomie and largesse, Sandy's brains, and Raoul's flair. In a further complication it is revealed that Paula had a drunken encounter with Bruce out on the dunes under full moon, several camps ago.

Figure 11. Raoul Manon
(Sloth)

The soul of Raoul is being permanently struggled over in a tight contest between the twin devils of his innate laziness and his boundless self-regard. Raoul's basic attitude to life is "let's party before we all die." A gay, irresponsible, but talented chef, Raoul's only material contribution to the campsite is a set of dumbbells brought over on his bicycle – both designed to keep the 'body beautiful' in shape. He refuses to cook (he's on holidays) and brings absolutely nothing useful to add to the pool of goods necessary to keep a camp of six people functioning for a festive week. Like most years, Raoul pretty much expects to 'sponge' off the others for the entire time, rewarding his fellow camp mates with his amusing take on everything. It is revealed that Raoul also had a mad fling with Margot several camps ago, and tries to use this grubby skeleton in her large closet to blackmail more money out of her for his failing restaurant in the Valley, hoping as always to get something for nothing.

In addition to these individual moral failings, and as their supply of edible goods soon reduces down to a bottle of tomato sauce and a slab of 'Fourex', the characters in *On Shifting Sandshoe's* begin experiencing real hunger probably for the first time in their lives. When Bruce finds a packet of soggy chips washed up on the beach, true to his nature, he at first tries to hide them, then refuses to share a single chip, threatening to swallow the entire packet in one go. However, under pressure from the group, including Diane's withering temper, Bruce relents and proposes a winners-take-all game of 'bastard ball' (their private version of beach volleyball), and proceeds to choose the best players for his own team, leaving Margot and Sandy with the crippled Diane. When even the chips aren't enough, however, the final desperate struggle for food sees them ingesting wild mushrooms which soon appear to have been hallucinogenic.

Figure 12. 'Blinky'
(Gluttony)

In this fragile, altered state, and the delirium that follows, the group, riven by the consequences of their individual and collective transgressions, plumb new depths of depravity as the camp mascot, a rare blue koala who they've nicknamed 'Blinky,' becomes impaled on a beach umbrella, a final mortal sin that confirms their descent into hell. Well within the tradition of a medieval morality, *On Shifting Sandshoes* restages the familiar adage that "the wages of sin are death," even if it is an innocent animal in this case who pays the supreme price.[36]

Aftermath

The following morning, in the sobering, harsh glare of daylight, the five Brisbane friends and the outsider from Melbourne, gather their tattered belongings and prepare to catch the barge home again, knowing full well that nothing between them will ever be the same again. In this sense the cyclone that floods and wrecks their campsite can be read as biblical also in its cleansing effect, forcing change, restoring normality and making a kind of redemptive renewal possible – placing *On Shifting Sandshoes* again well within the morality tradition.

---

[36] Although Blinky's 'innocence' may be contested by the evidence that Koalas do tend to lie around a lot on tree branches chewing gum leaves all day, whose high eucalyptus content subsequently drives them towards a constant state of irritable rage, thus embodying within their species hood the sins of sloth, gluttony and anger.

Predictably, Leonard Radic responded to all this in *The Age* in his review "not exactly incisive or innovative theatre," lacking the "Shakespearean resonances of Michael Gow's *Away*" which he found *On Shifting Sandshoes* partly resembled. And although, as "light comedy farce" it worked "well enough" for him, if there were "any subtleties in the script," Radic felt that "neither the director Mark Shirrefs nor the actors [had] locate[d] them."[37] Other critics were less harsh. Jennifer Ellison in the *Bulletin* found the characters were "intentionally stereotypical" but the humour "largely wholesome," and spoke of the "glee with which audiences can watch this show knowing that it's them and not us having to live through this abominably awful experience."[38] Either way, *On Shifting Sandshoes* made a healthy profit for TheatreWorks during its extended première run, and the 2009 production in Mullumbimby enjoyed a similar popularity with Byron Shire audiences. It also received an Awgie (Australian Writer's Guild Award) for the best Australian play of 1988.

Conclusion

The point of the caricature, exaggerated characters and incredible events, arose out of an intention to disturb the celebration of an official historical national moment. The Medieval tradition of bawdiness and irreverence is present also in the 'crude' way that the characters are constructed and thrown together. As A. C. Cawley points out

most of the English moral plays freely combine comic scenes and persons with a serious rendering of life. They commit what Milton has called 'the Poet's error of intermixing Comic stuff with Tragic sadness and gravity; or introducing trivial and vulgar persons.'
"[39]

Whether poetic error or not, *On Shifting Sandshoes* deals with 'vulgar' persons partly because it also grows from TheatreWorks community outreach agenda. One which insisted that these people were not in fact trivial. If the play lacks Shakespearean resonances this is because its genealogy is medieval, not Elizabethan. Radic's post-Renaissance perspective misses the point that *On Shifting Sandshoes* emanates from a tradition two centuries older than Shakespeare and the closed in, disjunctive Elizabethan stage/auditorium tradition. Its intentions are allegorical, not Freudian, bawdy – in a mobile and robust playing style. To answer the initial question therefore: *On Shifting Sandshoes* is a comic farce precisely because it is a morality play. Subtlety was never the point. Like any good morality it also reinforces the idea that the concept of 'sin' marks out a bedrock moral default position beneath which men and women cannot afford to sink without compromising their fundamental humanity. Redemption becomes possible because Bruce's environmental destruction has been checked, Margot's vanity stripped bare, Diane's anger quelled, Sandy's lust unrequited, Raoul's laziness shaken by bankruptcy, and Paula's jealousy extinguished thereby restoring some sort of natural balance both to them as individuals and the place in which they caused took place.

---

[37] Radic, Leonard, "A camping holiday that goes wrong." *The Age* 23 November 1988, Print.
[38] Ellison, Jennifer, Theatre Review *The Bulletin* 6 December 1988, Print.
[39] Op. Cit. (xv)

MELBOURNE'S LOCATION THEATRE MOVEMENT (1979-1994)

Paper for "Melbourne Theatre in the 1980s" Conference
Melbourne University 7/11/2012

Really Moving Drama

Melbourne's Location Theatre Movement 1979 to 1994

Paul Davies   University of Queensland   paulmdavies@bigpond.com

If the 1980s could be said to be bracketed by the assassination of John Lennon in the streets of New York at the beginning, (effectively marking the end of the dream of the 60s) and bracketed at the end, by the fall of the Berlin Wall, (marking the beginning of the nightmare of the New World Order). Which we don't seem to have quite woken up from two decades later.

The 1980s for TheatreWorks, were bracketed by the inauguration of the company in February 1981, and the death of Caz Howard in 1990, whose tragically early passing marked the end of its first iteration.

So I wanted to tell the TheatreWorks story partly to honour Caz's memory - and Peter Sommerfeld's - and all the other theatreworkers we've since lost .To celebrate the achievement of the company they helped found and kept going against all the headwinds.

I also undertook this study because I also wanted to understand the source of that strange kind of exuberance that I'd felt standing in the middle of *Storming Mont Albert By Tram,* on one of its more boisterous nights, my hands covered in tomato sauce (more about that in a moment) the audience hooting with laughter all around me, like over excited sporting fanatics, cheering on certain characters and shouting others down..

It seemed that in those moments we had stumbled on something in the location plays that galvanized spectators like no other theatrical event I'd ever experienced. And I wanted to find out why and how this had come about.

The empowerment of an audience who is in on the joke, and complicit with the actors in a performative occupation of space is a wonderful thing to behold. And it was not only fun to witness and be part of, it was economically viable. *The Tram Show* for e.g. ultimately became self-supporting, playing over a dozen years to some 20,000 passengers in both Melbourne and Adelaide, across around 400 performances and generating in today's figures roughly a million dollars at the box office – while trambulating a distance that would have taken it almost halfway around the world.

It was the location play par excellence and its immediate and enduring popularity was instrumental in leading to an outbreak of similar plays in real places in Melbourne throughout the 1980s that included boats, buses, trams, gaols, houses, pubs, parks and gardens, shopping centres, factories, scout halls, footy club dressing rooms and courts of law.

These were works that now comfortably sit under the rubric of "site-specific theatre" and from all I can discover, they were at the cutting edge of what was happing globally in this field at the time – although the term itself has become problematic – and other descriptors such as these

site-generic, site-responsive, site-sensitive, location, locative, inter-active, space-specific, place-specific, site-based, site-suggestive, environmental, pop-up, immersive, ecological, placial, post-dramatic, live-art, interactive, metadrama, experiential and promenade theatre ?

Sometimes it feels a bit like a bad case of post-dramatic stress disorder…but all these terms also compete to describe what, for the purposes of this paper are essentially spoken word dramas produced in real places, found or otherwise.

While there are important and fine distinctions here between works appropriate to only one site and others that could be staged in a number of similar places, or even plays that are simply given a unique alfresco setting, like the many Shakespeare's in the park or the local quarry.

The more important questions are, I believe: how and why did Melbourne's location plays become so popular with audiences? Plays which were contemporary with other pioneering site specific works by now iconic companies such as Brith Gof in Wales and Necessary Angel in Canada…?

So the goal of this thesis has been to not only document an overlooked chapter in the Australian theatre story, but also to propose a set of critical tools with which we might more appropriately evaluate this new and still evolving form of theatre. In addition to the usual issues surrounding script, performance and direction, matters of authenticity (spatial relations) and complicity (audience relations) also need to be addressed. In other words, we now need to ask, I believe, not only were the script and performances any good, but how convincingly does a particular story inhabit its place of performance, and almost as a consequence, how readily does an audience go along for the ride.

Because, within the frisson that occurs when various social and narrative spaces collide, these qualities of authenticity and complicity shape a whole new set of resonances that open up not only between the actors and their audience, breaking through theatre's fourth wall, but within the audience themselves (what may be called the fifth wall) and between both parties and outside reality sometimes looking back in, which is a kind of sixth wall.

Thus in addition to sight and hearing, these new engagements can theoretically embrace all of our receptive potential, adding touch, taste and smell– and even a kind of sixth sense in what we might call in the absence of better evidence, the pheromone effect. All this can be available to the site-specific practitioner – part of the performative palette.

The 'art of theatre' to use Adolphe Appia's descriptor, is clearly a living thing, and as with any vibrant organism, its processes function in a state of constant evolution, all in response to the narratives, technologies and socio-political zeit or this case S-I-T-E-geist in which it unfolds.

The zeitgeist unfolding around TheatreWorks in the early 1980s, was the Community Theatre movement: the idea of taking theatre out into the suburbs and regions and holding the mirror up as it were, to the lives of ordinary Australians.

Enter a chorus line of 'mohair stockings'...

TheatreWorks' founding members (1980)

This group of unlikely suspects, all recent graduates from the VCA in 1980, (except for Chi who wasn't a voting member although present at most meetings unfortunately), incorporated themselves as a self- governing ensemble officially called The Eastern Suburbs Community Theatre Co (as one director observed, not exactly a monika designed to have people clamoring at the box office). But the group always traded as TheatreWorks and was officially reincorporated as such in 1986.

From interviews with the key surviving players and from my personal observation, Peter Sommerfeld and Caz Howard were very much the initiating partnership -- the spark as it were that set TW flame going, but within the ensemble there was also the very strong feminist triumvirate of Suzi Fraser, Caz and Hannie Rayson -- driving shows such as *Women of Three Generations, Herstory, Mary, Room To Move* etc. But it was always hard for the funding bodies to get their heads around the idea of an 'artistic directorate' and this democratic insistence probably held TW back from general funding for several years.

But right from the start the intention to reach into the suburban heartland and to do it in a non-hierarchical way. To quote from one of the many funding applications:

"to create work which is pertinent to contemporary Australian lives, and to issues at stake". A fairly Brechtian ambition in fact.

BY PAUL DAVIES

The short story is that over the succeeding decade – 1980s -- TheatreWorks, produced by my count, some 28 original plays almost half of which would be classically site-specific --the definitional instability of the term notwithstanding. These are just a handful of the location plays.

This experiment began for TheatreWorks members while they were still students at the VCA with *Fefu and Her Friends* staged in an art deco house in Elwood. It ran on into the 1990s with on-going productions of *The Tram Show* in its final iterations under the banner of The Really Moving Theatre Company.

In creating this body of work the company effectively enacted Artaud's 1930s call to "engulf" the audience. Later, Peter Brook would remove all the clutter by reducing the theatrical act back to its basic triad of performer, onlooker and stage, while Grotowski and Schechner began filling Brook's empty stage by mixing performers and onlookers in a common playing area, albeit still in a purpose-built 'laboratory' setting. What TheatreWorks, WEST, The Mill, Home Cooking, MRPG and other Melbourne and regional Victorian companies did in the early 1980s was take Grotowski and Schecner's experiment out of the laboratory and into the real world. And this is what makes them I would argue, quietly revolutionary. Certainly at the cutting edge internationally.

SOME MELBOURNE SITE-SPECIFIC COMPANIES OF THE 1980s

Year	Company	Play	Location
1979	VCA Women's Group	Fefu and Her Friends	Private House in Elwood
1980	The Mill Theatre	Clyde Company Station	Woolen Mill ?
1981	TheatreWorks	The Go Anywhere Show	Shopping Centres, Parks
1982	TheatreWorks	Storming Mont Albert By Tram	#42 Mont Albert Tram
	WEST	The Cup	Club Rooms ?
1983	TheatreWorks	Breaking Up In Balwyn	MV Yarra Princess
	WEST	Hard Labour Mate	Melbourne Gaol
1984	Home Cooking	Looking In/ Looking Out	Private House
1985	TheatreWorks	The Pub Show	Esplanade Hotel
	WEST	Vital Signs	Nursing Home
1986	TheatreWorks	Living Rooms	'Linden' Acland St.
	Anthill	Macbeth	A Warehouse
1988	TheatreWorks	Storming St. Kilda By Tram	#69 St. Kilda Tram
	Australian Shakespeare Co.	Wind In the Willows	Melbourne Botanical Gardens
1989	TheatreWorks	Full House/No Vacancies	'Linden' Acland St.
	Home Cooking	Edna For The Garden	Fitzroy Gardens
	TheatreWorks	Fabulous Tales	Blessington Gardens
1990	TheatreWorks	Storming St. Kilda By Tram	#69 St. Kilda Tram
	TheatreWorks	Not Waving	Club Dressing Rooms
	Red Shed	In Cahoots	Scout Hall

This is obviously still a work in progress, and curiously, even Austage still doesn't seem to list site-specific theatre as a genre category. There's installation and interactive, and site-specific shows up certain productions…

There were also productions in a magistrates courts such as John Clark and Ross Stevenson's *An Enquiry Into the Lack of Corruption in the Victorian Police Force* and I'm still working on the details there… But the important thing to note is that *Fefu* for example is being produced in an art deco house in Tennyson Street Elwood in 1979 two years before John Krizanc's internationally renowned *Tamara* and even Brith Gof's first site- specific play *Brawen* in Harlech Castle both premiering in 1981.

The point is that in their historical context these plays are not only globally significant, but in their spatial experiment, and the progression of spaces performatively occupied, they reveal a clear aesthetic evolution. Interestingly, most involve some kind of movement of either their stage their audience or both. So along with notions of authenticity and containerization, mobility also becomes a key organizing factor.

If we look at some of the site-specific companies recently active in the UK alone

Towards a Sitegheist ?

Prominent Site-Specific Theatre companies 1980 - 2012

From a growing list and in no particular order (additions welcome):

United Kingdom

National Theatre of Wales, National Theatre of Scotland, Brith Gof (Wales), Wrights and Sites, London Bubble, Out of the Blue (Dance), Red Earth, GridIron (Edinburgh), Forced Entertainment (Sheffield), Shunt, The Whalley Range Allstars, Dream Think Speak, Poor Boy (Scotland), STATION HOUSE OPERA (LONDON), ART ANGEL, Welfare State, International (Cumbria), Cotton Grass (Peak District), Storm (Coventry), Blast Theory (integrating web technology) IOU, Impossible Theatre, Creation Theatre Company (Oxford), Test Department, Hide and Seek, Theatre Absolute, Frantic Assembly, Punchdrunk, Wildworks, Poorboy, DREAMTHINKSPEAK, Lone Twin, Kneehigh (Cornwall) Moving Being, Walk the Plank, PICKLE HERRING THEATRE, Pentabus Theatre, Theatre Nomad, THE LION'S PART (LONDON), The Olimpias, Emergency Exit Arts, Sirens Crossing (Dance), Boilerhouse, Cerberus, The Common Players, Horse+ Bamboo, Kunstwerk-Blend, Riptide, Rotozaza, Foster and Heighes, in situ, Invisible Circus, Slung Low, Wilson+Wilson, Scarabeus Theatre, Coco Loco

As you can see there is a certain post-punk quality to the labeling, and it should be pointed out that not all of these groups are exclusively site-specific, and again, this is still very much a work in progress, but there can be little doubt the epicenter of the S-I-T-E-geist in theatre practice has now shifted to the UK and Europe.

National Theatre of Scotland and Gridiron's *Roam*
Edinburgh Airport (2007)

Scotland's was the first of the UK National theatres to go site-specific with their inaugural production of *Home*. And here they teamed up with another Scottish site-specific company, Grid Iron to produce another show in Edinburgh Airport in 2007.

Now Miwon Kwon and Nick Kaye argue that the European & American examples descend from mimimalism in the visual arts, in particular from performance art, which in itself can trace a genealogy back through political street theatre, happenings of the 1960s, and even the first explosions and Futurism out of the galleries and into the streets, at the beginning of the 20th Century, of DADA – not for the first or last time.

A Wall in Collingwood, Melbourne (1979):

Appropriating public space in *Exits* (47 mins) Davies, Laughren, Howard (198
Mingling real and fictional events on 11/11/1975

Melbourne's Site-specific practice derives as well, I would argue from the practices of independent film making, where dramatic scenes were performed in real places out of budgetary necessity as much as from a desire to appropriate public space for dramatic purposes. In TheatreWorks' case both Caz and I had previously worked on a film about the dismissal of the Whitlam Government

Exits mixed dramatically reconstructed scenes inside a semi-real time documentary account of *les événements* of November 11, 1975. So the idea of performing fictional scenes in real places was really nothing new. The complicating factor was to do it in real time in a properly contained space.

Tents as spatial containers:

TheatreWorks' *The Go Anywhere (within reason) Show*
Group Devised   (1980)

TheatreWorks first technically site-specific production (in the sense that the diegetic space of the story authentically inhabited its place of performance) was the *Go Anywhere (within reason) Show* in 1981.

This play, about a homeless middle class family, was spatially aligned with the place of performance in so far as the Dickens: Dick, Dolly, Darryl, Deidre and Desdemona were allegedly on an extended camping holiday to cover over their desperate financial plight. Thus the shopping centre, or church hall or school in which the Dickens tent was pitched and around which the performance took place, was potentially their place of abode for the night.

Robyn Laurie who directed the play had been witness to *les evenements de Mai 1968* in Europe, had studied Grotowski and Schechner over there and brought back a very physical style to the show, creating larger than life characters in the best *Commedia* tradition. However because of the dispersed nature of audiences in public places such as shopping centres, the element of containerization in *The Go Anywhere Show* was still a work in progress. As in most traditional theatre, audiences remained essentially separate from the action, looking on from outside a performative circle centered in and around the tent. To this extent their subjectivity was more assumed than fashioned.

The quantum leap in forming audience subjectivities was to make them complicit in the action with the performers as fellow passengers on a tram journey and *Storming Mont Albert By Tram* soon became the location play *par excellence*. It had a secure but permeable *container*, it *moved* through a constantly changing landscape, so mobility went with the territory, and the subjectivity of its audience was easily fashioned around their fellow passenger status but could also take on different forms in relation to a random outside gaze looking back in. Again they were in on the joke.

Breaking through theatre's 'sixth wall'

This photo was taken during a publicity shoot at the end of one performance with the cast lined up in the doorway. Traffic rules dictate passing cars must stop to allow passengers to safely cross the road. So the people in the car here somewhat gobsmacked by the odd array of characters popping out of this tram's doorway. This is what I call penetrating theatre's 6th wall.

Trams and busses were not only perfect theatrical containers, being both permeable and safely enclosed, they immediately implicated their audiences as passengers who can follow the action as it happens all around them and as it frequently leaves vehicle to invade the space of the street outside.

Additionally the proximal relations of cast and audience allowed a range of senses to be engaged. To give just two quick examples.

The sense of smell.

Blood on his hands:

(Ticket) Inspector Morris Stanley mistakes tomato sauce for real blood
Storming Mont Albert By Tram   Paul Davies   1982

This is the tomato sauce moment I spoke about before, where the ticket inspector now accidentally stabs the 'derro' character in an inept tussle over a retractable plastic toy knife, originally brought on by the punk. The inspector turns to face the audience with his hands smeared in a red viscous substance. The fact that the audience can already *smell* that it is tomato sauce amplifies their enjoyment of his discomfiture. Their Brechtian subjectivity tells them this is a performance and fake blood is to be expected. However, in a twist on the 'generic credibility' of fake bleeding (as identified by Nevitt 87), this is *really meant to be* tomato sauce, since it stems from the derro's meat pie (put under his coat to keep it warm and accidentally smashed up in there by Morris). As a result, with sauce all over his hands, the 'stage character' Morris acts perfectly within what is generically credible for a theatre performance and 'mistakes' the sauce for blood. The audience experience of this moment comes from the collision of, and disjunction between, all these sensory perceptions. Like an alternating current that creates electricity, complex, sensually rich, information exchanges are taking place as fiction resonates with(in) reality.

Another sense available to the SS practitioner is that of touch.

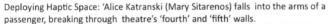
Deploying Haptic Space: 'Alice Katranski (Mary Sitarenos) falls into the arms of a passenger, breaking through theatre's 'fourth' and 'fifth' walls.

'Feelie' theatre or pheromone effect?

Storming Mont Albert By Tram   Paul Davies   1982

When the ticket inspector sacks the 'connie', Alice Katranski, for gross dereliction of duty– specifically, for failing to sell a ticket to the punk character. In her grief, Alice literally throws herself sobbing loudly onto the nearest passenger and that person responds here with what looks like sympathy, tempered by shock and hysterical disbelief that this could actually be happening to her. In fact, the audience member mirrors Alice's surrendering gesture by turning her own cheek onto the 'passenger' next to her, extending the hug. If Diderot's fourth wall in theatre is what separates an audience from the stage, then this moment in *The Tram Show* effectively breaks through a 'fifth wall' that obtains between audience members themselves. In this example therefore, the architecture of the inter-personal correspondence between performer and spectator, and between the spectators themselves, has shifted some distance from that which is normally available in a theatre that privileges vision.

Here a form of Boal's invisible theatre colonized the streets of Melbourne and on one memorable night event intersected with Rod Quantok's equally mobile show *Bus Son of Tram.*

Photo: *Australasian Post*

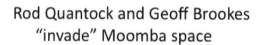

Rod Quantock and Geoff Brookes "invade" Moomba space

This surreal collision on the 26th February 1982 and I can pretty confidently claim that in no other city in the world at this time could the performative spaces of two separate plays collide like this -- like random black holes (or Foucauldian heterotopia) floating through the urban landscape. In a later interview for Really Moving Drama Rod alleges that the encounter was completely accidental but I'm pretty sure he kept his busses waiting for the ambush (it was our opening night) and in any case they blocked the tram tracks.

Text
and
the City

Route for *Storming
St. Kilda By Tram* 1988

Which of course meant that our story couldn't go forward until the tram itself did. Because of course the narrative itself, in another spatial parallel was intimately connected to the streets through which it moved.

What followed was an outbreak of site-specific practice in Melbourne that is only now being replicated in the UK and elsewhere. So in the time remaining just to give you quick overview of the range of shows produced in Melbourne at the time...

River theatre : "A floating piece of space" (Foucault)

MV Yarra Princess

ex-husband

An un-invited ex-husband (disguised as a gorillagram) waiting to gatecrash
Samantha's divorce celebration on board the MV Yarra Princess
Breaking Up In Balwyn   Paul Davies   (1983)

The Boat Show was the third example in the TheatreWorks' location theatre oeuvre
but it had a more artificial quality than its trambulating predecessor and was in much
less immediately contact with the outside world. A river bank is not as accessible to
a party boat as a city street is to a passing tram, and therefore the Boat Show, while
mobile, was much less permeable. Entrances and exits were therefore had to be more
carefully stage managed.

Re-enter the Greek French maid (Mary Sitarenos):

Connecting boat space with riverbank in
Breaking Up In Balwyn   Paul Davies (1983)

Such as the return of the Greek frenchmaid by means of a commandeered rubber dingy after interval.

Part of the problem of *Breaking Up In Balwyn* derives from the play being, in a sense, too "closed in on itself": an island both aesthetically and spatially. It was simply a bit too contained. The premise of the play was that it was a divorce celebration, a kind of inverted wedding party set aboard a boat hired for the occasion. Here the audience's subjectivity was framed by their being the invited friends and family of Samantha and Nigel, the gay divorcee and her new boyfriend.

Samantha (Hannie Rayson) floored by her friends' reception

Breaking Up In Balwyn   Paul Davies   (1983)

The Boat Show applied similar site-specfic strategies to the *Tram* in engaging senses of touch, taste and smell with which to fashion the audience's subjectivity and aid their immersion in the plays events. This involved serving drinks and 'divorce cake', in addition to showing home movies and exploring haptic space by mixing characters and 'guests' in an anti-bridal waltz.

Dancing with the actors:
Nigel takes an audience member for the 'anti-bridal' waltz

Breaking Up In Balwyn   Paul Davies   (1983)

Moving from tents to trams to boats and finally to houses, public and private, the next location play in the TW canon was *Living Rooms* in 1986

Play Houses: Occupying Space and Time

'Linden' at 26 Acland Street, St. Kilda
Members of the Michaelis family pose in their front garden (circa 1900).
Location for *Living Rooms* (1986) and *Full House No Vacancies* (1989)

Here, in contrast to the plays on public transport, the stages remained static while the audience moved. 'Linden', was a once grand Victorian mansion built over a century earlier by Moritz Michaelis, a prosperous leather goods merchant. Later it declined to a 26 room boarding house and by 1986 had been purchased by St. Kilda council for restoration as an art gallery.

In synch with this chronology, the three acts of Living Rooms were each set in one of the large, downstairs rooms, and evoke a key moment in the building's (and the nation's) history. These three periods and the characters that embody them, eventually collide in a surreal denouement (literally a collision of time and space) in the hallway.

Monika rips into Leon in the Hallway

Living Rooms   Paul Davies   (1986)

In this way the house itself becomes a palimpsest for distinctive historical formations and the audience's subjectivity is formed by different methodologies of viewing, casting them variously as ghosts or guests, scrutineers and hidden voyeurs, or simply fellow audience members attending 'a performance art event'.

Farewelling Lt. Deegan for the Boer War: The Drawing Room Act

Audience 'present' as guests at a patriotic send-off.   Photo: Ruth Maddison
Living Rooms   Paul Davies   (1986)

In one act, set during Linden's aristocratic heyday and located in the heterochrony of 1900, spectators were arranged around four sides of an open playing area sitting as largely unacknowledged 'guests' at a farewell party for Lt. Michael Deegan who is about to sail with the second Victorian contingent to the Boer War. The audience are present physically but absent from the narrative at the same time, positioning them within an ambiguous, almost ghost-like point of view: there but not there.

Waiting for Gough to end conscription: The Flatette Act

Audience as agents of
a panoptic gaze
hidden behind a scrim

Photo: Ruth Maddison

Living Rooms   Paul Davies   (1986)

A second act, set during Linden's boarding house iteration, is located within the heterochrony of 1972 on the eve of Gough Whitlam's election as Prime Minister.

Set in a 'Flatette' during Linden's boarding house decline, the audience are positioned behind a light scrim and thus rendered invisible to the actors and cast as agents of a panoptic gaze. In this way their mode of viewing is impeded or filtered, literally, by the scrim. Here they are also present as witnesses, but now in an even more extreme and distancing manner as if looking in on some form of social experiment, like trainee medicos observing an operation, or a team of detectives scrutinizing an interrogation through a one way mirror. Just as the Drawing Room Act delivered a colonial occupation within a heterotopia of elegance and wealth, the prevailing subjectivity in the Flatette is one of unease.

Monika and Leon waiting for a 'live performance' to start:
Actors and audience as fellow art patrons, attending a 'performance art event'

Photo:
Ruth Maddison

Living Rooms   Paul Davies   (1986)

A third act (but not necessarily witnessed in this order) is projected slightly into the future (from 1986) to the Bicentennial Year (1988), where Linden has finally been resurrected from its boarding house decline and transformed into an art gallery (as it currently remains). Here the audience were mixed with actors as fellow attendees at an historical exhibition, a self-described 'location theatre', or performance art event',

This late Twentieth Century make-over of Linden as a public gallery was emblematic of the re-gentrification that the surrounding suburb was currently going through, and which TheatreWorks itself, by virtue of its growing profile, had become a key cultural agent. Consequently, the building itself contained an embedded history within which the fiction of the play could resonate.

Audience perspective in a house in Fitzroy

Home Cooking's
Looking In...Looking Out   Andrea Lemon   (1984)

Two years before Living Rooms , Home Cooking had produced a play in a house in Fitzroy. Here the audience were essentially static but they could witness via windows mirrors and video, scenes that happened both inside and outside the house, in other rooms as well as out in the backyard.

Engaging a sense of smell (creating olfactory space):

The Gershwin Room
Esplanade Hotel
St. Kilda

Audience as fans of a rock and roll band

TheatreWorks'   *The Pub Show*   Peter Sommerfeld, David Swann   (1985)

A year after Looking In, TheatreWorks, by way of introducing itself into the St. Kilda community produced a play in the Gershwin Room of St. Kilda's iconic Esplanade ("Espy") Hotel. Like some local bands of the time *Eat The Rich* achieve a success beyond their ability to cope and here the audience get to watch them implode on stage as they worked their way through a typical pub concert.

Patrolling the liminal spaces between heterotopia

Trevor the pianist and Dug the bouncer in the Gerswhin Room
TheatreWorks' *The Pub Show*   Peter Sommerfeld and David Swann   (1985)

Here again characters were salted in among the audience as bouncers and even a groupie who claims to be pregnant to one of the band members as she quietly tries to sell the audience what looks like drugs.

The success of TheatreWorks' location plays was to establish a practice of site-specific theatre across Melbourne's alternative and community theatre companies (including WEST, MRPG, Gilgul, Home Cooking, The Mill etc. that persisted throughout the 1980s and even continues to this day.

And so to return to the place from whence we came and to perhaps know it for the first time …

Hullo My Name Is...
Nicola Gunn
TheatreWorks, September 2012

I find quite remarkable, that two months ago, three decades after our location theatre experiment started, I was able to attend a TheatreWorks supported event called *Hullo My Name Is...* written and performed by Nicola Gunn. where, upon arrival, I am given my own name tag as a ticket of entry and invested with the assumed role of someone needing to attend a Community Centre (which is what the TheatreWorks space as Parish Hall essentially is).

At one point, armed with a megaphone, Nicola leads us out of the building into the random reality of Acland Street for a short promenade where she reflects out loud to all and sundry on the pain of being an artist, even going down on one knee on the footpath to embellish a point. Back at the 'community centre' (Parish Hall) she singles out and then lies on top of an audience member, engaging haptic space to the maximum by deploying what she calls the 'body blanket' manoeuvre. Then she hands out art materials for a life drawing class and poses for us clad only in her radio microphone, all the while continuing a monologue that relates an unfolding story of love, identity, longing and the pain of loneliness.

Now I readily accept that this might not be everybody's idea of a great night out in the theatre. But I was amused, intrigued, and a little bit shocked (at the body blanket manoeuvre– perhaps more relieved that it wasn't me). I knew I didn't have to take part in any of this unless I really wanted to, and in any case I readily enough found myself holding hands with complete strangers while we all stood with eyes closed in a big circle (But I'm Byron Bay and do a lot of yoga so I'm fairly balance about haptic space – please feel free to hug me at any time. Passionate kisses might have to be negotiated)

In the best traditions of the site-specific genre, *Hullo My Name Is...* is a play about personal isolation that nevertheless creates personal connections not only between Nicola and her audience (at times quite intimately so), but also *within* the audience themselves, again smashing through theatre's fifth wall. As in earlier Theatre Works' plays I became part of a community of the audience, something not available to the individual spectator at a sight-specific event– whether screen based or live. Not surprisingly *Hullo My Name Is...* won the 2012 Fringe Award for best "Experimental Performance."

In summary, the point about all the plays under discussion are :

*They succeed in providing new ways of presenting & experiencing dramatic stories.
*They do this by fashioning different and subtle new subjectivities for their audiences.
*The organizing principles are: containerization, authenticity, complicity and mobility.
*Their proximal engagements also allow the deployment of a range of senses beyond sight and hearing.
*They can unfold in an unlimited number of spatial configurations.

And therefore,

*Offer ever more inventive ways of occupying space for performative purposes.
*They use existing spaces and are therefore relatively inexpensive to put on.
* Consequently, most of the investment goes into people and ideas
(instead of real estate).

Perhaps most importantly, they restore a certain Benjaminian aura to the theatre and the business of popular entertainment generally in an age where the **vision-**privileged/screen-dominated, digital revolution produces only virtual audiences for cyber spaces –the very antithesis of the social spaces under the microscope here.

(Although digital inter-connectivity has already been co-opted as a means of gathering in live audiences for performances. The United Kingdoms' Blast Theory company is internationally recognised known for this kind of work.)

In any case, if the 'art of theatre' is to find new expressivities, if it is going to be more than just a bunch of voyeurs gawking at a mob of exhibitionists, it needs to embrace the site-specific experience and profitably explore the infinite number of ways in which fiction can be playfully staged in real places. Thank you.

SIR DON V THE RATPACK
(Mapping the Performative Geography
of a Latter Day 'Happening') [40]
Paper for Australasian Drama Studies Conference 2009

This paper examines the creation and management of performance space in *Sir Don v. The Ratpack*, an item of agit-prop theatre produced by Mullumbimby's Gorilla Street Theatre (GST) outside the Brisbane Convention Centre on the 26th of November, 2009. The performance was staged to coincide with the Annual General Meeting of BHP Billiton, the world's largest mining company. Staged as a mock press conference, *Sir Don* was produced by a group of actors, activists and filmmakers drawn together by shared concerns about the huge expansion of uranium mining about to take place at Roxby Downs in South Australia. I argue that the 'energy' expressed in the polarised contest between actor/journalists seeking answers and the actor/chairman denying everything, creates a unique space of performance: effectively a heterotopia of alternate ordering. Like much site-specific practice, *Sir Don* is mobile, transgressive, and permeable. It unfolds in real time and its performative space is created and maintained by the act of pointing cameras and microphones towards a concentrated spot (the subject – Sir Don); who is thereby licensed to take this mobile scrum wherever he wants. Like the circle around a fight, this formation of spectatorship and participation can bend and extend, thicken and reform. It can even intercalate with the heterotopia of BHP's AGM: a ritualized, annual gathering of (mostly small) shareholders. *Sir Don* also draws in the social space of the nearby 'real demonstration' – otherwise kept at a distance by a strong police presence. This latter day 'Happening' deploys itself as a third space which mediates the divide between both points of antagonism: effectively bringing the 'real' demonstration *into* the realm of the corporate meeting. An 8 minute video

---

[40] In his seminal work on the subject, Michael Kirby defined a "Happening" as a "purposefully composed form of theatre in which diverse alogical elements, including non-matrixed performing, are organised in a compartmented structure." Michael Kirby, Happenings (New York: E.P. Dutton & Co., Inc., 1965) 21. "Matrixed" performance for Kirby refers to most traditional forms of theatre where characters, narrative, setting etc. are part of an "information structure" (13). "Compartmented for Kirby implies "the arrangement and contiguity of theatrical units that are completely self-contained and hermetic" (13). In the case of *Sir Don* therefore, we are dealing with both matrixed and non-matrixed elements, but *Sir Don* does exhibit 'compartmented structure in the form of the prepared journalists' questions which were rehearsed but asked in random order.

record of *Sir Don* can be viewed at
http://www.youtube.com/watch?v=cDD1q_sjor0 .

TheatreWorks' self-styled 'location plays' of the 1980s were early, local versions of
' site-specific theatre' – narrative dramas that took place in trams, boats, pubs,
houses, shopping centres, parks and gardens. Their immediate and popular success
lead to a breakout of 'location theatre' in Melbourne throughout the 1980s and their
influence can still be seen today.[41] Unlike comparable, contemporary productions
overseas which, according to Miwon Kwon, Nick Kaye and others trace their
genealogy back through minimalism in the plastic arts,[42] TheatreWorks' location
oeuvre came about as a result of specific, local influences, including the practices of
independent filmmakers and the strategies of Victoria's community theatre
movement to place themselves in the regions and suburbs in order to reach out and
find new audiences for theatre. Another influence was the prior participation of
TheatreWorks members in Happenings and street theatre performances in the 1970s

To inform this research and demonstrate the complex interconnectivity of invented
and found spaces that take place in a typical location play for the purposes of this
research, I helped reconstitute a contemporary example: *Sir Don v. The Ratpack.*
This was a largely improvised piece of 'agit-prop' mounted by Mullumbimby's
Gorilla Street Theatre (GST) outside the Brisbane Convention Centre during BHP
Billiton's Annual General Meeting on the 26th of November, 2009.[43] This
performance had elements of both the traditional 'Happening' and the classic site-
specific production.

Created out of the mines in remote Broken Hill, and now owned by shareholders
across the globe, what used to be called "The Big Australian" – BHP Billiton – is
currently the largest mining conglomerate in the world. Aware of a forthcoming
"International Convergence" planned for the corporation's 2009 AGM,
documentary filmmaker David Bradbury, along with a number of people active in
the environmental movement, were keen to promote their concerns about the
consequences of BHP's imminent, massive expansion of uranium mining at Roxby

---

[41] Glen Elston's productions of *Wind In the Willows* and various forest-located
plays of Shakespeare (*A Midsummer Night's Dream, As You Like It*) have enjoyed
a continuous run in Melbourne's Botanical Gardens since the 1980s.

[42] Miwon Kwon, One Place after Another, Site-Specific Art and Locational
Identity (Cambridge, Massachusetts: The MIT Press, 2004) and Nick Kaye, ed.,
Site Specific Art (London: Routledge, 2000).

[43] An 8 minute video record is viewable online:
http://www.youtube.com/watch?v=cDD1q_sjor0 . Viewed 23 February 2012.

Downs. This cohort came together around Mullumbimby's GST troupe with the intention of mounting a 'mock AGM' outside the Brisbane Convention Centre, using an actor to play the retiring chair of BHP, ('Sir') Don Argus. Here was an opportunity to explore how performance space can be produced in the Lefebvrian sense,[44] and then deployed like a Foucauldian heterotopia[45] to interact creatively with the various other social spaces that surround it. This, I argue, is key to reading the appeal and flexibility of place-based performance.

The public space available outside Brisbane's Convention Centre discloses a wide, fan shaped stair case leading up to the entrance. It suggested the layout of a neo-classical Greek amphitheatre and to exploit this historically charged cultural geography I calculated that rather than stage a static board meeting, a more mobile performance piece could start in what would be the 'orchestra' (here the footpath), and flow up through the 'audience space' (the steps) towards the wide glass entrance to the building. The trajectory of such a performance therefore would subvert the normal configuration of the classic model by taking the action from the stage *into* the arena of its reception – a tactic for breaching the fourth wall that some TheatreWorks location plays had also applied.[46]

Drawing on the TheatreWorks experiences it seemed to me that mobility was the key to any successful alternative performance outside BHP's AGM. In an echo of Lefebvre's point about space being produced by the energy deployed within Michel de Certeau describes how " the street geometrically defined by urban planning is transformed into space by walkers".[47]

One way to achieve mobility at the planned International Convergence was, I argued, to constitute a mock door-stop press conference outside the AGM, using 'journalists' instead of 'investor/protesters' at a static board meeting. This would

---

[44] As outlined in Henri Lefebvre's *La Production De L'espace*. Trans. Nicholson-Smith, Donald. (Oxford: Blackwell, 1991) where Lefebvre describes how all human space can be linked to Fred Hoyle's physical theory of space "as the product of energy" 13.

[45] The general theory of heterotopia is outlined in his lecture reprinted as Michel Foucault 'Of Other Spaces', *Diacritics* 16 Spring (1986).

[46] Most notably Peter Sommerfeld's *Dee Jay View* (1984) staged in a former cinema where the dramatic action took place in the raked auditorium, while the audience were seated where the screen would normally be.

[47] Michel de Certeau, The Practice of Everyday Life. Trans. Rendall, S. (London, University of California Press, 1988) 117.

allow the GST troupe to raise the relevant issues (as journalists) and to move all over the steps in any direction dictated by the central interviewee: the actor (Mike Russo) playing 'Sir Don.' After all, mobility as a common element of site-specific performance derives, among other things, from the earlier street theatre need to keep pace with a larger (moving) demonstration, and to minimise arrest, essentially – to move on, but keep performing.

The convention of the door-stop press conference is essentially an improvised (non-matrixed) contest between a random assemblage of paparazzi with their various notebooks and digital recorders on the one hand, and the person they're seeking answers from on the other – the latter sometimes flanked by minders, security, police, lawyers etc. The heterotopia of this performance circle, the social space of a media discourse, is 'created' in the Lefebvrian sense, largely by the act of journalists pointing cameras, questions and other recording devices in the direction of the interviewee, invariably a celebrity, politician, or person of current public interest. Sometimes these 'targets' attempt to hide their identity and avoid the press, in other cases they are happy to promote their own take on events and bask as it were, in the limelight of media attention. Like Lefebvre and de Certeau, Mike Pearson and Michael Shanks agree that "events create spaces"[48] In this case, the 'democratic circle' is something they observe forming around a public fight. This circle is key to understanding the mechanics of any space of contest, with the proviso that, in the mobile press conference scenario, there is generally a single combatant on one side (answering/avoiding questions) and any number of media players (opponents) on the other, throwing the questions out. The live 'audience' for this 'fight' is, in a very direct sense, also deeply implicated as one of the combatants (setting aside the intended audience witnessing these events via the subsequent media and print broadcasts). In most examples of this familiar engagement, the assumption is that the journalists are seeking the truth (or some further complication of the public narrative, a denial, exposure, or trip-up etc.); while the targeted subject aims to subvert the truth or at best avoid making an embarrassing public mistake. Whether this is correct or not, the basic combative nature of the press conference trope gives it its dramatic potential. This allowed the GST troupe to shape a piece street theatre around the kinds of questions people wanted to ask BHP Billiton's chief executive, and thereby draw attention, on a public stage as it were, to the environmental consequences normally glossed over by both the company, and an often compliant or disinterested media.[49]

---

[48] Mike Pearson, Michael Shanks. *Theatre/Archaeology* (London: Routledge, 2001) 21.

[49] As Queensland's disgraced former premier, Sir Joh Bejlke-Peterson famously boasted, attending a press conference for him was like "feeding the chooks," a not-so-covert reference perhaps to its acknowledged disinformative function.

Over a number of rehearsals the environmental impact of BHP's activities world-wide was analyzed and potential questions workshopped as the beginning of a 'text' (matrix) for the performance. This involved researching the mining industry generally, and uranium extraction in particular, so that eventually the issues to be dealt with could be organized thematically under headings like: 'Toxic Dust', 'Yellowcake,' 'Water Pollution,' 'Global Warming,' 'Legal Issues,' 'Effects on Indigenous Populations,' 'Industrial Relations,' 'Health and Safety,' 'Nuclear Proliferation,' etc.[50]

It was resolved that each 'journalist' would take a set of questions relating to one of these themes and fire them at the hapless 'Sir Don' in random order, much like real journalists would do in the circumstances (since most journalists and their media organizations often have not-so-hidden agendas anyway). Thus, as a rudimentary 'script' developed, characters within the Ratpack were designated as the 'Personal journo' (Don Argus, the real chair of BHP, was about to retire), the 'Yellowcake journo,' the 'Legal journo,' the 'Water journo,' 'Indigenous Affairs journo,' and so on. Meanwhile Sir Don, in the time honoured tradition of such events, would give a set of standardized, fairly meaningless, bland and ineffectual replies – literally dodging questions as he worked his way up towards the entrance to the Convention Centre (while maintaining the illusion that he was in fact the chairman of this vast multi-national en route to its AGM). Such a tactic allowed Mike Russo and Scott Davis (playing Sir Don and his minder) to lead the Ratpack virtually all over the steps, up or down, as the impromptu 'press conference' went where ever it felt like. In this way, Mullumbimby's GST plotted to get its message across to any interested shareholders arriving for the meeting and perhaps even to draw in the 'legitimate' media, and hence score points in the even greater contest for media 'space' on the evening news.

Applying Lefebvre's contention that social space can be generated by the energy deployed within it, the space of the moving press conference is thus 'vectored' into being by the focus that multiple cameras and other recorders have when they are all pointed towards the same person. Another way of expressing this is to say that energy itself originates with the interaction of polar opposites (points of alternate ordering). To return again to the metaphor of Physics, electricity for example, is created by an interchange between positive and negative terminals (direct current) or spinning magnets (alternating current). The polar opposites involved in a meta/physical confrontation, such as GST's 'press conference,' are the combatants

---

[50] Some of this material included publications such as: Friends of the Earth. BHP Billiton Alternative Annual Report: Undermining the Future (n. pub., 2009).

themselves. In the adversarial stance taken, lies the 'charge' that is required to 'detonate' performative space into being. All fights whether staged or impromptu (matrixed or non-matrixed) are also a kind of performance, with narrative through lines, moments of tension, physical engagement, and sweaty endings. Even common military parlance, language of the ultimate pugilists, speaks of a *"theatre of operations."*

Pearson and Shanks outline the spatial forces at work here.

> As a fight breaks out the crowd parts, steps back, withdraws to give the action space. Instantly they take up the best position for watching, a circle. It's democratic, everyone is equidistant from the centre, no privileged viewpoints. There may be a struggle to see better but the circle can expand to accommodate those who rush to see what's happening. Or it thickens. A proto-playing area is created, with an inside and outside, constantly redefined by the activity of the combatants, who remain three dimensional...The size and ambiance of the space are conditioning factors. Then just as quickly the incident ends, the space is inundated by the crowd and there are no clues what to watch. [51]

After 15 seconds of opening credits on the YouTube video,[52] the performance of *Sir Don v. The Ratpack* is inaugurated at the 18 second mark by the 'Personal Journo' with the line "There he is!" pointing towards where Sir Don and his minder are just arriving on foot. As Steward advises "[h]ave an elastic beginning for your script, allowing time for a crowd to gather". [53]Clearly, the GST budget did not stretch to the provision of a limo for Sir Don's arrival and anything less would have undermined the all important element of *authenticity*. Consequently, this opening line was designed to draw attention to Sir Don's arrival on foot and act as the trigger point for other 'Journos' who at this point just happened to be milling around nearby in small, discrete groups. This allowed the GST actors to remain initially distinct and separate from the larger demonstration which was kept well behind police lines in the background. If GST's performance of *Sir Don* had

---

[51] Theatre/Archaeology 21

[52] This opening sequence was not generated by GST directly. Instead it includes footage of the evacuation of a nearby office building – part of a fire-drill – that just happened to occur immediately after the live performance of *Sir Don* a few blocks away.

[53] Dwight. Steward, Stage Left (Dover, Delaware: The Tanager Press, 1970) 21

originated from within this larger, real demonstration kept at some distance by the police it is doubtful that it would ever have made it even to the intended starting point at the bottom of the steps. In this sense, the heterotopia of the performance was able to carve out its own spatial niche separate from the other, larger events taking place (the heterotopias of the real demonstration and that of the AGM).

The effect of the opening line delivered by the 'Personal Journo' was to identify the character playing 'Sir Don' and thereby draw the rest of GST's Ratpack into play as the constructed space of the press conference starts to gather shape out of the 'energy' of the oppositional performances brought into being on the footpath. Within a few more seconds the first questions about Sir Don's imminent retirement are fired by the 'Personal Journo' and the video cuts to a high shot looking down (22 second mark).

Figure 1.
Members of GST's 'Ratpack' confront 'Sir Don' upon his arrival.
A giant white elephant of the 'real' demonstration can be seen in the background (top right).[54]

Figure 1 shows the 'Ratpack' initially forming as a circle around the be-suited Sir Don and the minder to his immediate left: the 'Ghost of Peter Garrett.'[55] This

---

[54] Traditional street theatre tactics also employed large, hard-to-ignore puppets to make concise political points.

[55] Peter Garrett was Federal Minister for the Environment at this time and in his previous career as a rock musician had famously produced many political and environmental protest songs of his own.

uncanny player was also a archetypal accompaniment to the cult of celebrity: the private 'body' guard/personal minder. Everybody present seemed to understand and accept 'Peter Garrett's' role immediately, including the police and other security personnel, none of whom questioned the legitimacy of this character's silent but intimidating presence – a composite of his sunglasses, mysterious briefcase and small earphone – apparently connecting him to a larger, over-arching panoptic space of surveillance. As the 'press conference' makes its way up the steps it starts to draw in players outside the GST troupe, including BHP officials, glimpsed in a somewhat flummoxed state in the background (and no doubt wondering who this important person is). Indeed, at the 30-40 second mark a man in a light coloured coat, apparently connected to BHP and obviously concerned that one of his VIPs has been unintentionally accosted by the press contingent, seems to be voluntarily attaching himself to 'Sir Don's' security detail.

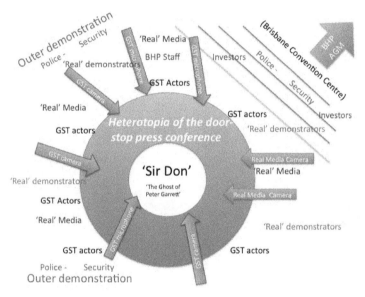

Figure 2..

A Map of the performative geography of *Sir Don v. The Ratpack*

Figure 2 shows how performance space is created in *Sir Don* using cameras and microphones which focus the outer edges of the circle towards the centre. In this way the arena of the press conference, with Sir Don marking its centre point, is given precedence over other spaces (such as the real demonstration nearby, and the AGM inside the Convention Centre). However, the journey of *Sir Don v The Ratpack* as a piece of agit-prop is precisely to move from the realm of the demonstration *into* the alternately ordered space of the AGM, illustrating Foucault's point about the permeability of heterotopia.[56]

At 1 minute 30 seconds into the video record other participants in the demonstration, 'real demonstrators', apparently ignorant of the nature of the constructed 'performance' occurring, are also drawn into the press conference, including an indigenous activist immediately behind Sir Don. After questions about the water supply for Roxby Downs (1 minute 40 seconds), questionable practices involving the military in West Papua working on behalf of BHP (2 minutes 30 seconds), carbon neutrality (3 minutes), BHP's toxic legacy (3 minutes 30 seconds) and nuclear proliferation, the subject turns to yellow cake – a refined form of uranium ore. By now the 'democratic' circle encasing Sir Don has grown considerably and forms an unbroken loop around him. At the 4 minute mark, Sir Don makes a weak joke about how he "wouldn't mind some yellow cake with his morning tea" since he's "feeling a bit peckish" and draws a suitably disgusted response from some of these genuine activists.[57]

At the 4 minute 30 second mark, some of these 'real demonstrators,' whether aware of the larger pretence or not, start throwing their own questions at the hapless 'Sir Don'. One asks about environmental destruction and social dislocation. At this point all three social spaces present around the Convention Centre, GST performers, real demonstrators, and attendees at the AGM are now sharing the same frame. The collision of heterotopia is therefore complete.

As this roiling intercalation of separate social spaces with their separate agendas, moves randomly towards the doors of the AGM, like Pearson and Shank's circle round a fight, the shape of the press pack expands and contracts, elongates into an ellipse then spreads lengthways up the steps as journalists and onlookers jockey for a better view or greater access to questioning – shape shifting but always focused on Sir Don. By the 5 minute 20 second point 'Sir Don' (no doubt surprised that he had managed to get this far), calls to his minder and together they step blithely through the police line guarding the front doors into the space of the official AGM. By this stage most of the real demonstrators have peeled off assuming, not unreasonably, that their entrance would be blocked. However, the constructed space of GST's

---

[56] 'Of Other Spaces': 26.

[57] Indeed, as soon as the circle of the press conference began forming on the footpath there were loud boos and hisses directed at 'Sir Don' *and* GST's Ratpack. Clearly, from the point of view of the 'real demonstration' both Media pack and Company representatives were perceived to embody two halves of the same problem.

door stop press conference, having gone through this crucial portal, now superimposes itself (collides) into its oppositional place of ordering: the foyer area of BHP Billiton's AGM. Although the ranks of the 'Ratpack' are now thinning, a determined few maintain their hot pursuit, their private, internal anxieties about getting this far reflected in the nervous question framed by the "Radiation/Health Journo at 5 minutes 40 seconds.

Questions about the health of BHP's workers continue as the mock press conference hovers under signs welcoming shareholders into the meeting and visually trumpeting the company's many achievements. Clearly, by this stage, GST's constructed heterotopia has gone about as far as it can and matters reach a climax as the questions turn to 'Sir Don's' own health. This was the designated trigger question to end the performance. At six minutes 30 seconds, as he tries to answer, Sir Don appears to suffer some kind of breathing difficulty, and asking for water, soon collapses to the ground, causing another layer of confusion (7 minutes) as real doctors (including anti-nuclear activist Dr. Helen Caldicott – also an investor/protestor) start discussing the need to call an ambulance (Figure 3).

Figure 3.
Sir Don 'collapses' inside the space of the AGM and is attended by doctor-shareholders

By now the heterotopia of the mock press conference as superimposed itself on the space of the AGM and at this point the Happening comes to an oddly anti-climactic denouement as Sir Don, (doubtless sensing the problems that could flow from a real ambulance being summoned), soon miraculously recovers, gets to his feet, and calmly walks back out of the building through its glass doors. Again, as Pearson and Shanks predict, the spectatorship gathered around a fight can just as effortlessly fade away – as happens here. "The incident ends, the space is inundated by the crowd and there are no clues what to watch".[58] Clearly the performative space created by the Happening can evaporate just as readily as it is formed.

In truth, nobody in Mullumbimby's GST imagined the ruse would work so convincingly that Sir Don and the combined Ratpack would be able to simply walk past a vigilant police line and enter the foyer of the building where the audience for the AGM was already gathering. This other audience, now drawn into GST's invasion of their space, consisted of a constellation of small investor/shareholders, fund managers, corporate staff, police and security personnel. There was clearly risk involved at this point in the form of bringing in real emergency services. As TheatreWorks location plays also demonstrate, problematic issues are always present when fictional elements are inserted into real locations and distinct social situations. Fortunately, the performance of *Sir Don* ended before anything untoward happened, or real emergency services became involved. But that concern was there. In this case, Dwight Steward's warning about having a definitive conclusion to one's street theatre performance clearly applies.[59] The collision of created spaces (mock press conference into AGM) becomes fraught as a result of the intervention of real people (doctors in fact) confronting from their point of view, a real (medical) problem.

Having previously only glimpsed this problem of a conclusion, I recall suggesting that Sir Don should have a penultimate light-bulb moment when the torrent of questions about the palpable damage done by his company would see him undergo a 'road-to-Damascus' moment and admit to the error of his ways, precipitating some kind of personal crisis. And although Sir Don's collapse *was* taken seriously at the time by those present who were not party to the pretence, this sort of narrative conclusion seemed rather 'in-authentic' and fairly unlikely, given both the character involved and in the context (and it was). And so GST's management of the space of its mock press conference worked to expectations in terms of the questioning and the drawing in of other demonstrators, investors, staff and security, but it failed Steward's important test of providing a convincing or satisfactory exit from the scene.

Applying a new critical toolkit.

---

[58] *Theatre/Archaeology* 21.

[59] *Stage Left* 24.

This raises the question of how *Sir Don v. The Ratpack* measures up in terms of the main set of assessment items proposed for site-specific theatre in my doctoral thesis *Really Moving Drama* .

> *Authenticity.* That the performance had an aura of authenticity is reinforced by the ease with which onlookers and other players were so readily drawn in to the ruse. A door stop press conference involving some important person is entirely to be expected around the fringes of events like the Annual General Meeting of a major corporation. All the props, cameras and recorders, were genuine and mostly working.

> *Site Generic or Site Specific.* Although the action was planned for this specific convergence of forces and personalities and was designed with BHP Billiton in mind, it is possible that a similar piece of street theatre could take place outside, or on the fringes of, equivalent corporate or political gatherings. The form of the press conference could similarly be used to illustrate partisan points in an ongoing discourse.

> *Appropriate in Other Settings?* It follows from item ii that staging a mock press conference would be appropriate in any setting where media are expected to gather.

> *Mobility.* Above all this was perhaps the key element in the conception and execution of *Sir Don*. The constant moving about of journalists and subject, the hankering, restless, nervous deployment of cameras and microphones, the urgency of the questions (time is money), all mimicked what happens in a real door stop press conference. These temporary media events are *expected* to move. This adds to the performance a measure of danger and unpredictability.

> *Relations between performers, audience, and outside world.* As can be seen from the video record the relations between the GST performers and their target audience – the real media and the BHP investors attending the AGM, was fluid and intermixed. As the event proceeds all these parties become involved. In the wake of the performance a number of national television articles referring to it appeared in at least two newspapers.[60] To this extent some elements of the intended

---

[60] (Tony Grant-Taylor, 'BHP Predicts Strong Demand for Coal Sales', *Courier Mail* (27 November 2009): 78 and the author, "BHP Billiton Hit by Gorilla attack', *The Byron Shire Echo* (1 December 2009): 17

story were promulgated to a much wider audience than those present around the Convention Centre.

Proximate or Ubiquitous? In the course of *Sir Don,* emotions run high in a quite tight circle that forms around the main character and his minder. Although, in the tradition of the door stop, Sir Don and the ghost of Peter Garrett are given due deference and kept in the centre of the action. This engagement then became ubiquitous as it spread in a wide trajectory up and around the steps of the Convention Centre towards the entrance.

Active or Passive Audience Role. Some onlookers remained passive (one suspects they were investors or neutral by-standers), others, obviously more politically committed, became quite active as they began to throw in their own questions. As we saw in some cases they also became quite upset with Sir Don's flippant responses.

Transgression and Complicity. The performance clearly transgressed a police line designed to protect the larger board meeting from any attempt at disruption. In this sense the mock press conference and its various hangers-on, became complicit in a strategy to occupy space they were officially prohibited from.

Permeability of Spaces. As the action proceeds the space of the real demonstration blends into the space of the mock conference, which in turn moves into the foyer of the Convention Centre and mingles with the periphery of the AGM. The problem identified above in relation to ending the performance occurs inside the Convention Centre's foyer where the invented space of the door stop effectively fizzles out for lack of narrative content (i.e. contest/questions).

Other Senses. No other senses were involved apart from sight and hearing although a certain amount of jostling and jockeying for position (haptic) space was involved in the constitution of the media ring, with various 'journalists' cramming together for optimal viewing and interrogating space.

Real Time Setting. Consistent with most site-specific productions, the action unfolded in real time and lasted for approximately 15 to 20 minutes in total. The video record is therefore an edited version containing about half the total exchange that took place. This length surprised the GST participants since in most rehearsals, the improvised questioning on various rehearsal staircases rarely ran to more than 5 minutes.

With the exception of the unresolved, potentially risky and odd ending, *Sir Don v The Ratpack*, satisfies most of the criteria required for a reasonably successful site-specific Happening. Its usefulness as a example of street theatre was recognized by at least the editors of the *Byron Shire Echo*.[61] It also succeeded in getting its anti-nuclear message across into at least a few of the mainstream media outlets present.

In summary, the 'heterotopia' of a performance space, can be created merely through the focused energy of a performance. The challenge lies in managing that space once it has been 'produced'. This brings into play the relationship between such a space and all the spaces, imagined or real, that surround it. The permeability of these various other spaces ensures that collisions and exchanges (of energy, people, narratives) is almost certain to take place. This gives site-specific performance both its special potential and its most serious limitation: the possibility that the underlying deception can be problematic. Controlling risk through the intercalations and superimpositions that occur when a play is produced on location is perhaps the most important criteria for spatial management. And if public liability requirements are to demarcate an official limit to some forms of site-specific practice, then management of risk becomes even more crucial.

---

[61] In the edition following the International Convergence, *Sir Don* is described in GST's hometown local paper as "one of the most effective and entertaining forms of protest" *The Byron Shire Echo* (1 December 2009): 68.

"THE WRECK"
or
"THAT SINKING FEELING..."

Treatment for a 1920s melodrama staged 'on location'
in the Cape Byron lighthouse precinct*
7/12/2012

(Photo *Time and Tide*)
Figure 1. The S.S. Wollongbar washed up on Bilongil Beach,
Byron Bay, circa May 1921.

*Based on the workshop: 'Fieldnotes for Performance' by Noelle Janaczewska
Held at the Geoffrey Rush Theatre, University of Queensland 23/8/2012

Miranda.

> If by your art, my dearest father, you have
> Put the wild waters in this roar, allay them.
> The sky it seems would pour down stinking pitch,
> But that the sea mounting to the welkin's cheek,
> Dashes the fire out. O, I have suffered
> With those I saw suffer ! A brave vessel,
> Who had no doubt some noble creature in her,
> Dashed all to pieces ! O, the cry did knock
> Against my very heart! Poor souls, they perish'd...

Prospero

> Be collected;
> No more amazement ; tell your piteous heart
> There's no harm done...
> The direful spectacle of the wreck, which touch'd
> The very virtue of compassion in thee,
> I have with such provision in mine art
> So safely ordered that there is no soul—
> No, not so much perdition as an hair
> Betide to any creature in the vessel
> Which thou heard'st cry, which thou saw'st sink.

The Tempest. Act I Scene II

Background

Like the shipwreck in *The Tempest*, there was no loss of life when the mini-liner, the S.S. Wollongbar, pride of the North Coast Steam Navigation Company, foundered off Bilongil beach in Byron Bay on the wild and stormy night of the 14th of May, 1921. Fortunately, only its cargo of butter, bacon and bananas was lost.

"Wollongbar" is a local, Bundjalung word meaning "hole in the ground" and was clearly not a very propitious title for modern steamships, given that the Wollongbar II, quickly built in Scotland as a replacement for the ill fated Wollongbar I, was also sunk, this time by a Japanese torpedo off Crescent Head in 1942.

Shakespeare's play was similarly inspired by an actual shipwreck,[62] and like many lighthouse stories, *That Sinking Feeling* also involves at its core, a pivotal and troubled relationship between a father and his (wayward, headstrong, brave, independent, self-willed) daughter.[63]

This project is projected to encompass a merging of 'tourist-theatre' with site-specificity in performance practice. Over time, the play could be remounted to coincide with peak holiday seasons, and become, like many popular location plays, ultimately self-supporting (think London's *Mousetrap*). The intention here is to fashion a 1920s style melodrama (think Noel Coward), and produce it in a building authentically related to that time and story. In this way *That Sinking Feeling* would take its audiences of traveller/tourists on a (literal) journey back through Byron's remarkably colourful history to the night of one of its most dramatic events: the foundering of the S.S. Wollongbar off Bilongil beach. Here the ship's structural skeleton, known locally as "the Wreck", remains today like a waterlogged 'ghost vessel' – an uncanny from the past that continues to haunt an unknowing present... *That Sinking Feeling* seeks to lift the veil and produce a more knowing audience...

EXEGESIS

---

[62] In Shakespeare's case (and in another demonstration of how the conquest and occupation of space in the New World furnished the imagination of the Elizabethans), the *Tempest* is said to have been inspired by the 1609 wreck of the Sea Venture, carrying the newly appointed Governor of Virginia, Sir Thomas Gates, to his posting in the North American colony. Fortunately, his honour was later found alive and well, washed up and semi-marooned in the Bermudas. This connection is outlined in *Shakespeare's Comedies* Peter Alexander ed. London. Collins. 1951: 27. Print.

[63] Despite the title, *That Wreck* as a new site-specific play, will be more a combination of House and Bus Shows than anything relating specifically to action on boats. My current doctoral research into TheatreWorks' location plays of the 1980s and their implications for theatre practice going forward convinces me that site-specific theatre today stands on the cusp of some exciting breakthroughs. It offers the 'art of theatre' novel and popular ways for engaging audiences across a range of senses and sensitivities, providing experiences unmatched by mechanically or digitally reproduced drama (film internet etc.).

In addition to discoveries made in the course of my research for *Really Moving Drama*,[64] the idea for *That Sinking Feeling*, and its potential staging strategies, also derive from a workshop conducted by Noelle Janaczewska at the University of Queensland in August 2012. This looked at creating performance from 'writerly' investigations into landscape.

In her introductory notes to the workshop, Noelle drew attention to the notion of 'psychogeography' which she "think[s] of as the writer as walker" [65]. In a web published example of psychogeography, Will Self describes a plane trip from London to Glasgow with amusing complaints every traveller will recognise, offering self-reflexive moments superimposed over an meditation on the nature of plane travel.[66] W.G. Sebald's novel, *The Rings of Saturn*, also recommended by Noelle, is essentially a long and rambling walk through coastal East Anglia, whose various buildings and landscapes project the walker/subject into a range of interconnectivities between history, people and place.

These two examples of "writers walking" provide a strategy for enacting a site-specific play in the present moment, while locating its narrative heterotopia and, what Foucault would call its associated 'heterochrony',[67] in another time period. Psychogeography potentially therefore, allows an audience to view (re)enacted historical events through the lens of the present (as created by actor/guides in character and framed by the found architecture of the place of performance).

Joanne Tompkins notes that *Suitcase*,[68] a play notionally set in the 1930s, was produced quite successfully in present day Liverpool Street Station, London. The play commemorated the 70th anniversary of the Kindertransport, the emergency evacuation of Jewish children out of Nazi Germany just prior to the Second World War. The performance presented the stories of some of those children who passed through this very station (in the 1930s timeframe), while the busy modern transport hub continues to swirl around them. Here is a site specific work in which, as Tompkins shows, the intercalation of distinct historical moments *into* the present, becomes not only possible and plausible, but as a result of the disjunction of these

---

[64] Davies, Paul. *Really Moving Drama*. Brisbane: University of Queensland: Fryer Library 2013. PhD Thesis (pending). This thesis principally focuses on TheatreWorks location plays of the 1980s

[65] Janaczewska, Noelle "Fieldnotes for Performance" 23/8/2012. TS. In my personal case, the fieldnotes for *That Sinking Feeling* derive from the writer as cyclist.

[66] Self, Will. Psychogeography – London to Glasgow, *The Independent*, London 29/12/2007. Available on line at http://www.independent.co.uk/voices/columnists/will-self/will-self-psychogeography--london-to-glasgow-766092.html (accessed 28/11/2012)

[67] Foucault, Michel. "Of Other Spaces." *Diacritics* 16. Spring (1986): 22-27. Print.

[68] Tompkins, Joanne. Theatre's Heterotopia and the Site-Specific Production of Suitcase *TDR: The Drama Review: A Journal of Performance Studies* 56. 2 [T214] (2012 Summer): 101-112.

temporal and narrative overlays and correspondences, *actually heightens* the temporal and placial resonances – adding to, and enhancing the total experience.

The notion of psychogeography derives from a group of left intellectuals and activists known as the Situationist International, and is best expressed in the work of Guy Debord. His idea of "constructing situations" is something which resonates with current site-specific theatre practice.[69] It seems perfectly in keeping that the Situationist International can itself can trace a genealogy back to the radical occupations of public and private spaces conducted under the banners of Dada and Futurism, and became a key ideological player itself in *les événements de May 1968.*

The challenge with *That Sinking Feeling* will be to fashion the subjectivity of its audience as "witnesses" to the historical events the play seeks to portray. A further reference suggested by Noelle, is Tim Etchells' *Certain Fragments,* an account of his company Forced Entertainment, the British site-specific group best known for its Bus Show, *Nights in This City.* Etchells notes that the formation of the idea of witness is "present everywhere in the contemporary performance scene" and "leaves us above all, unable to stop thinking, talking, reporting what we've seen…borne on by our responsibility to events"(18).[70] *Nights in This City* (and its predecessor in Melbourne, Rod Quantock's *Bus, Son of Tram*) offers a solution to the problem of getting the audience up to the lighthouse (with its limited parking space) and also an opportunity to engage in the psychogeographic exercise of having a tour guide/character overlay the passing landscape with descriptions of how it used to be, including the recounting of certain key incidents: the destruction of the two jetties, an attack by a pack of sharks leaping "like AFL players" at the strips of blubber hanging off harpooned whales as they're hauled ashore. Then the sharks turn on each other as they are hit by bullets fired by a whaler with a rifle, shooting into the pack to discourage them from destroying the Humpback…

This brief overview of the town's history could also touch on the radio-toxic legacy of sandmining, and the equally calamitous use of DDT in the cattle industry. There are stories about the many burnings down and rebuildings of the many hotels, of the night a humpback whale slithered down the main street, having slipped off a railway wagon –
adding considerably to the already heightened dislocation of drinkers exiting the nearby Pier Hotel.

A short (mobile) history of 'The Bay'

The initial ride up to the lighthouse therefore, provides a lens for uncovering Byron's diverse and at times, bizarre history. The account would start with its

---

[69] See Guy Debord. *The Society of the Spectacle.* New York: Zone Books, 1994.
[70] Etchells, Tim. *Certain Fragments Contemporary Performance and Forced Entertainment.* London: Routledge, 1999. Print. Etchells refers specifically to the characters in Brecht's poem who are witnesses to a traffic accident and stand around discussing what happened (18).

evolution as a Dreamtime Eden for the Bundjalung, through to the era of colonial exploitation and deforestation, the spread of the banana and dairy farms across a formerly pristine rainforest, appearing in patches first cleared by the cedar getters. This was quickly followed by an economic crisis when those soils were quickly depleted. Always, there is the boom/bust economy. This includes the coming and the closing of the economies of whaling and sandmining. Mainly the cattlemen prospered. But later their abattoir sites would be ritually cleansed by a Buddhist monk and new era would dawn in the bay. This saw the coming of alternative 'lifestylers' with their counter-cultural ambitions, and their dreams of self-sustainability. Here was an era of once again (following in an ancient local tradition), of treading lightly on the landscape. Alas, this (re)discovery of the magic within the place in itself triggered another era of excessive success, destroying the whole point of being 'here' in the first place. This is present era of the young traveller, the 'backpackers' who arrive by their hundreds in an age of jumbo jets. And so once again, a delicate balance is shifting out of kilter... the dream clouds again.

One question framing this inquiry as a dramatic work might then be: at what point and for what reasons, does a local community attitude shift from that of exploitation (the era of colonialism) back to nurture and regeneration (the era of self-sustainability, pre- and post-colonial). Thus, the attitudes of the characters in the play, at the historical moment of 1921, can be display micro examples of the larger shift in social attitudes. This includes outspoken female characters influence by the emerging feminist consciousness of the suffragette movement (in essence over women's right to vote). In this way the audience might even be taken down a moral path.

As Etchells points out in his account of Forced Entertainment's Bus Show

Nights In This City (1995) was a guided tour of the city [Sheffield] with its audience and performers on board a bus – a guided tour which avoided facts in search of a different truth. Slipping through the centre of the city and out of control – off the beaten path, playing always to the difference between on-route and off-route, centre and periphery, legitimate and illegitimate. Playing always to the different histories written in urban space – the official historical, the personal, the mythical and the whole city as a sounding board. (80-81)

All this and more is possible with such an iconic and historically significant place like Byron Bay. The 'guide character' in *That Sinking Feeling,* a key player in moulding and maintaining the community of the audience, is Dorothy "Dotty" Hunter, the wife of the Main Lighthouse Keeper, a spiritualist and leading member of the local Theosophical Society, with an uncanny ability to channel key figures from the past along with their memories of Byron's earlier days. 'Dotty' by name and dotty by nature, her waywardly guided tour up to the lighthouse precinct becomes a kind of mobile 'séance which carries the audience from the mundane via the historical, up to the "special world" at the top of the cape: the heterotopia of May 14, 1921.

Equally, the bus trip back down to town at the end of the performance can function as a kind of epilogue to the events just witnessed in and around the Lighthouse, an accounting by Dotty again of how the characters all ended up, a kind of future projection on to the site-specific narrative just witnessed, offering the wisdom of hindsight. This circularity of bus trips up and back, the rounding of the narrative journey with a literal journey, in a sense mimics the circularity of the turning light beam itself, an emblem of both unconditional protection (providing safety for all) and of 'enlightenment' in all its forms and connotations, the symbolic source of something higher and other.

The Lighthouse

(Photo: Annette Flotwell)
Figure 2. Cape Byron Lighthouse

A concrete block tower built in 1901 (the same year as the federation of the Australian Colonies), Cape Byron's iconic lighthouse features widely on innumerable cards, posters and photographic representations of the town. Its light shines through French crystal set in British steel, currently boasting the strongest light beam in Australia. The mechanism which weights a total of four and half tons is too heavy to stop so it is kept constantly turning in a bed of 850 pounds of mercury.[71]

---

[71] Ryan, Maurice and Robert Smith. *Time and Tide Again, A History of Byron Bay*. Lismore: Northern Rivers Press 2001. Print. 59.

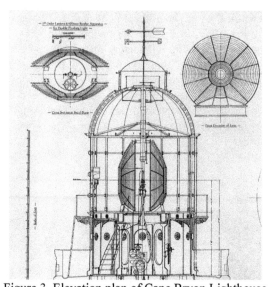

Figure 3. Elevation plan of Cape Bryon Lighthouse
showing light mechanism and circular balcony
NSW Dept of Public Works. (National Archives of Australia; A10182,CN 02 047)

Performatively speaking, the lighthouse building offers balcony spaces for the formal addresses (by a superior class) as if looking down from a symbolic castle (with its faux parapets), onto a crowd gathered below. Internally, two small rooms frame a remarkable spiral staircase, as well as a circular external parapet at the top. Off to one side is the signal box building which housed the flags used for semaphore signalling (also a possible site for dramatic action).

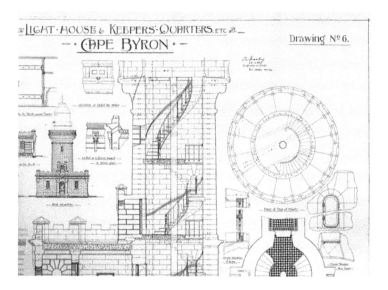

Figure 4. Cape Byron light house interior showing the circular stairwell, including side elevations and plan view of tower. (National Archives)

Byron Bay in 1921 [72]

Figure 5. Jonson Street Byron Bay circa 1921.

Byron Bay in 1921 seems reminiscent of some small, recently built town in the American West. I imagine the five musicians (centre left) still carrying their instruments (having just arrived on the Wollongbar from Sydney), are taking a stroll down the main street looking for refreshment or accommodation, or the pub where they're going to perform that night....

At the time in which the play is set (1921) the town of Byron Bay had a population of 1700 with another 3000 in the surrounding district. [73] Thanks to its jetty and a relatively calm, north-facing bay, it had become a major sea port on the New South Wales Coast. However it still lacked basic infrastructure such as electricity, decent roads, sewerage etc. It was essentially a pretty shabby industrial town with a working class population to service the local dairy factories, sawmills and abattoirs. There was some small tourist activity catered to by the various hotels, but the town was a long way from becoming the tourist Mecca that it is today. The period setting of the play would be established through performative style (a melodrama typical of the period) as well of course, by costumes worn by the cast as well as the 'set design' of the Main Cottage's rooms – the building itself being innately historically authentic.

---

[72] For most of the historical references here I draw on *Time and Tide*.
[73] *Time and Tide*. 67.

Staging strategies for relating story (shipwreck/daughter) to place (lighthouse).

As outlined in my research for *Really Moving Drama,* authenticity (spatial relations) and complicity (audience relations) are key elements in creating the diegetic (or narrative) world of any site-specific play. This fabricated social space, in line with Foucault's (and later Heathertington's) notion of the heterotopia, works as a place of 'alternate ordering' by being both permeable and contained at the same time.[74] I argue that what location theatre demonstrates for heterotopia is how the balance of these opposites can be kept in play by mobility (of audience or stage or both).

The Cape Bryon light house can therefore be *authentically* engaged as a site of action for the sinking of any ship in the Bay in 1921. Actors extend the connection by mimicking the mores and protocols of early Twentieth Century settler behaviour in a play based on a typical drama style of the time (melodrama). The *complicity* of the audience in the sinking of the Wollongbar is initially shaped by their historically layered bus ride to the site, and then conditioned by their investment on arrival as fellow guests at an engagement party of the lighthouse keeper's daughter. Here the narrative of the play taps into a common literary and cinematic trope: that of the courageous young woman who keeps the lighthouse flame alive in the constrained absence of her father. [75]

---

[74] Hetherington, Kevin. *The Badlands of Modernity: Heterotopia and Social Ordering.* London: Routledge, 1997. Print. 8-9.

[75] Examples include, not only the *Tempest* but feature films such as Willy Rozier's. *Manina, The Lighthouse Keeper's Daughter* (1952) – Brigitte Bardot's first starring role – and more recently, the Australian feature, Shirley Barette's *South Solitary* (2010). Arielle North Olson's best selling children's book, *The Lighthouse Keeper's Daughter* (illus. Elaine Wentworth. Mystic Seaport. Mystic CT. 2004), one of the best known versions of the trope is based on true events where a young girl kept the light burning in a lighthouse off the coast of Maine while her father, the keeper, was kept away by a violent storm.

(Illustration: Elaine Wentworth)

Figure 6. *The Lighthouse Keeper's Daughter* from the children's story by
Arielle North Olson (1987)

Figure 7. John Taraheteff's "The Lighthouse Keeper's Daughter" (2009)
A surreal visual interpretation of the lighthouse daughter trope.

Figure 8. Willy Rozier's *Manina, the Lighthouse Keeper's Daughter*
(1952, 86 mins.)

Manina was Brigitte Bardot's first major screen role.

The lighthouse-daughter trope often involves shipwrecks and wild storms, and the complication of a fraught relationship with an outsider/sailor/shipwreck survivor (of which Shakespeare's *Tempest* may also be read as distant narrative cousin)[76]. All of which is made worse by the overbearing presence of the father. Thus the trope often assumes a headstrong daughter's inability to cope with the adjacent 'normal' society of the town and/or her father's equally headstrong nature. A more recent example is the Australian Film, *South Solitary* (Shirley Barrett 2009).

King Lear also bears some resemblance in the father/daughter conflict aspect.

Figure 9. Poster for *South Solitary* (Shirley Barrett. 120 mins. 2009).
Co-incidentally, this version of the trope is also set in the 1920s.

Treatment

Within the lighthouse precinct the audience will be welcomed by the senior lighthouse keeper (Capt. Henry Hunter [ret.]) and invested as invitees to the engagement party of his daughter Lucinda (recently of Sydney) to Reginald Wareham Esq. (of nearby Suffolk Park). We learn that Reg is currently a supercargo on the S.S. Wollongbar and is soon to be made assistant lighthouse keeper to Capt. Hunter here at the Cape Byron lighthouse. This public service position provides a secure financial underpinning to the proposed nuptials. Needless to say, the parents are very happy with the arrangement but as the play shows, the daughter is most emphatically *not*.

Fieldnote Oct. 14 2012: On one trip (cycle) up to the lighthouse I consider the potential of placing this formal welcoming speech on the balcony of the lighthouse, with Captain Hunter using an acoustic megaphone and having Reg as his semaphore signaller 'texting' the speech with flags and wild arm movements. This has comic potential in the *commedia* tradition and will help technologically reinforce the heterochrony of 1921. Right from the start, the vaguely castle-like structure of the balcony (Figure 2) allows us to impose the Keeper as a colonially dominant and formal figure, looking down on his guests (subjects) from high above. I turn and look out across the bay to the township itself stretched out along the coast below and imagine bells ringing out in a time of crisis, a storm, a ship being wrecked on the beach! We would expect an animated crowd gathering next to the jetty, lifesavers, the police, children absconding from their bedrooms, all transfixed by the unfolding accident. Some might flock to the jetty as voyeurs, some hurry there to help. And so we introduce another form of pre-digital, communication: town and church bells, warning bells. Soundscapes projected across landscapes. The sound folds the community together into the crisis. In the same way, the lighthouse itself, (from the point of view of standing below it looking back at the town), seems to draw the land to this point on the peak of the cape. 'Cavanbah', its Bundjalung name, means "meeting place" . Then and now, a meeting place for people from disparate groups; originally for the two northern branches of the Bundjalung nation, and today for backpackers from all the nations on earth (if the accents in Woolies are any guide). I wonder if we could convince a restaurant or someone at one of the churches, to ring a bell at the same time each night –All in aid of the psychogeographic illusion?

From Capt. Hunter's formal welcome speech (with toasts proposed and reciprocated), the audience are taken down to Capt. and Mrs. Hunter's cottage to be inducted as 'guests' into the party proper. At the main door each audience member is given a fictional name drawn from the family names of known settlers in the district at this time. These 'guests' are announced to the party generally by Molly who is standing by the front door for this purpose. Here the play would draw on staging strategies deployed in other 'House Shows' as discussed in Chapter 6 of *Really Moving Drama*[77].

Fieldnote: October 17, 2012: On another cycle to the lighthouse I buy plans for the Keeper's cottages on sale at the National Parks' tourist shop inside the cottage itself. Here I am able to measure and count the rooms available for a performance in the Main Cottage. Conscious of the need to maximise audience numbers, I calculate that we are confronted by six medium sized rooms (three on either side of a central hallway) with each room capable of seating about 15 to 20 people around the walls (as in *Living Rooms*).

---

[77] Davies, Paul. *Really Moving Drama*. Brisbane: University of Queensland, 2013. PhD Thesis (pending).

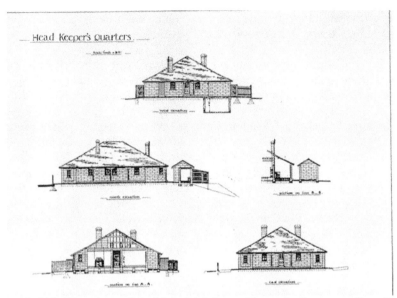

Figure 10. Side Elevations of the Main Lighthouse Keeper's Cottage at Cape Byron.
(National Archives)
The architectural style is in the manner of a settler cottage
of the time (1901), authenticating story with place.

Site-specific staging strategies for creating the diegetic heterotopia (space of the story).

This architectural template of the main lighthouse keepers cottage gives the production an audience of roughly 80 -100 people, divided into four or five sub-groups and sequestered at any given time into several of six possible rooms. The problem of how to fashion the subjectivity of the audience as guests at a 1920s' engagement party raises the possibility of formally dividing them into separate groups as in *Living Rooms* or allowing them to follow individual characters through the story as it were, by literally following them *through* the house as such. This was the spatial strategy deployed by Necessary Angel's production in 1981 of John Krizanc's *Tamara*. I'm proposing here a kind of third option: less formal than *Living Rooms*, but also less random and anarchic than *Tamara*. This would involve deploying the strategies of any social gathering (party) where information exchanges can be dispersed across discrete groups of people– usually focused around key, expressive individuals. These groupings within the larger gathering of the party would allow the rooms to be occupied as 'performative 'cells' in which subsets of the audience would be gathered for each Act and thus be in a position to 'overhear' the dialogue much like conversations at a party. These short scripted exchanges (scenes) would be of around four to five minutes duration. Such scenes could be repeated in different rooms so that all the audience become party to parts of the narrative – but perhaps not the whole story. To satisfy Tim Etchells' notion of fashioning 'witnesses' to the action, I imagine the role of the audience as partly voyeurs and partly 'ghosts' who are present but not totally visible to the actor/characters. Sounds (shouting, music, bells) would also carry from room to room and occasionally draw the focus to what's going on in the house as a whole (and the performance as a kind of meta event).

Thus scripted (and repeated conversations) would take place between characters as they moved from room to room and (re)appear in different couplings. Perhaps sometimes they would appear singly – performing monologues, effectively. At the end of each short scene characters would exit a room to be replaced by another coupling from the basic mix of dramatis personae (father, mother, daughter, fiancé, daughter's best friend etc.). Thus scenes between mother and daughter, father and daughter, daughter and fiancé, daughter and best friend, fiancé and father, will take place in each room and be repeated by the actors as they carry these scenes around the four 'performative cells'. Such exchanges taking place in each of four (or five) rooms would require a core cast of at least eight or nine. And again, like *Tamara* not everybody in the audience might view the same set of events, or even get a complete picture of the story in one attendance. Such an outcome with *Tamara* lead to the phenomenon of many people making multiple attendances to cover for themselves, the narrative gaps.

Temporally speaking, each of the three main Acts in the keeper's cottage therefore, (with its sub-sets of four, five-minute scenes), exists with its own separate heterochrony. At the end of the First Act (the initial sequence of four/five scenes), audience groups swap rooms and a Second Act again unfolds as various couplings within the core cast, effectively building on narrative information already supplied in the sequences of the First Act. Breaks between Acts allow the heterochronic clock to be reset as audience subgroups mingle throughout the house to share gossip, speculate on outcomes, create mischief, even perhaps to reshape themselves into a differently composed audience sub-group for the Second Act. The Third Act concludes with the major dramatic crisis – the sinking of the Wollongbar. A Final (Fourth) Act, reveals the dramatic effect of the sinking on everyone concerned. As with other House Shows examined in *Really Moving Drama*, the audience will continue to be present as 'guests' but also, in a sense, their subjectivity is fashioned as voyeurs. They become privy to certain backstories, and therefore begin to view the events of the play from something approaching the perspective of Etchells' 'witnesses'—engaging the moral imperative as they accumulate knowledge of characters and their various intentions – all of whom will have secrets to hide that become their points of vulnerability. The characters will also express confidentially certain irresistible desires (while clearly overheard by others).

Narrative could also be conveyed through an engagement with certain 'parlour games' appropriate to the social mores of the early 1920s (see further research). I am wondering here about the origins of 'charades' for example, or 'blind man's bluff'. Séances were also popular that this time as was singing familiar songs round a piano (sing-a-longs) – all strategies for moulding sub-sets within the various audience groups, and thereby further containing and manipulating the social mix within each room. Such engagements also dissolve the barriers between actor and spectator (without needing to go so far as creating August Boal's 'spectactors').[78]

Jerzy Grotowski and Richard Schechner both explored these proximal relationships in dedicated theatre laboratories.[79] Here their experiments can be applied to performances in the real world.

Narratively speaking, the crisis of the storm (enhanced by sound effects and incoming wet costumes), and the consequent foundering of the S.S. Wollongbar on the beach below, will draw all audience groups outside to a critical emergency response scene. Ideally this penultimate scene would be set inside the lighthouse building itself and thereby offers a panoptic view of the unfolding maritime drama. We can fictionally speculate that the lighthouse, with its commanding view and its communication systems (primitive as they were), would have been a major focal point for any response by the local emergency services (life saving, fire, ambulance, police and shipping crews). In a 1920's Australian country town, without a basic electricity service, primitive phones and telegraph machines, large bells and signal flags fill the communication gap.

Here again, in this crisis scene, our audience (like the formation of 'witnesses' Tompkins observes happening in *Suitcase*), enact for themselves a process of psychogeography. This enables them to impose their own interpretation of the historical events of the play onto the present day landscape. Their view of real and imagined events below the lighthouse can be shaped by the 'actor/guides' in character.

Dramatis Personae

In the tradition of TheatreWorks' location practices, and especially given the rapid entrances and exits required to keep the momentum of the dramatic events rotating through the various rooms of the cottage, I would again cast the characters in the style of the *commedia della'arte,* with the familiar ensemble of larger-than-life archetypes: the irascible, but hopeless 'capitano' (Captain Hunter), the quartet of Innamorati (Lucinda, Berny, Reg, and Monroe), the zannis creating mischief (Molly and the Musicians), the grand but deluded dame (Mrs. Hunter). In this sense *commedia della'arte* merges with melodrama.

In the best traditions of the melodrama the characters will also carry a debilitating secret, to be revealed at the worst possible moment and embellished by gossip spread throughout the play. Again, well within the *commedia* tradition, characters (especially the Innamorati) will manifest passionate but conflicting desires at cross purposes to their real intentions (Lucinda for Berny, Reg for Lucinda, Monroe for Lucinda, Molly for Monroe etc.).

See Boal, Augusto. *The Rainbow of Desire, the Boal Method of Theatre and Therapy.* London: Routledge, 1995. Print. 42.

79

See Grotowski, Jerzy. *Towards a Poor Theatre.* London: Methuen & Co, 1968. Print. And Schechner, Richard. *Environmental Theatre.* New York: Hawthorn Books, 1973. Print.

Captain John Hunter (ret.). Late 50s/early 60s (but looks older). John Hunter ran away from school to sea at fourteen and for a time sailed with the 'last pirate', a real life scoundrel named Bully Hayes. Hayes, an American, was immortalised in the short stories of Louis Becke who himself sailed with Hayes and was regarded as the first Australian writer to focus on the Pacific cultures and the impact of European colonial expansion into them. This association with Hayes is Captain Hunter's secret, his current pompous, upper class façade is revealed as a sham once the true facts are known. With Hayes (like Becke), Hunter was actually implicated in running guns to both sides of the Samoan Civil War and supplied slave labour (known as 'kanakas') to the Queensland cane fields. Many of these crimes will be drawn from Becke's own stories, especially his first and best known collection, *By Reef and Palm.*[80]

Lucinda Hunter. 30-ish. Capt. Hunter's daughter. Lucinda, is the 'bright spark' around which the action of the play unfolds. Like many lighthouse children Lucinda was sent to boarding school rather than have her education suffer on account of the isolation of lighthouse life. In Byron at last, she was able to go by pony to the local primary school where her life-long friendship with Berny (Berenice Armstrong) started. Their separation due to Lucinda's later boarding school absence in Sydney, was filled by a regular and passionate correspondence. After completing secondary school Lucinda stayed in the city where she worked as a seamstress and later in a more white-collar job as the secretary for a medium sized law firm. Here she soon fell in with the fast crowd, relishing Sydney in the roaring twenties. This was a time of hedonism and the inevitable relaxation of social behaviours in the wake of the First World War. This climate of change allowed certain 'liberated' women to challenge the contemporary patriarchal paradigm. It is partly to redirect her life from this 'wayward' path that her parents (particularly her father) have pushed Lucinda into the engagement to Reginald. However, in the tradition of the lighthouse daughter trope she is strong willed, passionate, independent, capable and somewhat driven.

Reginald Wareham Esq. Early 40s. Reg is at least ten years older than Lucinda and the son of settler parents. The Warehams were virtually 'given' hundreds of acres of Bundjalung land in a government handout to the better class of convict and other free settlers around 1860-70.[81] Reg has recently been a supercargo on the S.S. Wollongbar (an overseer/account role relating to the documentation of cargo–

---

[80] Becke, Louis. *By Reef And Palm.* Sydney: Angus and Robertson, 1955. Print. See also Becke, Louis *Bully Hayes: Buccaneer.* Sydney: NSW Bookstall Co., 1913. Print. There is a major scholarly work on Becke by A. Grove Day: *Louis Becke.* Melbourne: Hill of Content, 1967. Print. Personally, Becke is a distant relative being an uncle of my paternal grandfather Colwyn Davies. By the end of the 19th Century Becke was regarded as the 'Rudyard Kipling of the Pacific' (A. Grove Day, cover notes to *Louis Becke*).

[81] Under the Robertson Land Act of Free Selection, property around Byron could be had for one pound per acre, of which only five shillings needed to be put down (*Time and Tide* 15-16).

Becke himself worked as such for Bully Hayes). Reg is also unusual in that he seems to have survived the War (World War 1) without any visible or invisible scars. Yet he is nudging middle age and has never married. He is a decent enough fellow and is truly concerned for and affectionate towards Lucinda, behaving at all times with perfect respect and attention. Unsurprisingly, Lucinda recoils from what she sees as his dull, plodding, settler mentality and couldn't imagine anything worse that living out the rest of her life with him in the assistant lighthouse keeper's cottage, barely thirty yards from her parents home. The engagement therefore is being thrust upon her and as the engagement party looms Lucinda hasn't quite been able to wriggle out of this unwanted huge new commitment.

Mrs. Dorothy Hunter (late 50s). Lucinda's mother. And like her daughter, she is not a typical, subservient sea captain's (later lighthouse keeper's) wife. In fact 'Dotty' as her family only half jokingly call her, is a (hyper)active member of several local societies including the Theosophicals, and the Spiritualists, where she displays in frequent séances, an uncanny ability to get in touch with 'the other side'. She also plays piano for a jazz band which tours around the Northern Rivers, playing mostly in pubs and community halls (raising funds for charity). Dorothy also plays improvised music on the piano for the silent films shown at Byron's Literary Institute: an all purpose cinema, meeting place and community hall. It is easy to see where Lucinda gets her crazy/manic energy from.

Berenice (Berny) Armstrong. 30-ish. The same age as Lucinda, Berny is a typical country girl of the time. Brought up on a dairy and banana farm, she has milked cows, confronted pests and weeds, cut timber, butchered her own meat, shot pigs and wallabies, kept chooks and grown all her own fruit and vegetables virtually since she could walk. In fact, Berny's dad had her riding a pony before she could technically stand upright. She remains an expert horse breaker. Like Lucinda, Berny dreams of liberation from the limitations of her rural backwater. She doesn't dislike the country life but knows something is missing and Lucinda's apparently dazzling progress in Sydney is a constant reminder of her own stuck predicament. However, unlike Lucinda, Berny lacks both the financial means and the education to do much about her current situation. To overcome this she gambles all her nest egg on shipping three tons of butter on the Wollongbar to Sydney (and ultimately to England where Byron Bay butter is a prized item in the High Street). Alas, this a-typically risky gesture by Berny is destined to end in grief.

Monroe Dalgety. 40-ish. Monroe is one of Lucinda's city pals who has sailed up from Sydney with her travelling party on the S.S. Wollongbar a few nights ago – all travelling together for her engagement celebration on the Cape. Monroe is a charming but slightly dodgy character who claims to have worked as a journalist and magazine writer, but is secretly on the run from agents of a powerful Sydney bookie reputed to be connected to Squizzy Taylor. Lucinda is attracted to his debonair, gallows humour and for Monroe's part, the feelings are more than reciprocated. He is in love with her but can't seem to ever quite admit it. A confirmed bachelor, it may well be that Monroe is deep down, also a commitment-phobe. Meanwhile, true feelings suppressed, he offers Lucinda a sympathetic (if not completely reliable) shoulder to cry on, and is someone to whom she can unload the anxiety of her looming marriage to Reg. Like Reg, Monroe is old enough to have fought in the War but accounts of his military exploits keep changing and seem frankly contradictory. Capt. Hunter distrusts him on sight and treats him with a barely disguised contempt.

Other Minor Characters include **Molly (19)** an Irish serving girl who works the drinks and party food. Here the heterochrony of 1921 is maintained by engaging sympotic space (sense of taste) with typical menu items from the period that might include lamingtons, Anzac biscuits, corned ox tongue and roast beef sandwiches, plum pudding, savoury anchovies on toast, apple pie etc.[82]

Also present would be at least **Two Musicians: Tom** and **Betty Thurgood (40s)**. This couple are regulars with Dotty Hunter's jazz band, and together the trio provide both dance and background music for the party, including 'sing-a-longs of popular numbers round Dotty's piano (with her 'shandy' [a mix of lemonade and beer] perched permanently on a little shelf to the right of her piano). Tom and Betty are also both excellent tango dancers (the latest craze sweeping Europe from South America), and perhaps coach audience members through some simple tango routines. Meanwhile, the minor characters also make poignant asides on the main action – in the manner of Baynot and Mutton's interventions into the action in Jack Hibberd's *Dimboola* (1969). These two were an early example of the practice of site-specific theatre salting characters in among the audience. In *Dimboola* Baynot and Mutton critique the whole event with lewd asides while essentially freeloading on the food and drink provided. Tom may also double as a Morse code operator when news comes, via the telegraph of the evolving emergency with the S.S. Wollongbar.

Storyline

According to the generic orthodoxy, the main action of the play focuses on a troubled father/daughter/son-in-law triangle. In this case, it is more a question of a troubled father/daughter/daughter-in-law triangle.

Prologue: Bus ride to the lighthouse.

At the historic Byron Railway Station the gathering audience present their formally printed invitations to Dotty and board a double-decker bus (almost reminiscent of Sydney busses of the 1920s). Here they commence a detoured ride up to the engagement party while passing points of historic interest along the way. Dotty, gives a potted history of Byron's key moments reminiscent of Forced Entertainment's *Nights In This City*. He she applies a psychogeographic approach: imposing story on place as, like a human crystal radio set, she 'channels' characters from the past who ('through' Dotty) give graphic descriptions of the main events in

---

[82] *Time and Tide* contains a Menu card fro dinner on the Wollongbar's sister ship the S.S. Orara (94).

the formation of the town. The bus ride finally delivers the audience to the lighthouse proper, just in time for Capt. Hunter's formal speech of welcome delivered from its first floor ramparts and relayed to the crowd below by Reg using semaphore. This was an early form of text messaging involving coloured flags and a lot of arm movements between parties visible to each other. With field glasses and binoculars information could be sent over many miles (or battleships).

Act One: Setting the scene.

After the audience are taken down to the Main Cottage we hear more about the pending nuptials between Lucinda and Reginald. But we 'overhear' that Lucinda feels under pressure from her parents to "settle down", and now deeply regrets that (in a fit of near apoplectic stress and anxiety), she agreed to go through with it all. Reg, for his part, comes across as a decent enough fellow quite happy to make Lucinda his wife, have a family, and settle down to the domestic routines of an assistant lighthouse keeper and one day (soon probably) taking over his father-in-law as head keeper of the light. All of which equates to a form of living hell for the now metropolitanised and crypto-suffragette, Lucinda. Meanwhile, we find that Monroe himself carries a flame for her. The First Act climaxes with Lucinda re-encountering her old friend Berenice. All this information is carried in short scenes deployed through the various audience groups in different rooms.

Act Two: What's really going on.

After a short break that allows the audience to mingle and swap gossip, the second Act reveals that feelings between Lucinda and Berny have only increased since they last met, demonstrating a classic example of "absence making the heart grow fonder". Berny reveals all her financial hopes are riding on a cargo of butter from her farm which was loaded this morning on the S.S. Wollongbar for shipment to Sydney; and from there by refrigerated steamship to the Old Country, where Byron Bay butter is a prized item. Lucinda realises this would give her dear friend sufficient financial freedom to set up a life of her own, further facilitating any future relationship them. Throughout this scene, as the passions rise in inverse proportion to the barometric pressures, constant references are made by Capt. Hunter to a troubling plunge in the readings. A big storm is on its way.

Act Three: The storm.

After another short interval for refreshments the storm finally breaks (an illusion enhanced by lightning and sound effects (hail on roof, wind etc.). Wet costumes and a lot more shouting add to the building crisis. In the heat of the moment Lucinda calls it off with Reg – just as word arrives from the jetty (via Tom's telegraph in a back room) that the Wollongbar is breaking free from its moorings under the growing and relentless North Easterly gale. The captain of the ship has decided to make a run into the bay to stop her from foundering on the beach. Reg, his hopes and dreams in tatters, volunteers immediately to rejoin his old crew and face whatever the storm might throw against them. Lucinda begins to regret her harsh rebuff as he heads heroically out into pelting rain and hail. As the party waits with baited breath, updates arrive by telegraph of the dramatic action taking place in the bay. Tom, through telegram after telegram, delivers a blow by blow description of the fate of the Wollongbar. A sudden crisis in the lighthouse itself, the kerosene (paraffin) fed lamp is in danger of going out! Capt. Hunter calls for volunteers among "his guests" to hurry up there with him to help lift more supplies to the top (Reg has mismanaged his stock taking responsibility on his first day). At the same time, as the Wollongbar crashes unstoppably towards the beach, Capt. Hunter is struck by lightning. Unfortunately he had been getting a better view of events via his telescope at the top (while relaying each act in the drama to the audience helping lift kerosene tins up the internal staircase).[83]

Act Four: Aftermath

Capt. Hunter is shaken needless to say, but not stirred, and continues to rail against his daughter's 'betrayal'. While Berny's financial independence, in the form of three tons of butter, is currently mixing with the rest of the cargo of bananas and bacon washed up on Bilongil Beach. Reg is, at first, mistakenly thought to have been critically injured in the sinking. However he soon returns to the lighthouse, battered but basically okay. All he had to do at the end was jump overboard into about three feet of surf.

As Capt. Hunter is rushed to hospital by horse and cart, the events of this turbulent night reach their conclusion. Reg reluctantly accepts that Lucinda and Berny are going to move back to Sydney together -- for a time anyway. They will be followed by Monroe looking for a place to stay (a refuge from his relentless debt collectors.) Finally, Dotty by way of following her husband down to the hospital packs the audience into the bus for a lift back to where they started from (the railway station).

Epilogue: The Bus Ride Home

On the way down, stepping out of the heterochrony of the play and back into an indeterminate present, Dotty fills everyone in on the fates that befell the characters after that fateful night. She explains how Berny and Lucinda remained together and eventually returned from Sydney to run Berny's family farm after her own parents passed away. Monroe was found in a shallow grave on St. Kilda beach in Melbourne. And Dotty herself was reconciled to her daughter after Capt. Hunter finally died of a heart attack. Reg himself never married, but remained in touch with Lucinda and Berny and even helped out when they adopted a child together.

The ride home goes past the carpark overlooking the wreck of the S.S. Wollongbar as it stands today: its rudder and rear superstructure, and sometimes its boilers rising above the low tides off Bilongil beach. It still sits there as marker for today's board riders catching waves around it. Finally, Dotty draws everyone's attention to the Julian Rocks lying a little further out into the bay. In a moving speech she draws parallels between the story of Lucinda and Berny and the Dreamtime legend of the

---

[83] Lightning strikes were a not uncommon workplace hazard for lighthouse keepers and one such took place in 1920 (*Time and Tide* 59-60)

wife fleeing by boat with her lover from a jealous husband. Enraged, the husband threw a spear that sank their canoe, turning the lovers and their boat into the two rocks we see today (another form of shipwreck). Nevertheless, Dotty reassures us, these lovers from different clan groups, happily remain joined together – just under the waterline…

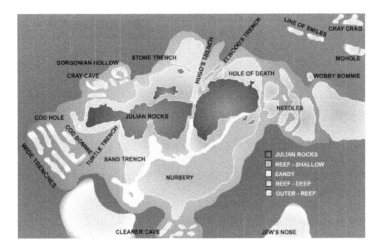

Figure 1I. Map of Julian Rocks showing two islets joined under the waterline.

Figure 12. The Julian Rocks today. A marine park and refuge for sea life.[84]

---

[84] This and other images are available at
http://www.google.com.au/search?q=julian+rocks+marine+reserve&hl=en&client =safari&sa=X&tbo=u&rls=en&tbm=isch&source=univ&ei=bB_AUJDsFs2jiAeW sICgCg&ved=0CF8QsAQ&biw=1112&bih=806

Other works consulted.

Carleton, Stephen. *Staging the North, Finding, Imagining and Performing an Australian Deep North.* PhD Thesis. University of Queensland: Fryer Library, 2008. E-copy.

Gilbert, Helen and Joanne Tompkins. *Post Colonial Drama, Theory, Practice, Politics.* London: Routledge, 1996. Print.

Kaye, Nick, ed. *Site Specific Art.* London: Routledge 2000. Print.

Kwon, Miwon. *One Place after Another, Site-Specific Art and Locational Identity.* Cambridge, Massachusetts: MIT Press, 2002. Print.

Lefebvre, Henri. *La Production De L'Espace.* Trans. Nicholson-Smith, Donald. Oxford: Blackwell, 1991. Print.

McAuley, Gay. *Space in Performance.* Ann Arbor: University of Michigan 1999. Print. Pearson, Mike, Michael Shanks. *Theatre/Archaeology.* London: Routledge, 2001. Print.

Taussig, Michael. "The Fetisization of Field Notes http://www.egs.edu/faculty/michael-taussig/videos/the-fetishization-of-field-notes/ (viewed 2/9/2012)

Tompkins, Joanne. *Unsettling Space: Contestations in Contemporary Australian Theatre.* Studies in International Performance. Ed. Reinelt and Singleton. New York: Palgrave McMillan, 2006 Print.

Turner, Cathy. "Palimpsest or Potential Space? Finding a Vocabulary for Site-Specific Performance." *NTQ* 20:4 November (2004). Print.

Wilkie, Fiona. "Out of Place the Negotiation of Space in Site-Specific Performance." PhD. University of Surrey, 2004. Print.

THEATRE IN THE SPACE AGE
Between Sight- and Site-Specific Futures
Paper for English Media Studies and Art History
University of Queensland. 19/10/2012

Theatre In The Space Age

Between Sight- and Site-Specific Futures

Storming St. Kilda By Tram   TheatreWorks   1988

Photo © Ruth Maddison
Figure 1 A case of the blind leading the myopic?
(Ticket) Inspector, 'Morris Stanley' (right), ignorant of the real situation,
makes a charitable donation into a stolen guide dog.

Since this is primarily a story of space and place its especially important that I acknowledge the Turrbal people as the traditional owners of Meanjin, the country where we gather today. And also to acknowledge my personal elders, Joanne and Stephen, for the guidance and opportunity to undertake this research and whose own work in the areas of theatre and spatiality gave me the frame for what follows.

It seemed almost too serendipitous that a world renowned theatre scholar and a working playwright were available as mentors in the place where my career in letters started as an English Honours student. And so here I am again, hopefully to know the place for the first time.

I should also declare that I was a participant in some of the plays discussed here both as an author and actor; and in a way this thesis could be read as an exegesis for work performed 30 odd years ago. I basically wanted to understand what gave rise to the kind of exhilaration that I'd felt standing in the middle of *Storming Mont Albert By Tram,* on one of its more boisterous nights, playing the over zealous ticket inspector, my hands covered in tomato sauce which I'm pretending to think is someone's blood and the audience, hooting with laughter all around me at my mock shock (more about that scene in a minute). I wanted to examine what forces were at work in a play that could cause an entire audience to sometimes react like over excited fans at a footy match, cheering on certain characters and shouting others down. I felt with TheatreWorks' location plays we had stumbled on something that galvanized spectators like no other theatrical event I'd experienced. The empowerment of an audience who is in on the joke, and complicit with the actors in an occupation of space made possible by their shared disbelief that what they're watching isn't scripted is truly a wonderful thing to behold. And it was not only fun to witness and be in, it was genuinely popular: such that *The Tram Show* in its final iterations ultimately became self supporting, playing over a dozen years to some 20,000 passengers, in both Melbourne and Adelaide, and generating in today's figures around a million dollars at the box office while travelling a distance that would have taken it almost halfway around the world.

These were plays that now comfortably sit under the rubric of "site-specific theatre" although the term itself has become problematic – other descriptors such as site-generic, site-responsive, site-sensitive, location, space-specific, environmental, and even promenade theatre also compete to describe what are essentially spoken word dramas produced in real places, found or otherwise. Space, appropriately enough, prevents me going into the fine distinctions here between works appropriate to only one site and others that could be staged in a number of generic places, or plays that are simply given a funky setting, outside somewhere, like a quarry or a botanical gardens.

And far be it for me to stoop to such unscholarly behaviour as google-ing something, but when I typed in "sight and site specific theatre" recently I was surprised find close to 16 million hits, and then to my utter astonishment the fourth item in the list read

> EMSAH Seminar: Friday 19 October Room 601 Michie Building. Theatre in the Space Age: Between sight and site-specific futures. Contact Stormy Wehi. With the abstract attached.

I thought gee- that EMSAH office team – they really are Miracle Workers, that award last year was no fluke, because thanks to Stormy 4th in 16 million means we must now be rating in the top 0.000,000,25 percentile. Without even paying google to be there.

The other point being that with 16 million hits there can be little doubt that the Site-geist as its been dubbed…in theatre practice has finally arrived, and is now happening anywhere and everywhere as Brisbane's recent "Anywhere" Theatre Festival literally attests. It seemed to me, standing in the middle of *Storming Mont Albert By Tram* 30 years ago as if Shakespeare's prediction voiced by Monsieur Jacques in *As You Like It* that "all the world's a stage" had finally been realized.

Yet if we do a proper scholarly search and go through something like the MLA data base it appears that there are only 75 available items on the topic of site specific theatre. The first two of which were articles by Joanne. Gold and Silver medals to EMSAH again! I rest my case. But the point is also that theory still runs a distant second to what appears to be an exponentially expanding practice.

It is perhaps no accident that just as the discovery and occupation of the New World furnished the imaginary of the Enlightenment, the conquest and occupation of extra terrestrial space fuels the theatrical imaginary of the second Elizabethan period, because space is theatre's foundational building block. And as Foucault expressed it over 40 years ago (in 1967), in perhaps a prediction of the internet, that we live in the epoch of space

> "in the epoch of simultaneity … the epoch of juxtaposition…of the near and the far, of the side by side, of the dispersed. We are at a moment, he believed, "when our experience of the world is less that of a long life developing through time than that of a network that connects points and intersects with its own skein."
>
> Michel Foucault ("Of Other Spaces" 22)

To which one might infer that also that we live in the epoch of space travel, of cyberspace, of all forms of social and physical spaces and the associated anxieties of their occupation, something Joanne deals with in the Australian context in *Unsettling Space*.

The goal of my research therefore has been to draw out the lessons learnt from a range of TheatreWorks shows in tents, trams, boats and houses throughout the 1980s, works that appeared at around the same time as early site specific groups such as Brith Gof in Wales and Necessary Angel in Canada. I wanted to not only document an overlooked chapter in the Australian theatre story, but also to propose a set of critical tools with which we might more appropriately evaluate this new form of theatre. In addition to the usual critical issues surrounding script, performance and direction, matters of authenticity (spatial relations) and complicity (audience relations) also need to be addressed. In other words, we now need to ask, I believe, not only were the script and performances any good, but how convincingly does a particular story inhabit its place of performance, and almost as a consequence, how readily does an audience go along for the ride. Because, within the frisson that occurs when various social and narrative spaces collide, these qualities of authenticity and complicity shape a whole new set of interconnectivities that open up not only between the actors and their audience, but within the audience themselves and between both parties and outside reality sometimes looking back in. So in addition to sight and hearing, such new engagements can theoretically embrace all the senses, adding touch, taste and smell to sight and hearing– and even a kind of sixth sense in what we might call the pheromone effect. (see Alice Miller "Pheromones and Human Behaviour" Ph D Thesis. Sterling University, Scotland)

The 'art of theatre' to use Adolphe Appia's descriptor, is one cultural activity where space is the basic canvas, primarily involving the placement and interaction of bodies in space for the purposes of storytelling. In director parlance this is called "blocking." It goes without saying, that the 'art of theatre' is itself a living thing, and as with any vibrant organism, its processes function in a state of constant evolution, all in response to the narratives, technologies and socio-political zeit or this case site-geist in which it unfolds. (end of puns, I promise)

If we step back a moment and ask ourselves "[W]here does this nightly practice of large groups of people sitting down in darkened auditoria to watch mimetic displays of human behaviour on illuminated stages come from?" what has been somewhat disparagingly described as a bunch of voyeurs watching a pack of extroverts, we may trace a genealogy, at least for western performance traditions, back through the high point of the dedicated Elizabethan theatre buildings, to biblical stories enacted centuries earlier on the backs of wagons to a basically illiterate audience gathered in town squares; or even to that critical moment a millennium before that, when the first Greek actor emerged as an individual from the chorus around him and began the process of dialogue. Indeed, the practice of theatre might just as easily have originated in the nocturnal storytelling of our pre-historic ancestors sitting around the primeval campfire, recounting a no doubt exaggerated version of that day's quest for food. What remains common through all these iterations of the form is the dynamic interplay between narrative, character, witness and place of performance.

Appia, who wanted to develop actor-audience relationships in order to create a 'people's theatre' away from the 'guilded frame' of the proscenium arch (qtd Wiles 236-237) also argued that "[e]very work of art must contain a harmonious relationship between feeling and form, an ideal balance between the *ideas* which the artist desires to express, and the *means* he has for expressing them..." (29).

Underpinning everything else, theatre is always the art of the possible and its means of expression necessarily arrive out of the technologies available.

Now, in the face of the challenges posed to theatre by cinema in the early part of the 20th Century, various theorists and practitioners have tried to distinguish live performance from its mechanically reproduced cousin. To characterize theatre's effect and ensure its relevance, they naturally sought to emphasise its essential 'liveness', what might be called the Benjaminian 'aura' of each unique performance.

The Dadaist project, in one sense a reaction to the catastrophe of the First World War, saw a kind of anarchic counter-performance taken out of theatres into art galleries and once again out into the streets. At around the same time and in the wake of the Russian revolution, agit-prop ensembles like gangs of theatre commandos staged impromptu performances on trams in Leningrad and Moscow, short playlets that highlighted the need for personal hygiene or the evils of religion. Just over a decade later in France in the 1930s and 40s Antonin Artaud began calling for audiences to be 'engulfed' by his theatre of 'cruelty'. While Bertholt Brecht wanted them to be conscious of their participation in an essentially fabricated process, to stand back and think for themselves. By the 1960s Peter Brook had cleared the traditional, purpose-built stage of all un-necessary clutter in order to reduce theatre back to its essential 'empty stage', a triad of actor ,watcher and performance space: this soon became the pared back place that Grotowski and Scheckner were beginning to occupy by mixing audiences and actors on the same common playing ground – albeit in a self-styled theatre 'laboratory'. These were still dedicated theatre spaces, studios and the like, but they were much more flexible than the proscenium binary of stage and auditorium which had persisted since the Elizabethans and on through its canonization in the Enlightenment with Diderot's formulation of the idea of the fourth wall in his quest for a kind of ultimate naturalism. Naturalism still provides the basic game plan here but it is of an entirely different order.

Meanwhile, the visual arts themselves exploded out of the gallery and gave birth to the hybrid 'performance art' tradition – or live art as it is now described. Such a breakout challenged theatre practitioners to do the same. So that finally, by the 1980s, in the wake of the 'happenings' and the agit-prop occupations of public space in the political upheavals of the 1960s and 1970s, the idea of producing plays in 'real' spaces saw Grotowsky and Schechner's laboratory experiment finally taken out into the real world.

In Australia, in the 1980s, this early site-specific movement was centered on Melbourne, and grew from the success of plays on busses, trams, boats, in goals, pubs, gardens, courts of law and houses, public and private. A decade later it also flourished in the United Kingdom where site-specific performances continues to expand across a number of dedicated companies including now both the National theatres of Scotland and Wales.

Towards a Site-Geist?

Prominent site-specific theatre companies (as at 2012) - from a growing list (and in no particular order) - include:

United Kingdom
National Theatre of Wales, National Theatre of Scotland, Brith Gof (Wales), Wrights and Sites, London Bubble, Out of the Blue (Dance), Red Earth, GridIron (Edinburgh) Forced Entertainment (Sheffield), Shunt, The Whalley Range Allstars, Dream Think Speak Poor Boy (Scotland), Station House Opera (London), Art Angel, Welfare State, International (Cumbria), Cotton Grass (Peak District), Storm (Coventry), Blast Theory (integrating web technology) IOU, Impossible Theatre, Creation Theatre Company (Oxford), Test Department, Hide and Seek, Theatre Absolute, Frantic Assembly, Punchdrunk, Wildworks, Poorboy, dreamthinkspeak, Lone Twin, Test Department, Kneehigh (Cornwall) Moving Being, Walk the Plank, Pickle Herring Theatre,Pentabus Theatre, Theatre Nomad, The Lion's Part (London), The Olimpias, Emergency Exit Arts, Sirens Crossing (Dance), Boilerhouse, Cerberus, The Common Players, Horse+ Bamboo, Kunstwerk-Blend, Riptide, Rotozaza, Foster and Heighes, in situ, Invisible Circus, Slung Low, Wilson+Wilson, Scarabeus Theatre,

Ireland
Corcadorca (Cork) Semper Fi, Papan Theatre

Netherlands
Dogtroep

USA
Lucia Neare's Theatrical Wonders (Seattle, USA)
Nu Dance Theater (New York, USA)
Peculiar Works Project (New York, NY, USA)
Play Grounds - Wood Stove House (Lancaster, PA, USA)
Scrap and Salvage (San Francisco, USA)
Skewed Visions (Minnesota, USA)
St. David High School (Arizona, USA)
Supernatural Chicago (Chicago, USA) Supernatural Chicago's website

Theater Anew - Established plays in unique performance venues (San Francisco)
Third Rail Projects (USA)
Walkabout Theater (Chicago, USA)

Canada
Necessary Angel, Dummies Theatre (Montreal), FIXT POINT (Toronto) Swallow-a-Bicycle Calgary, Electric Company Theatre (Vancouver) Litmus Theatre (Toronto)

Australia
Urban Dream Capsule (Melbourne- Myers Windows) Back to Back (Geelong) Legs On the Wall (Australia) TheatreWorks (Melbourne) Gilgul (Melbourne) West (Melbourne) The Mill (Geelong) Home Cooking Company (Melbourne) Australian Shakespeare Company (Melbourne)

Festivals
Anywhere Festival (Brisbane)
Acco Festival (Israel/Palestine)
LIFT (London International Festival of Theatre)

As for the Australian context, Julian Meyrick, in an overview of Melbourne Fringe Festival productions from 1988 to 1995, cites a total of 47 works produced outside purpose-built theatres, and finds that after 1990 the selection of sites becomes to include "a fabric warehouse, a textile factory, a deserted brewery, Luna Park funfair, and even a shopping mall. He adds that it is "a rare international festival now which does not have its quota of site-specific work," although the values behind the investment of such venues are "more conventional" and that they are often 'read' as theatres even when they do not resemble them (2000: 170-171)." Rachel Fensham, in her 1991 article "Location, Location Location: Australian Theatre on Safari" observes that from the early 1970s the Australian Performing Group (the Pram Factory) took to the streets and mounted performances at pop festivals, political rallies and work sites, enacting a belief that "[s]hifting theatre out of doors was a political act because theatres were thought to be 'politically bankrupt and impotent." (245). Surely, there can be no greater confirmation of a movement's success than to find newspaper articles already announcing its demise.[85] In a post *News of the World* world, it may well be the newspapers themselves who should be worried about longevity.

---

[85] Honour, Philip. "Is It Really Curtains for Site-Specific Theatre?" Opinion. *Guardian* 24 August 2007. Print.

All this in an age which has coined the term "dramality" to describe that strange hybrid of performative behaviours, conscious or otherwise, that now occurs under the panoptic gaze of television's 'reality' shows.

So this paper proposes that the 'art of theatre' stands today at a kind of cross roads, offering several ways forward. It can take a right turn as it were into ever more spectacular (*s-i-g-h-t*-specific) large budget, mostly franchised musicals (whose narratives are now routinely plundered from successful feature films– the final surrender to cinema). Or it can continue straight ahead, unfolding in large, state subsidized theatre buildings, another form of (*s-i-g-h-t*-specific) practice where no matter how marvellous the text, performance or direction, any extended creative possibility will always be hostage to real estate and external funding.

Both these options, right turn or steady as she goes, privilege **s-i-g-h-t** (and hearing) as the primary sense organs, an approach David Wiles finds inherent in the Western dramatic tradition.

> The Italian Renaissance prioritized vision…The dichotomy of soul and imprisoning body implies, as in Plato's simile [of the cave], a system of representation which invites the viewer to penetrate an interior. Plato and the idealist tradition in antiquity held that vision was an additive process, with the eyes emitting rays or spirit, and this theory of optics supported the notion that the eye was a privileged instrument, allowing the soul to probe where the body could not follow. (216)

Fair enough. And no doubt visually accented theatre will continue to find an audience, even if the accompanying husbands are mostly snoring by interval.

Alternatively, theatre practitioners can take a left turn, as it were, into the ever burgeoning world of performance in real places where the potential for engagement with an audience and with the place of performance is greatly enhanced, where spectators become complicit with the actors, not only in the events unfolding all around them, but also in a transgressive occupation of public or found space – if only via their passive presence at the event.

Figure 2. *Storming Mont Albert By Tram* (Paul Davies) 1982
The penultimate 'bomb scare' scene.

Thus audiences and characters in TheatreWorks *Tram Show* were to all intents and purposes fellow passengers on a # 42 Tram so that at first glance it would be impossible to tell looking at figure 7.3 who is an audience member and who an actor – except of course here the actors are pretending, while the audience are reacting with genuine emotion.

LeFebvre, Foucault and later Heatherington and others give us the means to unpack what is going on here as various social spaces collide. Borrowing from Physics and Hoyle's theories, LeFebvre argued that such spaces can be created by the energy deployed within them. Therefore, we might usefully read what is occurring in a site-specific play as a process whereby the imaginary space of the text as enacted by the performers makes symbolic use of its location, a real tram, in order to produce a coherent system of meaning (a story about tram travellers); both by using language (dialogue) and by means outside of words (larger than life gestures, physical interaction, smell, touch etc.).

While warning of the hyper-complexity involved, what differentiates social spaces from those of "natural space" for Lefebvre, is the fact that they can not only be juxtaposed (as Foucault would have it) but they can, continuing the astro/physical metaphor, be "intercalated, combined, superimposed, they may even sometimes collide" (88). Such a collision for Kevin Heatherington relates to the 'shock effect' of heterotopia, something that derives from their different mode of ordering (*Badlands* 42). For Heatherington, heterotopia "are established through the juxtaposition of things not usually found together and the confusion that the resulting representations creates" (*Identity, Space, Performance* 131). Interestingly for this study and the influence of agit-prop street theatre in the formation of site-specfic performance, Heatherington also finds that Lefebvre's analysis of everyday life "provided some sort of theory" for *les evenements de Mai 1968* "before they actually happened" (*Identity, Space, Performance* 66). It is worth noting that Foucault's lecture "Of Other Spaces", Brooks' *The Empty Space,* and Grotowski's *Towards A Poor Theatre* are all published in roughly the same 18 month time frame as both the Paris occupations of 1968 and the first moon landing.

What is clear is that audiences in a site-specific play therefore can be engaged across all five, possibly even six senses. In a TheatreWorks location play you literally get to *feel* the actors.

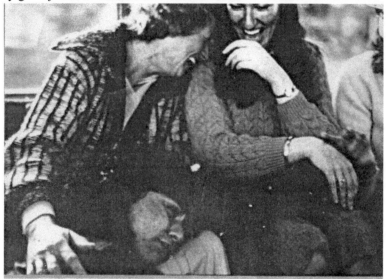

Figure 3. *Storming Mont Albert By Tram* (Davies 1982)
'Feelie' theatre or the pheromone effect?
Conductress Alice Katransky seeks comfort from a passenger
on news of her sacking.

'

This image depicts a moment in the original *Tram Show* where the ticket inspector Morris Stanley, has just dismissed the conductress, Alice, for dereliction of duty. In her grief Alice literally throws herself sobbing onto the nearest passenger and that person responds with what looks like sympathy tempered by shock and hysterical disbelief that this could actually be happening to her. In fact the audience member mirrors Alice turning her own check onto the 'passenger' next to her. If Diderot's fourth wall in theatre is what separates an audience from the stage, then this moment in *The Tram Show* effectively breaks through the 'fifth wall' that obtains between audience members themselves. In this example therefore, the architecture of the inter-personal correspondence between performer and spectator, and between the spectators themselves, has shifted some distance from that which is normally available in a theatre that privileges vision.

Now there have been prior attempts to imagine how the experience of drama might become more all engaging.

About half way through Aldous Huxley's *Brave New World* the 'savage' character, ironically one of the last few real human beings left on the planet, is taken to a 'feelie', to what the 'movie' has effectively become in Huxley's dystopian future. Here sunk in his pneumatic stall the savage witnesses characters in a kind of three dimensional projection, a 'synthetic talking, stereoscopic feely with scent organ accompaniment'. The characters in the feelie are "incomparably more solid-looking than they would have seemed in actual flesh and blood, *far more real than reality,*" At one point it depicts a, quote "gigantic Negro locked in the arms of a golden-haired, young brachy-cephalic Beta-Plus female."

> The savage started. That sensation on his lips! He lifted a hand to his mouth: the titillation ceased; let his hand fall back on the metal knob; it began again. The scent organ meanwhile breathed pure musk. Expiringly a sound track super-dove cooed 'Oo-ooh'; and vibrating only thirty two times a second, a deeper than African bass made answer: Aa-aah.' 'Ooh-ah! Oo-ah!' the stereoscopic lips came together again, and once more the facial erogenous zones of the six thousand spectators in the Alhambra tingled with almost intolerable galvanic pleasure. 'Ooh...'
> (Aldous Huxley, *Brave New World* 135)

Now, I'm not suggesting that going to a TheatreWorks location play was anything quite like that. For a start we rarely had the space available to play to houses of more than a 100 people, and certainly there weren't too many erogenous zones involved so far as I can discover or recall, but the total experience of a location play *did* involve senses of feeling, taste and smell.

Figure 4. Storming Mont Albert By Tram (Davies 1982)
'Blood' on his hands.
Ticket inspector Morris Stanley (Johnnie Walker) stares horrified
at what he thinks is the derro's blood.

To return to that moment in *the Tram Show* where the ticket inspector who has sacked Alice earlier, now accidentally stabs the derro character in an inept tussle between them over a plastic toy knife. The Ticket Inspector emerges from the altercation with his hands covered in a red viscous substance. He immediately, assumes this is the derro's blood and that he has seriously wounded, if not actually killed the man. Morris wallows in a Macbeth-style shock/horror exit, staring incredulously at the 'blood' on his hands, displaying them both to the audience and to nonplussed motorists waiting for him to cross the road as he flees in despair from the tram.

However, the substance is in fact, merely tomato sauce from the derro's pie (put under his coat to keep it warm). But the fact that the audience can already *smell* that it is tomato sauce amplifies their enjoyment of Morris's discomfiture. They know he's acting, they know the blood is fake, but they also accept that his *character* is *not* pretending. In this example *The Tram Show* plays with an inherited stage tradition regarding the depiction of blood in performance, something identified by Lucy Nevitt who found that it could

"…easily fail to achieve its intended effect through a failure of credibility" because "spectators know it is not real and so always judge it against that knowledge: stage blood effects need to overcome the fact of their unreality, not by genuinely seeming to be real, but by meeting an expected standard of generic credibility – by seeming to *try* to look like blood. (87; original emphasis)

Nevitt goes on to note that "[b]lood effects in theatre tend to be reserved for moments of high narrative tension" (88). The result of this moment in *The Tram Show* is to drive the annoying ticket inspector off the tram, apparently guilty of manslaughter, never to be seen again. Thus *The Tram Show's* Macbeth moment co-opts the convention of 'fake' bleeding and takes it to a point of comic absurdity. It is altogether another order of suspended disbelief. In this way the comedic potential of the Ticket Inspector's delusion is enhanced and extended, and eventually capped by the derro himself, left behind on the tram and angry that his 'lunch' is now ruined and demanding to know who's going to replace it, but Morris Stanley is no longer there to blame.

David Wiles makes the point

Neither Appia nor anyone else in the twentieth century had an easy answer to the question of how to make the actor-audience relationship closer, once the proscenium arch had gone. What sort of activity was now expected of the spectator? How should the seats be arranged? What degree of merging between actor an spectator was possible? How was interaction to be reconciled with aesthetic distance (236 – 237)

Yet tantalizingly, Wiles history of Western performance space stops short of the outbreak of site-specific practice that takes place in the UK, particularly in the 1990s and early 2000s.

Tim Etchells, of Forced Entertainment, echoing Foucault's description of the present epoch as belonging to the 'near and the far, of the side-by-side, of the dispersed' (Open Spaces 22), hits a note of warning, however.

Theatre must take account of how technology…has rewritten and is rewriting bodies, changing our understandings of narratives and places, changing our relationships to culture, changing our understandings of presence. Because to fall back on theatre's oldest rubric–an actor in front of an audience–is not something one can do lightly, not something one can do without understanding the complexities of what we might mean when we say 'actor' and what we mean when we say 'in front of'…presence is now always complicated and layered, a thing of degrees, and in these strange times one can feel closer to a person, sometimes when they are further away than when they are fully and simply before us. (*Certain Fragments* 97)

Here's Foucault's prediction of the near and the far again. The sense of 'engulfment' in a theatre experience that Artaud was calling for (also curiously around the same time as the sensual immersion of Huxley's 'feelies'), was something that TheatreWorks aimed for – or perhaps more accurately, stumbled upon – in their determination as a community theatre company to take theatre out to people and explore all sorts of potential new interconnectivities– not just in subject matter, holding the suburban stories up to the people who lived them, but also in an exploration of site-specific performance across a progressive staging of plays in tents, trams, boats, pubs, houses and gardens. This is a progression in itself reveals a certain systematic intention to explore and innovate. The end result in the more successful versions, was an immersion of the audience in the dramatic experience which I would argue pushed out the boundaries of what was theatrically possible. Here presence and space were tangible things.

If we look at the TheatreWorks location *oeuvre* as a coherent and evolving body of work therefore what it gives back to Foucault's hypothesis of the heterotopia are concrete examples of how such spaces CAN be created and managed as places of alternate ordering. Above all the key lies I would argue in notions of "containerization" and "authenticity": how best to define the 'borders' of the narrative space so that it is both permeable and safely cocooned from the risks involved when engaging with an outside reality. The process always involves a suspension of disbelief. How successfully the narrative space 'authentically' inhabits its place of performance, clearly enhances an audience's experience of the event. It is not so much a question noted by Miwon Kwon and first asserted by US site-specific artist ???? that to move the work is to destroy the work, but rather, the question in the theatrical context might be more "could this story conceivably happen here?"

The result in TheatreWorks case was a succession of plays that started with scaffolding on portable stage, lead to the insertion of tents into shopping centres, leapt onto trams, then across onto boats and finally into houses both public and private.

What they offer the concept of the heterotopia is their demonstration of the ease and multiple inventiveness with which such spaces can be created and managed inside real places for dramatic purposes. The key lies in containerization: how to make space of performance permeable but "safe" at the same time. Here the audience is absent and present at the same time. It is present in an embodied form inside a real moment. It is also invisible as an audience to any outside reality looking back in. Thus the tension between presence and absence (embodiment and the imagination) can be the energy flow that conditions the audience experience of the play.

What follows therefore is a brief history of the plays and various audience roles and methods of containerization: managed not only to extract money and make the exercise financially viable but to also to minimise risk…

Miwon Kwon, Nick Kaye and others source the origins of site-specific performance overseas in minimalism and site-specificity the visual arts but they derive in Australia I would also argue from the practices of independent film making where dramatic scenes were performed in real places out of budgetary necessity as much as from a desire to appropriate public space for dramatic purposes. In TheatreWorks case both Caz Howard and I had previously worked on a film about the dismissal of the Whitlam Government in 1975.

Figure 5. *Exits* (Davies, Laughren, Howard 1980)
Appropriating public space in independent film.

Exits mixed dramatically reconstructed scenes inside a semi-real time documentary account of *les événements* of November 11, 1975.

Another influence in TheatreWorks drive towards site-specific practice was its agenda as a community theatre company to reach out and produce plays in the suburban heartland it chosen to occupy.

One of TheatreWorks' early community projects, *Couch 22* (1983) involved engaging with some of the (largely hidden) community of unemployed young people in the otherwise affluent eastern suburbs. It took the form of a documentary film based on interviews performed *alfresco* in places like Camberwell Junction. Here props such as a couch and carpet were used to literally occupy public space for performance purposes

(photo Liz Honybun)
Figure 6. *Couch 22* (1983) Occupying suburban space
Paul Davies directs CUSH members from behind the camera

Figure 6 shows members of C.U.S.H. (Camberwell Unemployed Self Help group) filming on location in busy Camberwell Junction. Here the TheatreWorks cast and crew have taken 'the couch' of the title and used it to occupy a corner of public space, deploying or assuming the licence of a film crew to re-position what is usually a private space (a living room) on public land.

Even before company officially existed, while still students at the VCA, the prospective TheatreWorks ensemble used a purpose built scaffolding set for Hannie Rayson's first play *Please Return to Sender* (1980).

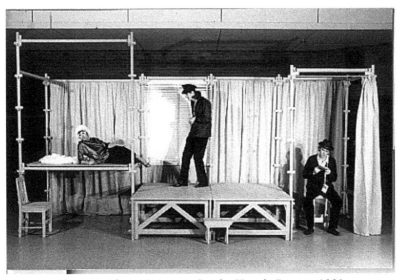

Figure 7. *Please Return to Sender* Hannie Rayson 1980
Scaffolding as spatial container

This was a gender-reversal story where a male postman becomes pregnant and is forced to consider an abortion. It was designed tour the company through the eastern suburbs, its chosen community of operations. While the demountable set not un-reminiscent of Brith Gof's 19?? production of Twi Bydwyd, which used a scaffolding set based on a design by Bernard Tscumi to stage simultaneous performances of three separate scenes in three transparent rooms.

Please Return to Sender may have been an idea for portable theatre space but it was clearly structured along the lines of the traditional proscenium arch and in practice wasn't all that mobile. So this was not a site-specific play according to Fiona Wilkie's definition, because while it might have satisfied the criteria of "performance occurring in a non-theatre venue" (1) it was not a play in which "site was a vital element, instrumental in developing the theme or form of the work" (2). However Wilkie herself concedes that such a definition omits the potential for "movement" "transience" and "playfulness".

Transience and playfulness and movement were much better organized in TW's next production *The Go Anywhere (within reason) Show* which ditched the clunky scaffolding approach in favour of a more portable certainly much more lightweight tent.

Figure 8. Tents as spatial containers
The Go Anywhere (within reason) Show (Group Devised 1981)

Here the play, about a homeless middle class family, was more thematically aligned with the place of performance in so far as the Dickens: Dick, Dolly, Darryl, Deidre and Desdemona were allegedly on an extended camping holiday to cover over their desperate financial plight in Malcolm Fraser's recession of the early 1980s. From day one TheatreWorks' mission was to celebrate and disturb. Thus the shopping centre, or church hall or school in which their tent was pitched and around which the performance took place, was potentially their place of abode for the night. Although the strict convention of authenticity to site was broken by certain pantomimed interventions such as a television news broadcast, the play demonstrated the potential for this kind of theatre to be mobile and reasonably popular. However because of the dispersed nature of audiences in public places such as shopping centres, the element of containerization in *The Go Anywhere (within reason) Show* became a work in progress. The audiences were still essentially separate from the action, looking on from outside a performative circle centered in and around the tent.

The breakthrough step was to make them complicit in the action with the performers: Wilkie's notion of 'playfulness'. *Authenticity* (spatial relations) and *complicity* (audience relations) collided for the first time in *Storming Mont Albert By Tram*. Here a form of Boal's invisible theatre colonized the street.

Apart from the aforementioned biblical scenes enacted on the backs of medieval wagons and certain agit-prop raids on trams in Leningrad and Moscow after the Russian Revolution, the world's first truly moving, spoken word drama on a wheeled vehicle was arguably TheatreWorks' second site-specific piece *Storming Mont Albert By Tram*. It was in many ways the par excellence example of the emerging form, a perfect container that was safe, familiar and permeable. It combined authenticity with mobility in a package was easy to understand and relate to.

The tram was not only a perfect container it immediately implicated its audience in the events of the play as passengers who could follow the action as it happened all around them and as it frequently left the tram to invade the space of the street when characters got on and off.

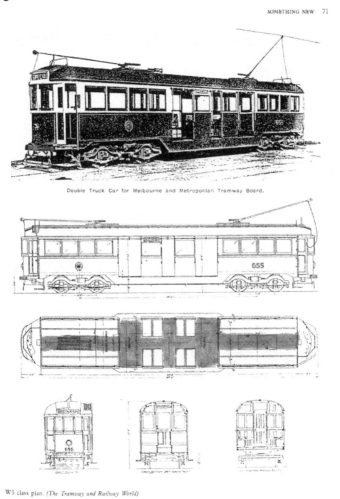

SOMETHING NEW   71

Double Truck Car for Melbourne and Metropolitan Tramway Board.

W3 class plan. *(The Tramway and Railway World)*

Figure 9. Floor plan and elevations of a W class tram
Green areas denote available performance spaces between seats

Unlike a traditional theatre set a tram did not have to pretend to be a tram. Here the element of disbelief was reserved for the second tier audience, the people outside the tram who are randomly caught up in its events as it passed them by.

Figure 10.
Scenes from *Storming Mont Albert by Tram*

The company experiment that had begun for TheatreWorks with a play performed around a moveable canvas tent made a quantum leap here – a spatial trajectory as it were onto a moving vehicle. Certainly, *The Tram Show* helped put TheatreWorks on the map both critically and financially, and its immediate success gave rise to an outbreak of site-specificity in Melbourne theatre practice that flourished for well over a decade.

The Tram Show was produced over a dozen years from 1982 to 1994 on various tram routes in both Melbourne and Adelaide, trambulating a distance that would have taken the play and its combined audience of some 20,000 people virtually half way around the world!

However, its sequel set on a Melbourne river boat was, while still popular with audiences less critically successful.

Figure 10. River Theatre *Breaking Up In Balwyn* (Paul Davies 1983)
An uninvited 'passenger' waits to board the MV Yarra Princess.

Part of the problem of *Breaking Up In Balwyn* derives from the play being, in a sense, too "closed in on itself": an island both aesthetically and spatially – without Foucault's call for it to be simultaneously "open to the infinity of the sea". The premise of the play was a divorce celebration set aboard a party boat hired for the occasion at which the audience were invited friends and family (in the style of Jack Hibberd's earlier wedding play *Dimboola 1969*).

Figure 11 Re enter Greek Frenchmaid, Lurlene
after being left behind at Interval

This third example of TheatreWorks' location theatre experiment had a more artificial quality than its trambulating predecessor and was in less vibrant contact with the outside world.

Figure 12.
Nigel engages member of the audience (party guest) in a dance

It had site-specific virtues of *mobility* and took place in *real time*, it also involved senses of touch, taste and smell (haptic and olfactory spaces). Here you could dance with the actors and share in toasts and divorce cake, but the play lacked a certain *authenticity* in its thematic premise: the idea of inverting the social ritual of the wedding reception and essentially turning it into a celebration of divorce and a privileged woman's search for freedom. As a result, *The Boat Show* was less successful in making its audience *complicit* as 'friends and family' of the gay divorcee, in the events that unfold during her floating party.

The final set of plays in the TW canon are the ones that took place in existing houses.

Figure 13. 'Linden' St. Kilda, circa 1900.
Members of the Michaelis family pose in their front garden.
Location for *Living Rooms* (1986) and *Full House/No Vacancies* (1989).

In the winter of 1986, *Living Rooms* was staged in 'Linden', a grand Victorian mansion built a hundred years earlier. The three Acts of *Living Rooms* are each set in one of Linden's large, downstairs rooms, and evoke a key moment in the building's (and the nation's) history. These three periods and the characters that embody them, eventually collide in a surreal denouement (literally a collision of time and space) in the hallway. In this way the house itself becomes a palimpsest for distinctive historical formations: Linden's bunyip-aristocratic heyday in 1900,

(Photo © Ruth Maddison)

Figure 14. *Living Rooms* – The Drawing Room Act, 1900.
Cuthbert toasts Michael's embarkation for the Boer War.
Audience present as unacknowledged 'guests' at a farewell party.

Here spectators are arranged around four sides of an open playing area. Here they sat as largely unacknowledged 'guests' at a farewell party for Lt. Michael Deegan who is about to sail with the second Victorian contingent to the Boer War.

A second scene is set in 1972 takes place in a 'Flatette' during Linden's boarding house decline. Here the audience are positioned behind a light scrim and thus rendered invisible to the actors. In this way their mode of viewing is impeded or filtered, literally. Here they are also present as witnesses, but now in an even more extreme and distanced manner – as if looking in on some form of social experiment, like trainee medicos observing an operation, or a team of detectives scrutinizing an interrogation through a one way mirror.

In this sense, Paul Bugden, whose rooms this is, resides in a place of secretive examination, a metaphorical prison. Indeed, issues of 'legality' and suppressed identity drive the Flatette Act given that Bugden as a conscientious objector is on the run from the Federal Police – signifying conscription and Vietnam, and yet another 'unsettling' moment in Australia's ongoing formation of nationhood.

(Photo © Ruth Maddison)
Figure 15. *Living Rooms* – the Flatette Act (1972)
A traveler frozen in time, Paul Bugden (Paul Davies) awaits the buzzer that will summon him to 'life'. Here the audience are 'hidden' out of sight, cast as agents of a panoptic gaze.

Finally projected slightly into the future (1988) where Linden has been transformed into an art gallery (as it currently remains).

(Photo © Ruth Maddison)

Figure 16. *Living Rooms* – The Gallery Act, 1988.
Monika (Caz Howard) and Leon (Peter Sommerfeld)
waiting impatiently for something to happen.
Audience mixed with actors as fellow witnesses to a 'performance art event'.

This late Twentieth Century renovation was emblematic of the re-gentrification that the suburb surrounding Linden was then going through Therefore the building itself already contained an embedded history with which the fiction of the play could resonate.

As Figure 16 indicates, the characters in the Gallery Act (Monika and Leon), were present within the audience (to begin with) but as their own conversation becomes more heated this well dressed, culturally articulate couple, seem to emerge from the audience as if they are 'real' people who have come to see (according to the program) an 'exhibition of location theatre' – which, in their particular room, doesn't seem to be working. They dutifully press their buzzer but no actors turn up – because of course, Monika and Leon *are* the play in this room. And so a 'performance art piece' *is* happening, although as 'characters', Monika and Leon never acknowledge this.

Thus while each House play managed the creation of its counter-site of performance in slightly different ways, common elements (of simultaneity, mobility and juxtaposition) across all these works are evident.

In contrast to TheatreWorks' earlier plays on public transport, the *Living Rooms'* 'stage' remained static while here it was the spectators who moved. Mobility therefore remains a key site-specific element. In order to locate the story inside the building it was notionally about, the performative strategy was to divide the arriving audience into three groups (of roughly 30 people each) by handing them different coloured floor plans of the house.

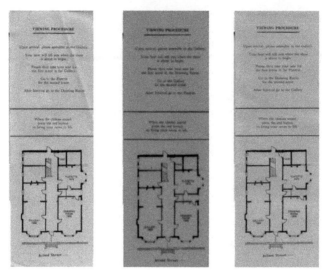

Figure 17. *Living Rooms* (1986)
'Viewing procedure' for the three audience groups: grey, orange blue.

These pamphlets explained how to 'animate' each room by pressing a buzzer located on the wall, and invited the various audience groups to view the play in one of three possible orders (Figure 17). This division enabled each thirty minute scene to be staged simultaneously (and repeated three times).

Finally, a short, concluding scene was staged on Linden's grand central staircase which drew all characters and all audience groups to a denouement in the hallway.

Figure 18. The Hallway Finale

These different modes of witnessing (voyeurs, detached scruntineers, fellow visitors to a gallery) allowed the *Living Rooms'* audience to become conscious of itself as an audience (albeit one composed of three sub-sets). They were engaging with and being engaged by the play in different ways. Their 'occupation' of Linden (a real and imagined place) therefore comes with a sense of trespass, of being complicit with the actors in an intrusion upon the histories and living spaces of others; of being in a private space where the legitimacy of their presence is at best questionable.

On one level they are all ghosts 'inhabiting' a troubled site and thereby constitute a collective uncanny, a post-colonial presence in a colonialised world. While complicit with the events taking place through their silent witnessing, the audience are also offered a shared experience, a sense of moving around as a group, of accessing the narrative sequence with different itineraries – something which again engenders the 'community of the audience' within the play. In *Living Rooms* they are on a journey together, through time and space. Such reconfigurations of the theatre-going experience engendered a sense of being *present* in a way that was greater than the sum of its parts. The result was the staging of a kind of meta- event, with sounds bleeding from one room/time/space into another and which, despite its experimental nature, again found a rapport with people not normally drawn to live theatre. Which brings us back to the future and hopefully to know the place for the first time. To the third way...

More than two decades after the TheatreWorks location experiment ended, I find it encouraging even quite remarkable, that only few weeks ago I was able to a TheatreWorks supported play called *Hullo My Name Is* written and performed by Nicola Dunn, where I'm given my own name tag:

Figure 19.
Audience identification tag

...and invested in the role of someone attending a Community Centre (which is what the TheatreWorks space as Parish Hall essentially is). Here Nicola Gunn, cast as an all purpose community worker starts organising activities, inviting us to play ping pong and other board games, or to plant seedlings in pots.

Figure 20. Nicola Gunn as a community worker (photo Joe Armao)
Hullo My Name Is TheatreWorks September 2012

At one point, armed only with a megaphone, Nicola leads us out of the building into the random reality of Acland Street for a short street promenade where she reflects out loud to all and sundry on the pain of being an artist, going down on one knee while standing on a traffic pedestal. Back at the community centre she lies on top of an audience, engaging haptic space to the maximum, enacting what she calls the 'body blanket' maneuver. Then she hands out art materials for a life drawing class and poses for us clad only in her radio microphone, all the while continuing a monologue that relates an unfolding story of love, identity, longing and the pain of loneliness.

Now I fully accept that this might not be everybody's idea of a great night out in the theatre. But I can assure you I was amused, intrigued, a little bit shocked, I also saw my image of a few minutes ago projected on a large screen at the back of the space, creating a slight temporal distortion. I knew I didn't have to take part in any of this unless I really wanted to, and in any case I readily enough found myself holding hands with a stranger in a big circle with our eyes closed. (But I'm from Byron Bay). *Hullo My Name Is* is a play about personal isolation that nevertheless created connections not only between Nicola and her audience (at times quite intensely so) but also within the audience themselves, again smashing through the fifth wall. In the best TheatreWorks tradition I became part of the community of the audience, something not available to the individual recipient of a **s-i-g-h-t** specific experience – whether screen based or live.

The point about all the plays under discussion here is
The do work
They establish new bonds with audiences
They don't cost much to put on.
They can be great fun to put on.
They restore a certain Benjaminian aura to the business of entertainment in an age where the sight based/screen dominated digital revolution produces only virtual audiences for virtual spaces.

And if the art of theatre is to find new expressivities, if it is going to be more than just a bunch of voyeurs gawking at a mob of exhibitionists, it has to embrace the site-specific experience, to negotiate the infinite number of ways in which fiction can be invisibly and playfully inserted into real places.

Julian Beck, of New York's *Living Theatre* spoke in the 1960s of his dream of a company of actors that could "stop imitating", and "move their audiences" so as to imbue them with "ideas and feelings that allow transformation and genuine transcendence to be achieved". Sadly Beck concluded however that "None of the actors" knew what he was talking about. (qtd Tytell The Living Theatre Art Exile and Outrage 161) Julian Beck's greatest misfortune well may be that he was ahead of his time. In an increasingly digitized world which has vastly upscaled our basic interconnectivity, and where people now spend so much of their working and personal lives alone and in front of a screen we find that all too sadly despite this enhanced ability to communicate we still don't have all that much to say. The cost has been a loss of physical contact, something that, despite the constant shape shifting is at the heart of its practice is essentially what the Art of Theatre has to offer.

TRANSITING THROUGH THE CULTURES OF SUBURBIA

How Theatreworks Discovered the "Community" of an Audience.

Australasian Drama Studies Vol 60 (April 2012). 138-156.

Keywords: Australian 'Next Wave' Theatre, Community Theatre, Location Plays, Site-specific Performance.

Abstract

"From Burwood to the Bay": A theatre company's transition through the cultures of suburbia.

In its first iteration as an ensemble of actors, writers and directors dedicated to "celebrating and disturbing" Melbourne audiences, *TheatreWorks* changed its base of operations from a tiny office at Burwood State College (in 1981) to the Canterbury Gardens Centre (1983) and finally to a Parish Hall in St. Kilda (in 1985), where in a rare feat of longevity, the company continues to support the production of innovative, original, work. This paper examines that transition from the outer suburbs to an inner urban demographic as a search for new audiences across different cultural sub-groups: middle class, upper middle class and the mix of younger, poorer but artistically literate interest groups to be found converging on St. Kilda in the 1980s. In a wider context, *TheatreWorks* was one of a number of small, professional companies that deployed themselves in a broad strategic formation across Victoria at that time. *West* went west, *TheatreWorks* east, the *Murray River Performing Group* north, *The Mill* south, and *Crosswinds* ended up somewhere in the middle. Additionally, there was *Anthill*, *La Mama*, *Melbourne Worker's Theatre* and *The Church* – all contributing to a vibrant theatre tradition since described by Geoffrey Milne and others as the 'Next Wave' movement. In addition to transitioning through these suburbs as a company, *TheatreWorks* also developed forms of site-specific practice which saw the staging of plays on trams, and riverboats, in pubs, houses and gardens. These 'location plays' with their energetic manipulation of diegetic and found spaces, drew in new audiences for theatre. The *Tram* and *Boat Shows* literally moved their audiences from their outer suburban starting points to the city and back. Other plays such as *Living Rooms* (produced in a former colonial mansion) explored the demographic changes in St. Kilda by ushering its audience through different historical moments in the same building. Thus, not only did the company itself 'move' in response to a changing aesthetic and cultural agenda, so too, did the audiences within each show.

TheatreWorks and the Community Theatre Movement

On the 23rd of February 1981, an ensemble of recent graduates from the Victorian College of the Arts, Drama School (Caz Howard, Peter Sommerfeld, Susie Fraser, Hannie Rayson and Peter Finlay) incorporated themselves as the 'Eastern Suburbs Community Theatre Company Limited' but the group was more colloquially known as 'TheatreWorks' and was re-incorporated as such (on 21st Februrary1986) after consolidating its move to the Acland Street Parish Hall in St. Kilda. Right from the beginning, the company was

committed to exploring how a group of professional actors/theatre workers can best serve the people of the Eastern Suburbs by providing an *accessible* form of *entertainment*, educational and leisure activity, through the services of a community theatre (emphasis added).[86]

A few years later these aims had evolved to include

creating work which is pertinent to contemporary Australian lives, and which reflects the energies of urban life, building a symbolic vocabulary which will serve and sustain people in their search for meaning and identity. We aim to make our work both celebratory and disturbing. 'Celebratory' in that a sense of wonder and curiosity is embraced and reflected in all aspects of our work. 'Disturbing' in that we do not see our role as passively reflecting the status quo, but as intervening against certain spurious images disseminated in the mass culture, thereby opening up new channels of perception. We also seek to explore new actor- audience relationships and thereby to maximise the possibilities of the audience/participants both *identifying with the work, and evaluating* the broader issues at stake. (emphasis added). [87]

The 'disturb' clause hints at an already uncertain relationship to the suburbs surrounding Burwood State College where the company had its first office. Equally important is the open-ended nature of TheatreWorks' embrace of this new audience – who would also be the chief source material for the narratives of ordinary life to follow: stories and characters that could authentically exist inside a tram, a shopping centre, a riverboat, pub, family home or boarding house, all of which became sites of TheatreWorks productions. Accessibility, complicity, mobility and connectivity would become key elements in the company's

---

[86] TheatreWorks' Archive (Brisbane: Fryer Library, University of Queensland) Artistic Policy Documents, 1981.

[87] TheatreWorks' Archive (Brisbane: Fryer Library, University of Queensland). Artistic Policy Documents, 1984.

performative style, especially as TheatreWorks pursued the exploration of its self-described 'location theatre' plays, works which would now be more commonly known as 'site-specific theatre'[88].

In a text-centric critical discourse not a great deal has been written about these plays given that the script was a relatively minor part of a process that encouraged improvisation and a good deal of physical business. Consequently, the public record has tended to overlook both the subtle management of social spaces, and the robust interplay of fiction and reality that is going on in these works.[89] I would argue that it requires a new critical approach to assess site-specific performance, and new criteria with which to interrogate its spatial manipulation. Such a tool kit would allow an appreciation of elements such as the engagement of multiple senses (olfactory space), the relation of text to location, exploration of actor-audience relationships and co-ordination and stage management of the fiction/reality interface.

Certainly nothing has been written about Melbourne's outbreak of site-specific theatre in the 1980s as a coherent body of work: the 'location theatre' sub-movement, as it were, within the larger 'Community Theatre' umbrella – which in itself was an integral part of the 'Next Wave' or 'Third Wave' of Australian theatre as described by Geoffrey Milne and others.[90] Increasingly, a rich archive of audio visual material is being produced and uncovered to counter the ephemerality of live performance – something with which to apply a new critique of these productions. TheatreWorks for one, has left a useful record of its location plays in the University of Queensland's Fryer Library, including film, video and audio recordings of plays and workshops as well as photographs, manuscripts, company documents and other published and unpublished materials.

However, the general oversight has allowed certain historical blind spots to emerge, an example of which can be found in Laura Levin's recent description of

---

[88] See Gay McAuley, *Space in Performance*. (Ann Arbor: University of Michigan Press, 1999). Also Mike Pearson and Michael Shanks, *Theatre/Archaeology* (London: Routledge, 2001). And Fiona Wilkie, *Out of Place: the Negotiation of Space in Site-Specific Performance* (University of Surrey, 2004). PhD thesis.
[89] There are of course, several worthy exceptions, including Geoffrey Milne's *Theatre Australia (Un)Limited: Australian Theatre since the 1950s*. Australian Playwrights. Ed. Kelly, Veronica. Vol. 10. (Amsterdam/New York: Rodopi, 2004). Also *Community Theatre in Australia*. In Richard Fotheringham, ed., (North Ryde NSW: Methuen, 1987), and John O'Toole's *The Process of Drama: Negotiating Art and Meaning* (London: Routledge, 1992) which has a section on *The Tram Show*: 'Renegotiating Expectations in Adult Theatre' 173-182.
[90] Ibid. 5-6. See especially the graph of the three distinct 'waves' of theatre activity on 5.

Nights In This City (a bus show by the British theatre group Forced Entertainment in 1995) as "the *celebrated prototype* for urban site-specific work" (emphasis added).[91] This production used two tour guides to take audiences on a bus trip around Sheffield which included certain staged events along the way. Yet more than a decade earlier, in 1982, Rod Quantock's 'celebrated' *Bus, Son of Tram* carried passengers on busses to improvised performances at sites around Melbourne by two 'tour guides', one (Quantock) carrying a chicken on a pole as a rallying point for his fellow travelers, the other (Jeff Brookes), holding a stuffed koala. The point being (and part of the motive for this article) is that we neglect our own history at the risk of it being overlooked.

TheatreWorks was the third example of a Community Theatre company to emerge from the Victorian College of the Arts. The formula of "theatre by the people, for the people, of the people"[92] had been pioneered by WEST in the western suburbs of Melbourne and the Murray River Performing Group after they headed north to Albury-Wadonga (both emerging from the VCA in1979). Earlier, The Mill Theatre had gone south-west to Geelong and later Crosswinds would occupy the centre (of Victoria) by basing itself in Wangaratta/Benalla.

Politically and demographically this movement can now be read as part of a strategic plan to capitalize on the momentum building behind a wider democratization of the arts across Victoria that followed in the wake of the Cain (State) and Hawke (Federal) Labour governments[93]. Peter Oysten who had instigated the do-it-yourself and keep -it-local ethos at the VCA Drama School, had come back from directing a regional company in the UK towards the end of the Australian 'Second' or 'New Wave' in 1975. [94] In this cultural/political climate Oysten's agenda was unashamedly nationalist.

It's important to find the Australian voice because this is who we are. Otherwise it's schizophrenic because we are a very naïve people – open and susceptible... So my attitude in starting the School of Drama at the VCA was that we would speak *our* words and I asked Sue Spunner to teach a subject called Australian History. I found a great number of students didn't know enough about the subject. And if

---

[91] Laura Levin , 'Can the City Speak? Site Specific Art After Poststructuralism', in D.J. Hopkins, Shelly Orr and Kim Solga, ed., *Performance and the City*. (New York: Palgrave Macmillan, 2009): 241.

[92] Geoffrey Milne, Personal Interview, TheatreWorks' Archive (Brisbane: Fryer Library, University of Queensland) 2010. CD.

[93] Indeed in the very person of Victoria's new Arts Minister, Race Mathews, there was a sense of a certain continuity with and restoration of Whitlamesque patronage for cultural activities across the board.

[94] The Duke's Playhouse in Lancaster.

you don't have a sense of where you come from and why you're here then how can you be responsible for expressing the dreams in theatrical terms? [95]

As Geoffrey Milne points out

The Second Wave was when we Australianised the Australian theatre. And got the situation up to the stage where Australia became the dominant content. It was largely a mono-cultural, nationalist project. There was a fertile national imaginary that encouraged the development of an Australian culture across the board.[96]

So if the Pram Factory and Nimrod had been about finding the Australian voice, the Community Theatre Movement was perhaps about getting lost in the multiplicity of voices that followed.

As Richard Fotheringham notes in his introduction to *Community Theatre In Australia,* and as TheatreWorks soon discovered, there can be many different kinds of community, based not only on socio economic indicators, but also on criteria such as age, gender, institutional, or work situations.[97] Consequently, inside this apparently amorphous suburban demographic, into which TheatreWorks had chosen to launch itself, there were in fact any number of different communities and the cultures associated with them. All of which begs the question: what constitutes a community? As Fotheringham himself concedes, the term is difficult to define.[98] One can talk about sharing something in common (a suburb, a workplace, ethnicity, the local football team etc.) but I would argue that a more critical ingredient in the formation of 'community' is 'identity' – something internal and subjective rather than being externally or objectively driven. And if we are to talk about the idea of a 'community of the audience' this self-referencing involves more than just groups of spectators seeing themselves across a thrust stage, something which Gay McAuley discusses in a recent article about Sydney theatre spaces.[99] With regards to *The Tram Show* for example, the audience becomes aware of itself not only as fellow passengers sharing a journey and facing each other across an aisle, but as a separate cohort within the larger random reality of the streetscape going past outside which sometimes enters back

[95] Peter Oysten, Personal Interview, TheatreWorks' Archive (Brisbane: Fryer Library, University of Queensland) 2010. CD.

[96] Geoffrey Milne, Personal Interview, TheatreWorks' Archive (Fryer Library, University of Queensland) 2010. CD

[97] Ibid. 20.

[98] Ibid. 20.

[99] Gay McAuley, 'The Sydney Trinity: Performance Space and the Creation of a Matrix of Sensibility', *Australasian Drama Studies* 58 (April 2011) 83.

into the frame of the play in the form of regular commuters expecting a normal ride.

An earlier example of a Community Theatre model can be seen in The Mill Theatre Company, set up as an offshoot of Deakin University in Geelong in 1979. Its founding artistic director, James McCaughey, explains that

Part of my ideological framework was that theatre was dead. It had to go into the streets and work places. If theatre is just going to be a ghetto thing, then I don't want to spend my life doing it. The mission was to explore what was the role and function of a professional theatre company in Geelong. And it sure as hell wasn't to run a repertory company. Theatre was an activity integral to all human life. I felt we had to look for ways (to enact plays) in different locations and societal frameworks, in which we could create the events with people. Or help them create the events.[100]

The Cultures of Suburbia

The term 'suburban' implies something '*less* than urban', lower in the hierarchy, bland, away from the centre of things, of minor significance, often co-joined to the idea of 'wasteland'. However, what TheatreWorks encountered was something that Donald Horne had identified almost a generation earlier. The quote from *The Lucky Country* that TheatreWorks' included on the opening page of its first pitch document to the funding bodies was Horne's assertion that

The profusion of life doesn't wither because people live in small brick houses with red tile roofs. It is the almost universal failure of Australian writers to realize this that causes them either to caricature Australian life, or to ignore it... Almost all Australian writers, whatever their politics, are reactionaries whose attitude to the massive diversities of suburban life is to ignore it or to condemn it rather than discover what it is." [101]

And this, I would argue, is essentially what the TheatreWorks' project set out to do: to discover who their audiences were, and to reflect that discovery back to them in order create a culture of live performance in the suburbs and the regions where there had been none, a process that was intentionally strategic. As Peter Oysten recalls, he "had a map on the wall of my office with the various population

---

[100] James McCaughey, Personal Interview, TheatreWorks' Archive (Brisbane: Fryer Library, University of Queensland) 2010. CD
[101] Donald Horne, *The Lucky Country*. (Ringwood: Penguin, 1964) 18. As quoted in TheatreWorks' Archive (Brisbane: Fryer Library, University of Queensland) Artistic Policy Documents. 1981.

densities, giving us an insight into where new companies could go…you must start from a sense of place."[102]

Strategic mobility was also inherent in the TheatreWorks' business plan because, in its first five years of operations (until the move St. Kilda in 1985), the company did not have a proper performance space of its own. Not surprisingly, in these peripatetic years, a certain restlessness characterized both the company and its activities. Plays from 1980 to 1986, all had a tour-able potential, designed to be produced in any available hall or class room, internal or external space. Initially, therefore, the elements of mobility and accessibility to be found in the early plays were the outcome of a certain corporate homelessness. The search for new performance spaces was leading TheatreWorks increasingly out into the open, to the streets, parks and public spaces (including public transport) that a long tradition of street theatre had already occupied, arguably tracing a genealogy back to the practices of medieval theatre with its miracle and mystery plays staged in public squares and mounted on the backs of wagons.

The agenda was two-fold: to situate the work in the eastern suburbs and to reflect that community back to itself. TheatreWorks also sought to do this in ways where the decision making was shared equally across the ensemble. This intention to reach into the suburban heartland and to do so in a non-hierarchical way (as an 'artistic directorate'), further blurs the demarcation between producers and observers, and prepares the way for any prospective audience to enter into the process as participants, something more than the passive voyeurs of a proscenium-arch theatre, seated alone and in the dark, peering through an invisible fourth wall.

TheatreWorks suburban audiences were not passive, never alone, and rarely in the dark. Nor was there any fourth wall to peer through since the audience for the site-specific plays had been taken through it to be effectively placed 'up' on stage with the actors. In the often confined spaces of these plays, other senses beyond those of sight and hearing could also be engaged including smell, taste and touch. Here audiences got to *feel* the actors – literally, they could fall into your lap, reeling from some dramatic moment, or ask you to dance (at Samantha Hart-Byrne's divorce party): the roar of the grease paint, the smell of the crowd.

All these factors, community outreach, corporate homelessness, performative mobility, new actor/audience relationships, the visceral component, all coalesced to create a form of site-specific production that was playful, inventive and popular,

---

[102] Peter Oysten, Personal Interview, TheatreWorks' Archive (Brisbane: Fryer Library, University of Queensland) 2010. CD

something unique to Melbourne at the time. What they also lead to was the formation of the community of the audience *within* the play.

Transitions

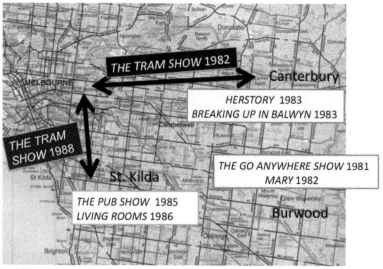

Figure 1. Occupying Suburban Space
Indicative TheatreWorks' productions 1981-1988

Figure 1 shows seven TheatreWorks plays that were sited in the three different municipalities (and effectively very different communities) in which the company positioned itself as it moved steadily west from Burwood towards the inner city.

And if a Community Theatre company is essentially about reflecting a local demographic back to itself, then this progression in search of audiences and stories, is reflected in the quite different content and style of the various productions that came out of the three main stopping points of Burwood, Canterbury and St. Kilda. These range from the *Go Anywhere Show* and *Storming Mont Albert By Tram* to *Mary* (all set in the outer east), *Herstory* and *Breaking Up In Balwyn* (in the more up market middle east) and finally, *The Pub Show* and *Living Rooms* in a much grungier but culturally literate inner-urban community.

Almost from the start there was a certain ambiguity about the outer eastern location in which TheatreWorks had chosen to situate itself. As founding member Hannie Rayson says

The suburban experience was something I was running a million miles from. That's why I'd come to live in Fitzroy, Collingwood, Carlton. I was never going back to the suburbs. But there I was. It wasn't like WEST [community theatre company]. That was something we felt keenly. They were attached to a community that they passionately wanted to represent and we didn't want to represent these [eastern suburbs] values at all. So there was a sense of slight wrong-footedness from the start.[103]

Other founding members had similar reservations. In Susie Fraser's words: "We felt a bit weird going out into the Eastern Suburbs. It was a long way away."[104] Mary Sitarenos also remembers, "when we went out there it was a bit of a desert."[105] And Peter Finlay confesses that he "used to call it Kafka country."[106]

Nevertheless, true to its community agenda, TheatreWorks set out to embody what they found in that 'desert' allowing us to read these seven early plays as reflecting the very different set of cultures thus embraced – all serving to highlight Horne's insight that the "profusion of life" can indeed flourish beneath those amorphous "red brick tiles."

Communities of the Homeless – *The Go Anywhere Show* (1981)

TheatreWorks first response as a company was to produce what Susie Fraser called their "calling card":[107] *The Go Anywhere (within reason) Show,* a play that set out to highlight ('disturb') the hidden unemployment making life difficult for many people in Melbourne's outer eastern suburbs in early 1981 – a contributing factor to the demise of the Fraser Liberal Government two years later.

The Go Anywhere Show enacted an early form of localized site-specific theatre which occupied public spaces and borrowed freely from the agit-prop, street theatre of the late 1960s/early 1970s. Director Robin Laurie (herself a key New Wave player at the Pram Factory), and most of the TheatreWorks' ensemble had been directly or indirectly involved in such activities. As the title implies, *The Go Anywhere Show* was designed to be produced in virtually any location (public or private) that was capable of containing, or attracting an audience. The narrative itself was semi-improvised around a number of set scenes, which were intercut

---

[103] Hannie Rayson Personal Interview, TheatreWorks' Archive (Brisbane: Fryer Library, University of Queensland) 2010. CD

[104] Susie Fraser, Personal Interview, TheatreWorks' Archive (Brisbane: Fryer Library, University of Queensland) 2010. CD

[105] Mary Sitarenos, Personal Interview, TheatreWorks' Archive (Brisbane: Fryer Library, University of Queensland) 2010. CD

[106] Peter Finlay, Personal Interview, TheatreWorks' Archive (Brisbane: Fryer Library, University of Queensland) 2010. CD

[107] Susie Fraser Personal Interview, TheatreWorks' Archive (Brisbane: Fryer Library, University of Queensland) 2010. CD

with a liberal application of physical comedy ('*lazzis*' in *commedia dell'arte* terms).
Sometimes the show would be booked by a school or community centre, at other
times it might be produced *alfresco* in a camping ground or shopping centre – as a
form of theatrical busking.

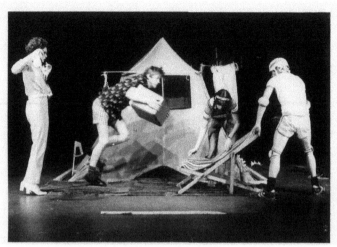

Figure 2. *The Go Anywhere Show* (group devised) 1981
The 'Setting up the Tent' Lazzo
L-R: Caz Howard, Peter Finlay, Hannie Rayson, Tony Kishawi

The performance space of the play was 'produced' in a Lefebvrian sense by the
erection of the tent.[108] What unfolded around this family 'home' was a narrative in
which we meet the Dickens family: Dick (father), Dolly (mother), Darryl (son),
Daphne (daughter) and Desdemona (auntie). The conceit behind the play depicted
the Dickens as a homeless, down-on-their-luck family, perpetually wandering the
eastern suburbs looking for a permanent address (much like TheatreWorks itself).
However, in order to keep up appearances, the Dickens pretended that they were
merely on a sort of "permanent holiday"; when in fact they were actually
unemployed and utterly impoverished.[109] Although Peter Finlay provided the
characters and Hannie Rayson some of the dialogue,[110] much of the humour of the
piece turned on the gap between appearances and reality: that middle class attempt
to stay calm and carry on while ignoring the dire reality of their situation.

---

[108] Henri Lefebvre, *La Production De L'espace*. Trans. Donald Nicholson-Smith,
(Oxford: Blackwell,
1991). See especially 13 where he links the production of space to physical theory.
[109] *The Go Anywhere (within reason) Show* (Group Devised) TheatreWorks'
Archive (Fryer Library, University of Queensland) MS.
[110] Peter Finlay, Personal Interview, (Brisbane: TheatreWorks' Archive: Fryer
Library, University of Queensland) 2010. CD

Communities of Commuters – *Storming Mont Albert by Tram* (1982 - 1994)

Figure 3. *Storming Mont Albert By Tram* (Paul Davies) 1982
The penultimate 'bomb scare' scene
Extreme Left and Right: Peter Sommerfeld, Mary Sitarenos

The story of an 'ordinary tram journey', but based on a real incident witnessed by its author, the original *Tram Show* was staged on a Number 42 tram as it proceeded along its normal route from the Mont Albert terminus to the city and back (interval was held at the Australia Hotel in Collins Street). Of all TheatreWorks' location plays this was by any measure the most successful staging of the site-specific idea, particularly in the integration of text and space.

The story unfolds around various characters as they enter and exit the tram in the guise of ordinary passengers (including an over zealous ticket inspector working 'undercover'). These people form the sort of temporary and often curiously intimate micro relationships that occur between strangers on any public vehicle. As they meet and spark off each other, their various backstories and anxieties unfold in front of an audience cast at first in the role of *de facto* voyeurs, much like anybody overhearing a conversation in public. While the journey proceeds the audience become drawn into the web of events more as accomplices with the actors in a set narrative that has been let loose within the random reality of the city going past outside. Here the audience also become aware of themselves as the object of someone else's gaze, but from a position of narrative privilege – in on the joke as it were.

Finally, after an attempted hijacking by a homeless alcoholic, the 'police' arrive, completely mis-read the situation, and proceed to arrest the wrong people. [111] Like Rod Quantock's bus show the piece revolved around the guiding/uniting spirit of the tram's conductress, Alice Katranski, as she struggled to cope on her first night on the job. [112] Like hospital waiting rooms and airport terminals, trams are social melting pots, one of the few places people from different strata of society can find themselves thrown together. Into this dramatic container TheatreWorks poured a forensic cross section of the different sub-communities it was uncovering in the eastern suburbs and with whom it was engaging in a premeditated act of celebration and disturbance. As well as the 'connie', the ticket inspector, and the homeless alcoholic, the dramatis personae include a slightly threatening punk, a single mother, a visiting Sydney filmmaker, and an upper middle class housewife who's never been on public transport before but reluctantly comes on board looking for the first class section.

The Tram Show became TheatreWorks' signature site-specific play and was reproduced half a dozen times on tram routes in both Melbourne and Adelaide over the succeeding decade. It ran to more than 300 performances and travelled a cumulative distance that would have taken it half way around the world! Figure 3 shows a moment in the play when the police character (back, centre) thinks he has just uncovered a bomb on board the tram (set in a more innocent time when the idea of explosive devices on public transport could still be regarded as a joke – witness the audience reactions).

What made the *Tram Show* so appealing, was not only the sense of inclusion (in that the 'community of the audience' was framed by their shared status as fellow

---

[111] Paul Davies, *Storming St. Kilda By Tram* (Sydney: Currency Press, 1982) 65. Quite often real police officers would also arrive having received reports of an 'incident' occurring on the tram. On entering however, and expecting trouble, they would instead be greeted by a bemused expectation from the audience that they were also part of the show. And perhaps a sense of shared guilt among the audience that they were partially responsible, another audience/community building element.

[112] It's worth noting that both these examples of 'really moving drama' were on in Melbourne at the same time (February 1982). And in a unique collision of real and invented spaces, Quantock timed one of his performances to block *the tram Show's* progress along Victoria Parade by parking his bus across the rails. What followed as the characters from both 'events' interacted with each other, created a kind of improvised meta performance as reported by Susan Spunner in the *National Times*: "Theatre on the Number 42" *The National Times* (April 11 to 17 1982). Such a bizarre interface of colliding social and narrative spaces could arguably only ever have occurred in Melbourne at that time – at the height of the site-specific craze in the early 1980s.

passengers with the actors), but also that the play achieved a certain 'authenticity' by manipulating the commonly understood protocols of public transport behavior and playing them up for comic effect. The narrative perfectly matched the location – arguably the *key* performance indicator of any site-specific play. Nor was it merely a three dimensional experience happening all around the audience (and sometimes above or below them), it was such a close engagement between performers and spectators that a certain olfactory space could also be engaged: the stench of 'derro' as he fell asleep on your shoulder, or took his socks off. Or the smell of tomato sauce from his meat pie that he mistakes for his own blood. Here you could also literally *feel* the actors as they bumped into you, or as the Connie appealed to you for sympathy, reeling from the dramatic shock of her sacking. The audience became aware of itself as an audience not just because in a tram they sit facing each other (more proximate even than McAuley's thrust stage scenario), but because they were the subject of another gaze: a random spectatorship looking back into the play from the street going past outside and into which the *Tram* narrative ebbed and flowed as various characters came and went.[113]

John O'Toole describes the "Brechtian ambush" that occurred just before interval where

the 'tram inspector' revealed that he was a fringe theatre worker (true), and only working on a tram because he was 'resting' (fiction but likely). He then hung out of the tram shouting humorous insults at the Melbourne Theatre Company and its real patrons until the tram had passed the building…This gentle metaxis of real and dramatic contexts was layered further by a Brechtian ambush of the whole convention, bringing the *medium* into the metaxis. Maintaining his 'officious tram inspector' persona, this actor simultaneously overlaid it with the real role of the TheatreWorks stage manager explaining the interval procedure for the audience, including prearranged drinks at a city hotel bar.[114]

---

[113] This precision required the script to conform to a strict chronology (much like a television script with its strict segment lengths). The length of scenes between character entrances and exits was based on timetables supplied by the Melbourne Metropolitan Tramways Board which proved more theoretical than practical. Consequently, as traffic flows became worse the length of the play expanded and often required improvisation between stops in order to keep the momentum of the story going. Clearly, the narrative itself could not progress until the vehicle itself did.

[114] John O'Toole, *The Process of Drama: Negotiating Art and Meaning* (London: Routledge, 1992) 180-181.

O'Toole accounts for this synchronicity of text and location as "a further layering of metaxis" which he defines as a "tension caused by the gap between the real and the fiction, and a recognition of that gap."[115]

For all these reasons, but especially in its marriage of space and narrative, and the extension of the theatre experience that results (for actor and spect-actor alike), *The Tram Show* became the benchmark site-specific piece against which others were measured (and sometimes found wanting). In many ways, the self described 'location plays' produced by TheatreWorks in the wake of the *Tram* were all various attempts to re-concoct the original magic formula. In all cases some kind of mobility was inherent: either the stage moved or the audience did (for example through the rooms of an old mansion in *Living Rooms*). In most examples there would also be an element of playful complicity in which the audience became aware of itself as a distinct cohort within the event: the 'community of the audience' within the play.

Communities of Ethnicity and Age – *Mary* (1982)

Figure 4. *Mary* (Hannie Rayson) 1982
Joy Dunstan (Gail), Mary Sitarenos (Mary)
Girlfriends across the suburban divide

---

[115] Ibid. 166

A year later, but still in Burwood, Hannie Rayson's second play, *Mary* deals with the Anglo-Celtic lower middle class as it finds itself sharing suburban space with an emerging migrant group, specifically the post-war, southern European 'New Australians' (Greeks and Italians mostly). [116] This ethnic community had started their upwardly mobile journey from the cafes of the inner city and the manufacturing industries of the western suburbs and now saw their second and third generations set off in search of a better life in Melbourne's vast eastern spread. In *Mary* there is also a clash of generational communities as the younger members of the different ethnic groupings shared a sub-culture related to the interests of their own age. Another feminist inspired 'TheatreWork', *Mary* was as much a play about what the daughters have in common as what the mothers don't.

Rayson says that when she began the process of writing *Mary* she was very conscious of the fact that

I was a fifth generation Australian attempting to write a play about the experiences of Greek women living in Melbourne. I was concerned on one level that the Greek community itself might regard my intentions with a degree of suspicion but also whether I could in fact truthfully tap into a cultural milieu so different from my own. With regard to the Greek community, my fears were dispelled rapidly..."[117]

Len Radic found the play " a study of the tensions and conflicts between new and old Australians," and compared it to Richard Beynon's *The Shifting Heart*.[118] Laurie Landray, in his review, quotes the Greek mother chastising her daughter Mary: "You're talking like an Australian – you got no respect" to which, Landray reported "the audience of Australians and Greeks, and Greek Australians breaks up with laughter."[119] In this moment Rayson manages to unite these disparate communities, Australia's new 'multicultural' paradigm, within the community of *Mary*'s audience.

---

[116] Hannie Rayson's first play *Please Return to Sender* was written and performed in 1980 while the TheatreWorks founding members were in their final year at the VCA. This play marked their inauguration as an ensemble within the VCA.

[117] Hannie Rayson, Personal Interview (Brisbane: TheatreWorks' Archive, Fryer Library, University of Queensland) 2010. CD

[118] Leonard Radic, 'On Opposite Sides of the Fence', *The Age* (16 December 1982).

[119] Laurie Landray, 'Showcase for *Mary*' *The Herald* (9 December 1982).

Communities of Class -- *Breaking Up In Balwyn* (1983)

Figure 5. *Breaking Up In Balwyn* (Paul Davies 1983)
Enter the Greek 'frenchmaid' (Mary Sitarenos)

By 1983 TheatreWorks had left its office in the outer east and moved closer to the city, to inner eastern Canterbury. Subtitled "a toast to money marriage and divorce," *Breaking Up In Balwyn* was a very different response by the company to the new, affluent and politically conservative community in which they now found themselves.

Designed to make theatre as soap opera, *Breaking Up In Balwyn* was written as a sequel to the *Tram Show*, and even recycled some of the same characters. In this case the public vehicle was the appropriately named, 'Yarra Princess' and the party/play was staged on board as the boat as it made its way from Melbourne's CBD up the Yarra River to the suburb of Toorak, home to some of the city's wealthiest people. The play took the form of a kind of inverted wedding ceremony, a divorce party in which Samantha Hart-Byrne 'celebrated' her separation from her shonky stock-broker husband, Michael.

Although it enjoyed a healthy box office, built largely on the profile and success of the earlier *Tram Show, The Boat Show* was less successful with the critics, its lightweight *commedia* style unleavened by the potential and tension of random interventions. And although the *Boat Show* employed the same site-specific tactic of a moving stage into which characters entered and exited as it went along, in this case there was less opportunity for the outside gaze to happen given the darkened, mostly empty river bank going past outside. It is also probable that audiences found their assignment as a boatload of Samantha's 'very dearest and best friends' less comfortable, particularly as it involved participating a subtle put-down of the whole idea of marriage. In this respect the 'disturb' element of TheatreWorks agenda became more dominant than the 'celebrate' clause, the result being that here the community of the audience became a more fraught proposition, the identity element lacking.

Structurally (and with a nod to Jack Hibberd's *Dimboola*), *Breaking Up In Balwyn* attempted to subvert the wedding reception formula by reconstituting its familiar outline but turning all this on its head with the presentation of (inappropriate) gifts, a grand entrance by the new divorcee, cutting a special cake, an anti-bridal waltz etc. The play almost caused a split in the company as Susie Fraser for one, felt that *Breaking Up In Balwyn* was trite and lacked any real point, she even wondered where TheatreWorks was going as a company.[120] Certainly, the audience felt less comfortable being guests at a divorce party than they did being passengers on a tram where the protocols and rituals of public transport behaviour were more familiar and accepted – even if some of the *Tram* characters were notionally more threatening.

One result of these internal divisions was that two years later TheatreWorks abandoned the outer and middle eastern suburban experiment and moved to its final destination in St. Kilda where, much like Nimrod before it, the company found its natural home in the city's red light district. But before that move there was one more show reflecting life in middle-eastern Camberwell.

---

[20] TheatreWorks' Archive (Brisbane: Fryer Library, University of Queensland) Minutes of Company Meetings. 1983.

Communities of Age and Gender– *Herstory* **(1983)**

Figure 6. *Herstory* 1983 (group devised)
Susie Fraser, Caz Howard

Soon after the company moved to the Canterbury Gardens Centre (in 1983), the community it chose to tease out and reflect was both generational and gender specific. *Women of Three Generations* was a large scale project which examined the history and experiences of women in the Camberwell City area over the previous century. The process involved script and performance workshops, oral histories, lectures, discussions, and the presentation of films by, for, and about women.

Applying the classic modus operandi of a Community Theatre production, *Women of Three Generations* was designed as the seed project for a later play, *Herstory,* which used these oral histories and dramatic explorations to knit together a piece of documentary theatre, using performance, slides and music to reflect the journeys of many different women over the preceding century. The project coordinator, or 'animateur' was Susie Fraser. The concept of the 'animateur' as it evolved through the VCA training process, described a person who was part dramaturge, part researcher, part producer/coordinator and workshop leader; in short the person who brings a particular project 'to life' ('animates') and who nurtures it through its various developmental processes. It was possible at the time at the VCA Drama School, under Peter Oysten's direction, to follow this career path through the College as an alternative to becoming an actor, writer or director in the more traditional sense.

As Fraser later commented in relation to the *Herstory/Women of Three Generations* project

There was a lot of stuff in the press at the time about our generation being the first feminist one and everything I read about the 1890s and 1920s [showed that those periods] had been important times for women and so it seemed arrogant to say we were the first…We went to the Baptist home for the elderly, got some fantastic women in their 80s and girls from Fintona [high school]. It was partly blue ribbon, (former Premier) Dick Hamer's daughter took part in it. Also a girl from prison who had had a baby adopted out. Quite big stories, and it did feel it was part of that consciousness raising. Some women found it very formative in making them think about being a woman. But we always wanted to gather it together as a thread… ‴[121]

Communities of Culture – *The Pub Show* (1985)

Figure 7. *The Pub Show* 1985 (Peter Sommerfeld)
Smoke and Mirrors: "Eat The Rich" play the Gershwin Room live
Stage L-R: Boris Connelly, Jeremy Stanford, Paul Davies

It's hard to imagine a more different style of show to *Herstory* than Peter Sommerfeld's *Pub Show* – ostensibly the story of the rise and fall of a local rock band as it implodes on stage during a session in St. Kilda's iconic Esplanade Hotel. Here the audience were invested with the role of rock fans and brought within the fourth wall of the performance as the action unfolded not only up on stage but throughout the venue (including under the tables) as various actors filled ancillary roles of bouncer, gaffer, drug pusher, police officer, pregnant deluded fan etc.

---

[121] Susie Fraser Personal Interview (Brisbane: TheatreWorks' Archive, Fryer Library, University of Queensland) 2010. CD

And here the community being reflected was an educated, young, inner urban, culturally literate one. The audience were thereby invested with the role of typical hotel patrons who might be found attending any number of St. Kilda's many live band venues. *The Pub Show* was a continuation of the site-specific tradition that had started with TheatreWorks Tent, Tram and Boat Shows.

The narrative involved a parody of the rise and rise of a semi-talented rock band called appropriately enough, given TheatreWorks' recent fraught relationship with Canterbury, 'Eat the Rich'. The strategy was to stage a kind of rock musical in a typical pub band venue, but to salt in the individual stories of the band members as it all comes out between the songs.

Communities of History and Place– *Living Rooms* 1986

Figure 8. 'Linden' circa 1900

The final production in TheatreWorks journey westwards through Melbourne is *Living Rooms* (Paul Davies 1986). And here the communities are both chronological and socio-economic.

By 1986, when this house based, site-specific play was produced, St. Kilda was going through it's third major demographic transformation. It had started life in the previous century as an aristocratic seaside retreat for Melbourne's newly wealthy 'squattocracy'. Here the fortunes made in the wool and gold industries spawned a series of spectacular mansions of which 'Linden' at 27 Acland Street was an outstanding example. Figure 8 shows members of the Michaelis family who had built Linden in the 1880s, at the height of the 'Marvelous Melbourne' period.

By the 1960s St. Kilda had declined to a much less salubrious red light district which saw many of its grand old buildings subdivided into boarding houses. However, by the 1980s it was going through a period of re-gentrification, as a new inner-urban professional class moved in. St. Kilda's night life and cosmopolitanism, as well as its proximity to the bay, and their offices in the city, were now all win-win situations.

The idea of *Living Rooms* was to embody these three demographic transitions by staging scenes from the different eras in three separate rooms. Thus, the very different communities occupying St. Kilda in the previous 100 years were reconstituted in the same place. Here the community of the audience was divided into three sub-groups who each rotated through the house as the scenes set in different historical periods were replayed simultaneously. All groups consequently witnessed the whole play but in different running orders, and each room required a different mode of witnessing: from fellow participants (Gallery), to voyeurs (Flatette), to invisible ghostly presences (Drawing Room). A final scene drew the all audience groups together for a denouement in Linden's spacious hallway, where the house itself gets to have a final say.

Photo © Ruth Maddison
Figure 9. *Living Rooms* (1986)
The Drawing Room Scene 1900: Kevin Cotter, Cliff Ellen

In the Drawing Room, set in 1900, the audience find themselves present at a farewell party for a young artillery officer heading off to the Boer War. Here the audience are arranged around the room as passive witnesses – present but curiously absent at the same time, not directly referred to by the characters. But *there* nevertheless, situated in amongst the fine crystal glasses and Rupert Bunny landscapes on the wall, ghosts effectively, within the story.

Photo © Ruth Maddison
Figure 10. *Living Rooms* (1986)
The Flatette Scene 1972: Cliff Ellen, Paul Davies

In the Flatette scene, set in 1972 (St. Kilda's down-market era), a conscientious objector on the run from the Federal Police, anxiously awaits the election of the Whitlam labour government and his consequent decriminalization as Australia's participation in the Vietnam War comes to an end. Here the audience look on, hidden behind a light scrim, observing the action as if they are detectives scrutinising an interrogation, or medical students observing an operation, effectively distanced from the action in a very deliberate way.

Photo © Ruth Maddison
Figure 11 *Living Rooms* (1986)
The Gallery Scene 1988: Peter Sommerfeld, Caz Howard (front row)

1 the gallery scene, set in the near future (the bi-centennial year of 1988), a newly rrived yuppie couple emerge out of the audience as their private argument ecomes more audible. They've arrived in Linden expecting to find an exhibition f 'living rooms' but find their particular room "isn't working."[122] Because of ourse, they *are* the play in this room. Here much like the *Tram* and *Boat* shows, 1e actors effectively invade the audience and pretend to co-exist with them – on 1e same playing field as it were.

s *Living Rooms* proceeds with each scene repeated three times, and the action leeding from one story to another, the rooms themselves become unstable ontainers of space and time. In addition, two actors move between the rooms urning up as different characters in different time periods. Sitting in one room the udience can hear shouting and other noises going on all around them and if 1ey've already been in those rooms may have some idea of what is going on. In 1is way they become aware of their participation in the play as a kind of 'meta vent'. In terms of staging, this was one of the most sophisticated site-specific lays that TheatreWorks undertook. And the company repeated the formula three ears later in the same building with *Full House No Vacancies* (Paul Davies, 989).

---

22 Paul Davies, *Living Rooms,* TheatreWorks' Archive (Brisbane: Fryer Library, Jniversity of Queensland) 1986. MS. 81.

Conclusion

Figure 12 Finally on the Map
TheatreWorks Artistic Directorate 1988
L-R: Paul Davies, Shirley Sydenham, Caz Howard, Wolfgang Wittwer

By the end of the 1980s, TheatreWorks, through its very presence in St. Kilda as an agent of cultural production, had become part of the change it was talking about, effectively part of the gentrification of the community it had chosen to stay with. Indeed, in a rare feat of longevity for any artistic enterprise, TheatreWorks continues to support the production of new work (much of it local), from its final destination in the Christ Church, Parish Hall. By 1988 the company was officially on the map, an indelible part of the demographic evolution it had set out to describe, celebrate and disturb. On its journey from Burwood to Port Phillip Bay it had revealed something of the complex web of life that failed to wither under Donald Horne's red tiled roofs. Partly as a result of this, TheatreWorks also became a key player in Melbourne's site-specific revolution throughout the 1980s, which lived on in the numerous productions in found spaces that took place the following decade. Julian Meyrick counts no less than 47 such works in the various Fringe Festivals from 1988 to 1995, and an additional 'extensive number' of shows in found spaces outside the Festival context.[123] Much of the enduring success of this form of theatre, which grows out of a certain community outreach ethos, resides in its ability to give audiences a sense of coming together in an act of self-identification (as an audience), which in turn allows, I would argue, for a heightened and more complex engagement with the drama they're witnessing.

---

[123] Julian Meyrick, 'Filthy Spaces: the Investment of Non-theatre Venues in Melbourne 1990-95', in Peta Tait, ed. *Body/s: Australian Viewings of Live Performance* (Amsterdam: Rodopi, 2000) 170-171.

DRAMATIC TALES STIR SUBURB!
Actors Believe What They Do!!
MELBOURNE'S REALLY MOVING THEATRE COMPANIES (1979-1994).
Australasian Drama Studies # 64 (April 2014)

Keywords: Australian 'Next Wave', Community Theatre, Location Theatre, Site-specific Performance, TheatreWorks

(photo Neale Duckworth, *The Herald* [29 May 1982]:11)
Figure 1. Left: Jan McDonald Artistic Director of WEST theatre company
Right: *Storming Mont Albert By Tram* TheatreWorks 1982. 'Daniel O'Rourke'
(Peter Sommerfeld) 'hijacks' the tram from Ticket Inspector 'Morris Stanley'
(Paul Davies)

An Inciting Incident

At approximately 9.17 pm on the 26th of February 1982 in Victoria Parade Richmond, two buses containing *Bus, Son of Tram* (heading north towards Fitzroy), blocked the tracks of a tram carrying the world premiere of *Storming Mont Albert By Tram* (heading east towards Hawthorn). For several minutes characters from both productions improvise an interaction out on the thin nature-strip between tram tracks and bitumen, while their respective audiences looked on. According to Suzanne Spunner "(p)assengers in all vehicles were stunned but sustained no injuries except for a debilitating contortion of the facial muscles." [124] It was a collision of mobile, performative spaces that arguably, could only have happened in Melbourne at that time (and not many places since). Like 'Foucauldian black holes' (performative heterotopia) the precincts of two distinct plays had coalesced in real time and the spark created by their enduring popularity helped foster an outbreak of site-specific work in Melbourne that lasted well into the 1990s and continues to the present.[125]. Spunner identified the "ancestry" of what took place that night in the "happenings and events of the late 1960s," and went on to point out that in both productions "the usual division between audience and performance is challenged, which gives rise to ambiguities that are confronting and often hilariously funny."

The Tram Show evolved over eight iterations from 1982 to 1994 on various tram routes in both Melbourne and Adelaide, attracting a total of around twenty thousand passengers and generating in today's figures, roughly a million dollars at the box office. Equally, *Bus Son of Tram* became a recurring and reliable hit for the Banana Lounge's Rod Quantock and Geoff Brookes who took their nightly audiences to police stations, private clubs, family planning clinics, the windows of expensive restaurants and whatever city-wide events happened to be taking place at the time, which in February 1982 included the annual 'Moomba' Festival.

---

[124] Suzanne Spunner, 'Theatre on the Number 42', *The National Times.* 11-17 (April 1982): 24.

[125] See Julian Meyrick, "Filthy Spaces the Investment of Non-Theatre Venues in Melbourne 1990-1995." *Australian Viewings of Live Performance.* Ed. Peta Tait. (Amsterdam; New York: Rodopi, 2000) 154-76. In this time frame (1990-95) Meyrick cites a total of 47 works produced outside purpose-built theatres, and finds that after 1990 the selection of sites becomes more varied to include "a fabric warehouse, a textile factory, a deserted brewery, Luna Park funfair, and even a shopping mall." He adds that it is "a rare international festival now which does not have its quota of site-specific work." (171).

* THE Herald Outdoor Art Show was closed for the night, but Rod's loud hailer opened it up.

LEFT and ABOVE: All the fun of the fair as the diners enjoy the attractions at the Moomba carnival.

(photo Barry Weller, *Australasian Post* [8 Apr. 1982]:3)
Figure 2. *Bus, Son of Tram* (Rod Quantock 1982)
Left: Geoff Brookes re-opens the Herald Art Show and takes a 'boat' ride.
Right: Rod Quantock pauses at Moomba's 'Fool's Window'.

This preference for performance in real places saw a number of spoken-word dramas staged not only on trams, buses and a riverboat ('really moving drama'), but also private and public houses (*The Pub Show, Living Rooms, Looking In/Looking Out, Full House/No Vacancies*), cinemas (*DJ View*), wedding reception centres (*Dimboola, Breaking Up in Balwyn*), parks and gardens (*Wind in the Willows, Tales From the Horses Mouth, Edna for the Garden*) camping grounds (*The Go Anywhere Show, Dick and Dolly Dickens*), a gaol (*Hard Labour Mate*), a woolen mill (*Clyde Company Station*), a carwash (*Macbeth*), and various courts of law (*A Royal Commission into the Absence of Corruption in the Victorian Police Force*).

(TheatreWorks Archive, Fryer Library)[126]
Figure 3. Posters for some indicative location plays of the 1980s

In Melbourne theatre practice the decade of the 1980s was the era of the professional, self-governing ensembles: WEST, Murray River Performing Group, The Mill, TheatreWorks, The Church, Melbourne Workers Theatre, Whistling in the Theatre, Anthill, Crosswinds.[127] These small, independent companies, with their fluid and overlapping memberships constituted a movement which Geoffrey Milne later dubbed the Second or 'Next Wave' (following on from the APG and Nimrod's 'New Wave' of the 1970s). Collectively, they created a body of work that by the late 1980s he would call "the golden age of Melbourne alternative theatre".[128] These plays were also contemporary with other pioneering, site-specific works by companies such as Brith Gof in Wales (with its first production *Branwen* in Harlech Castle in 1981), and Necessary Angel in Canada (with its

---

[126] Most of the TheatreWorks Archive (1980 – 1990) is now held at the Fryer Library at the University of Queensland. Links to an extensive range of digitized copies are available on line through the Library's data base @UQeSpace.

[127] Admittedly, and from time to time some of these companies were run by individual artistic directors but the zeitgeist of the time was ensemble and collective – taking inspiration from the Next Wave's predecessors: the New Wave's Australian Performing Group, Popular Theatre Troupe, and Nimrod.

[128] Geoffrey Milne. *Theatre Australia (Un)Limited Australian Theatre since the 1950s* (New York: Rodopi, 2004). 295. For Milne the seminal year was 1988. For TheatreWorks 1988 was also a high water mark with productions of *Storming St. Kilda,* Andrew Bovell's *After Dinner* and the Awgie award winning *On Shifting Sandshoes* (Paul Davies) – another tent show but done 'in house' in TheatreWorks' Parish Hall.

ground breaking production of John Krizanc's *Tamara* in a house for the Toronto
Theatre Festival also in 1981).

The following table presents a selection of Melbourne 's site-specific companies
of the 1980s and some of their indicative productions.

Year	Company	Play	Location
1978	The Mill Theatre Geelong	*The Wool Game*	Woolen Mill
1979	VCA Women's Group	*Fefu and Her Friends*	Private House in Elwood
1980	The Mill Theatre	*Clyde Co. Station*	Woolen Mill
1981	TheatreWorks	*The Go Anywhere Show*	Shopping Centres/ Parks/Streets
1982	TheatreWorks	*Storming Mont Albert By Tram*	#42 Mont Albert Tram
	WEST	*The Cup*	Racing Club Rooms
	Home Cooking	*Not Still Lives*	Art Galleries
1983	TheatreWorks	*Breaking Up In Balwyn*	MV Yarra Princess
	WEST	*Hard Labour Mate*	Old Melbourne Gaol
1984	Home Cooking	*Looking In/ Looking Out*	Private House/Gallery
1985	TheatreWorks	*The Pub Show*	Esplanade Hotel
	WEST	*Vital Signs*	Nursing Home
1986	TheatreWorks	*Living Rooms*	'Linden' mansion.
	Anthill	*Macbeth*	A Carwash
1988	TheatreWorks	*Storming St. Kilda By Tram*	#69 St. Kilda Tram
	Australian Shakespeare Co.	*Wind In the Willows*	Melbourne Botanical Gardens
1989	TheatreWorks	*Full House/No Vacancies*	'Linden' Mansion
	Home Cooking	*Edna For The Garden*	Fitzroy Gardens
	TheatreWorks	*Fabulous Tales From the Horses Mouth*	Blessington Gardens
1990	TheatreWorks	*Storming St. Kilda By Tram*	#69 St. Kilda Tram
	TheatreWorks	*Not Waving*	Footy Club Dressing Rooms
	Red Shed	*In Cahoots*	Scout Hall/ Parish Hall

Other Influences

As Spunner indicates, much of the audacity of occupying public spaces for performative purposes has a late 1960s' inspiration (vide *les événements de Mai 1968*). Another contributing factor was the manifest intention of Melbourne's alternative theatre companies to reach out into the suburban/regional heartland as avowedly 'community theatres'. Here they were able to engage with audiences not normally drawn to live drama; and in any case, purpose-built theatres were often neither available nor appropriate.

While European site-specific performance, as proposed by Kaye[129], Kwon[130] and others, can trace a genealogy back through minimalism in the visual arts, Melbourne's self-described 'location plays' derive more from a crossover of personnel and techniques with the local, independent, filmmaking scene. By the 1980s Melbourne's alternative cineastes were using the new, light-weight technologies (16mm film and crystal-sync sound) to 'locate' dramatic scenes in real places (if only out of budgetary necessity).

(frame capture: Paul Cavell)
Figure 4. *Exits*. Pat Laughren, Caz Howard, Paul Davies (1979).
Co-opting prior (graphic) occupations of public space
L-R: Paul Davies ('George'), Pat Laughren (the 'paper seller').

Exits for example, was made with TheatreWorks' actors and located all of its scenes in the streets, pubs and theatres of Melbourne, mixing documented

---

[129] Nick Kaye ed. *Site Specific Art*. London: Routledge, 2000.
[130] Miwon Kwon, *One Place after Another, Site-Specific Art and Locational Identity*. (Cambridge, MA: The MIT Press, 2004).

noments in the Whitlam dismissal in 1975 with a fictional narrative reflecting back on those events. As Figure 4 shows, certain scenes were staged in places that had themselves been overlaid by a prior 'graphic occupation' in the form of graffiti. Here the text of the existing message sprayed on a wall in Collingwood ("Past, Present + Futile") is co-opted, as 'found art design', into the 'theme' of *Exits*: the sense of the powerlessness of individuals to effect (or ensure) any real political change, and the consequent debasement of democracy that follows. This is, in essence, what 'George', the main protagonist of the film, alleges took place in 1975. *Exits* mixed dramatically reconstructed scenes inside an allegedly 'documentary' account of '*les événements de November Onze*'. So the idea of performing fictional scenes in real places was really nothing new. The complicating factor for live performance – in order to maintain a certain authenticity between space of play and place of performance (and to put the enterprise on a self sustaining footing by being able to charge a price for admission) – was to do it in 'real time' in a properly contained space. Finding, defining and occupying those spaces became a major preoccupation of Melbourne theatre practice over the succeeding decade and the fertile inventiveness with which it was done constitutes an important benchmark in alternative theatre practice.

Melbourne's location plays of the 1980s were works that would now comfortably sit under the rubric of "site-specific theatre" and, while still somewhat overlooked,[131] were at the cutting edge of what was happing globally at that time. Although the term itself has become problematic and other descriptors are also applied including: site-generic, site-responsive, site-sensitive, locative, inter-active, space-specific, place-specific, site-based, site-suggestive, environmental, pop-up, immersive, ecological, placial, post-dramatic, live-art, interactive, metadrama, experiential and promenade theatre – a case perhaps of 'post-dramatic stress disorder'.[132] These terms compete to describe what, for the purposes of this

---

[131] Notable exceptions to this historical blindspot include Richard Fotheringham's collection of contemporary articles in *Community Theatre in Australia*. North Ryde NSW: Methuen, 1987. See also John O'Toole's *The Process of Drama Negotiating Art and Meaning*. London: Routledge, 1992. and Rachel Fensham's 'Location, Location, Location: Australian Theatre on Safari." *Meanjin* 50. 2/3 Winter-Spring (1991): 241-51. Geoffrey Milne's encyclopedic *Theatre Australia (Un)Limited Australian Theatre since the 1950s*. Australian Playwrights. Ed. Veronica Kelly. Amsterdam; New York: Rodopi, 2004, also makes many references to these plays.

[132] For a working definition of 'site-specific' theatre I refer to Fiona Wilkie's "performance occurring in non-theatre venues in which site is a vital element instrumental in developing the theme or form of the work." Fiona Wilkie, *Out of Place the Negotiation of Space in Site-Specific Performance*. PhD. Diss. University of Surrey, (2004) 1-2.

article, are essentially spoken word dramas produced in real places (found or otherwise). It is true there are important distinctions to be made between works appropriate to only one site and others that could be staged in a number of similar places or even plays that are simply given a unique alfresco setting (like the many examples of Shakespeare's works done in botanical gardens or the local quarry). However, the more important questions here are: why did these plays happen when the did, and how did they become so popular with audiences? The short answers to which are: that they happened primarily because of the confluence of 60's political agit-prop, community outreach and 1970s independent filmmaking practice; and they succeeded because most of these plays inhabited their places of performance in 'authentic' ways. This authenticity validates the occupation of space that results, creating in turn a kind of 'harmonic resonance' for audiences and performers alike between work and site. Thus, site-specific sculptor, Richard Serra's famous assertion that "to move the work is to destroy the work",[133] infers an inviolable bond between location and creation, 'host' and 'ghost', site and play.[134] This connection, when it is validated in the performative setting, allows spectators to become *complicit* with the actors in an act of spatial transgression which in turn opens up sensory engagements beyond those of sight and hearing[135] – effectively pushing the theatrical experience into new territory (literally). Michel Foucault's (and later Kevin Hetherington's) use of the medical term 'heterotopia' to describe social spaces of alternate ordering provides a useful tool for mapping this common playing area. It also allows an understanding of the kind of energy released when certain fictional characters, with their invented ambitions and back stories, collide with each other in a real place (as happened in the original tram/bus 'collision'). A key attraction of site-specific performance lies, therefore, in the creative instability of the 'boundaries' between fiction and non-fiction, heterotopia and real world, that results.

Broadly speaking there were two types of location play: those that moved their audiences from place to place (trams, boats, busses) and those where it was the audience itself that moved – while the stages remained static. What follows is a brief outline of the range of Melbourne plays produced in the 1980s involving seven types of container (tram, bus, boat, tent, house, pub, cinema) each requiring a different performative strategy. Such a survey is necessarily more thematic than

---

[133] Kwon 73.

[134] These are terms applied by Brith Gof's Cliff McLucas (as qtd. In Kaye 128) and Mike Pearson, *Site-Specific Performance*. Basingstoke: Palgrave Macmillan, (2010): 37.

[135] Other senses which arrive largely as a result of the proximal relations of cast and spectators, include, smell, touch, taste, balance and even potentially a kind of 'sixth sense' as indicated in relation to the pheromone effect.

chronological, but outlines, albeit schematically, what I would argue was a conscious and evolving radical experiment with space in performance.

Perhaps the dominant example of the ambulatory-audience/static-stage template were the various 'house plays'. Here, in contrast to plays on moving vehicles, any interaction with an outside gaze was limited, offering little opportunity to bring in any sixth wall engagement between the event itself and an outside world. [136] To counter this limitation the house plays found different ways of immersing their audiences in the action, either as ghosts, as voyeurs, or fellow participants, enabling an engagement at least through a fifth wall (between audience members themselves). In addition, audiences could enjoy a kind of 'global awareness' of the 'meta-event' of the play as it unfolded in other rooms throughout the house, all around them (simultaneously and in real time). Here was another fatal intersection of Foucault's "time and space."[137]

House Plays (1979 – 1989)

If we discount Jack Hibberd's *Dimboola* which was originally staged in Melbourne's tiny La Mama theatre (but later enjoyed numerous site-specific productions in restaurants and wedding reception centres), arguably Melbourne's earliest 'site-specific' play was staged 'on location' in April 1979 by the Women's Theatre Group at the Victorian College of the Arts.[138] Directed by Ros Horin, this production of Irene Maria Fornés 1977 play, *Fefu And Her Friends*, was mounted inside a large, art-deco house in Tennyson Street, Elwood.[139] Like Necessary Angel's *Tamara* two years later, the Elwood house authenticates *Fefu's* staging as it evokes a 1920s aesthetic to accord with the play's narrative time-frame.

---

[136] If we take Diderot's fourth wall as a kind of invisible curtain hung across the proscenium arch (separating actors and dramatic action from an audience sitting opposite}, the fifth wall may be said to obtain between audience members themselves, and a sixth wall between the total event of the play (actors and audience) and an outside world sometimes looking back in. In the Tram and Bus shows kind of 'seventh wall' also came into play via the mirror effect of a tram's window at night, framing a viewer's perception of events with their own reaction.
[137] Foucault, Michel. "Of Other Spaces." Trans. Jay Miskowiec. *Diacritics* 16 Spring (1986): 22-27.
[138] This was a collective formed within the VCA and included three of TheatreWorks' founding members: Caz Howard, Hannie Rayson and Susie Fraser.
[139] It was tenanted at the time by fellow students from the VCA who made their home available for performances.

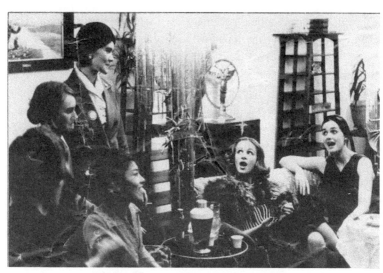

(photo: *Theatre Australia* June 1979)
Figure 5. *Fefu and Her Friends* (Maria Irene Fornés 1977)
VCA Production directed by Ros Horin April, 1979.
L-R: Caz Howard (back), Cathrine Lynch, Amanda Pile,
Amanda Ma, Lynn Howard, Hannie Rayson.

In *Tamara* the spatial strategy was for audience members to select a character and follow them through the story (and the house).[140] In Horin's production the audience were divided into four sub-groups who rotated (in different orders) through scenes performed simultaneously in four different rooms. This was to be the performative template for TheatreWorks' *Living Rooms* and *Full House/No Vacancies* some years later, although in *Fefu's* pioneering instance the site-specific location was a second option for Horin. Her first choice had been the Great Hall of the National Gallery of Victoria, but when this became unavailable the location shifted to the house in Elwood. As Suzanne Spunner noted:

The choice of a non-theatrical location did more than merely surmount the technical difficulties – the setting positively enhanced the production and measurably added to the final texture of the work...The effect of moving from room to room and seeming to chance upon actors in conversation, with the knowledge that at the same time in other rooms other conversations were taking place which one had already heard, or was about to become privy to, created an

---

[140] In Brith Gof's house play *Tri Bydwyd* (1995) the rooms were transparent (after a tubular design inspired by Bernard Tschumi) so that the simultaneous scenes could be witnessed all at the same time. This was not unlike Peter Sommerfeld's design for the set of TheatreWorks' (and Hannie Rayson's) first play, *Please Return To Sender* (1980).

intimate domestic atmosphere and cast the audience into the not unwelcome role of peripatetic voyeur.[141]

So here the subjectivity aimed for is unapologetically voyeuristic, yet the atmosphere was "domestic" and "intimate" – both conditioning and validating the emotional responses of the audience watching a play that happens to be taking place in a house. Significantly, Spunner draws attention to the 'meta-event' of multiple scenes continuing throughout the house, something that readily aids an audience's immersion in the play. In *Tamara*, as noted, audience members got to choose a particular character and followed them through the house (and the story from that character's point of view) – a factor which lead to the phenomenon of people returning to *Tamara* for multiple viewings, presumably in order to get more of the complete narrative picture.

Spunner herself was to join with Meredith Rogers, Barbara Ciszewska and Rosalind Hill to form the Home Cooking Theatre Company (in 1981 to produce Rogers' and Ciszewska's, *I Am Whom You Infer* at La Mama). This was another Melbourne based site-specific company which, in October 1984, produced Andrea Lemon's *Looking in...Looking Out* in a private home in North Fitzroy. Here the audience again became voyeurs, present but largely unacknowledged and to that extent 'absent', as the three women of the play, Woman A, Woman B, and Woman C (Meredith Rogers, Barbara Ciszewska and Mary Sitarenos) go about their rituals of domestic behaviour as if nobody else is in the room. The fashioning of subjectivity here and in other house plays does not *necessarily* imply *participation* in the sense of Boal's 'spect-actors',[142] rather it is as much about point of view: the moral, emotional and fashioned perspective of the individual viewer/witness.

---

[141] Suzanne Spunner, "Feminist and Feminine *Fefu and Her Friends.*" *Theatre Australia* (June 1979): 32.

[142] Augusto Boal, *The Rainbow of Desire, the Boal Method of Theatre and Therapy*. London: Routledge, 1995.

Figure 6. *Looking In...Looking Out* Andrea Lemon 1984.
Panorama depicting the mirror-enhanced, audience point of view.
Barbara Ciszewska far right.

The audience for *Looking In...Looking Out* remained essentially static but they could witness (via windows, mirrors and a video screen) scenes that took place both inside and outside the house: in other rooms as well as out in the backyard. The exterior scenes were visible through glass windows, aided by a large mirror so placed as to reflect the outside back in (hence 'looking in' while 'looking out'). In this way the thematic internality of the piece, with some scenes performed by the characters alone, is amplified by the spatial configuration of the 'stage': the domestic setting itself.

For TheatreWorks, the key house play was *Living Rooms* (Paul Davies 1986) which was produced in 'Linden', a once grand Victorian mansion built during the period of "Marvellous Melbourne" a century earlier. Later the building declined to a 26 room boarding house and by 1986 had been purchased by St. Kilda council for restoration as an art gallery. In synch with this chronology, the three acts of *Living Rooms* were each set in one of the large, downstairs rooms, and evoke a key moment in the building's (and the nation's) history. These three periods and the characters who embody them, eventually collide in a surreal denouement (literally a collision of time and space) in the hallway.

(photo Ruth Madison)

Figure 7. *Living Rooms* (1986): the Hallway Act. Surrounded by the 'ghosts' of an audience, Monika (Caz Howard) confronts her husband 'Leon' (out of frame to the left).

In this way Linden itself functions as palimpsest for three distinctive historical formations and the audience's subjectivity is formed by different methodologies of viewing, casting them variously as ghosts or guests, scrutineers and hidden voyeurs, or simply fellow audience members attending 'a performance art event' (the Gallery Act).

In one act, set during Linden's aristocratic heyday and located in the heterochrony of 1900, spectators were arranged around four sides of an open playing area sitting as largely unacknowledged 'guests' at a farewell party for Lt. Michael Deegan who is about to sail with the second Victorian contingent to the Boer War. The audience are present physically but absent from the narrative at the same time, positioning them within an ambiguous, almost ghost-like point of view: 'there' but 'not there'.

A second act, set during Linden's boarding house iteration, is located within the heterochrony of 1972 on the eve of Gough Whitlam's election as Prime Minister (again the Whitlam theme).

(photo Ruth Madison)

Figure 8. 'Paul Border' (Paul Davies) *Living Rooms*: the Flatette Act.
A traveller frozen in time awaits the audience buzzer
that will summon him to 'life'.

Set in a 'Flatette' during Linden's boarding house decline, the audience are positioned behind a light scrim and thus rendered invisible to the actors. In this way their mode of viewing is impeded or filtered, literally, by the scrim. Here they are also present as witnesses, but now in an even more distancing manner, as if looking in on some form of social experiment, like trainee medicos observing an operation, or a team of detectives spying on an interrogation through their one-way mirror. Just as the Drawing Room Act delivered a colonial occupation within a heterotopia of elegance and wealth, the prevailing subjective experience of the Flatette is one of deception and unease. A third act (but not necessarily witnessed in this order) is projected slightly into the future (from 1986) to the Bicentennial Year (1988), where Linden has finally been resurrected from its boarding house decline and transformed into an art gallery (as it currently remains). Here the audience were mixed with actors as fellow attendees at an historical exhibition, a self-described 'location theatre', or 'performance art event'.

This late twentieth century make-over of Linden as a public gallery was emblematic of the re-gentrification that the surrounding suburb was currently going through, and which TheatreWorks itself, by virtue of its growing profile, had become a key cultural agent for. Consequently, the building itself contained an embedded history within which the fiction of the play could resonate. The formula (although not the time frame) was repeated for TheatreWorks second house play staged in Linden three years later: *Full House/No Vacancies* (Paul Davies 1989). Here audiences were again subdivided into three groups and rotated through simultaneous, repeated scenes, in different orders, implementing a similar staging strategy to *Fefu* and *Living Rooms*.

(photos TheatreWorks Archive)
Figure 9. Character transitions in *Full House/No Vacancies*:
Clockwise from Top Left: Morrey mingles with arriving 'guests',
Freddie and Gareth cross to Rosie's room, Sheila returns to her room,
Rosie heads towards Freddie's room. Nick crosses to Sheila's,
'Cleaner'/Stage Manager (Paul Davies) keeps time with stopwatch.

A concluding scene brought together all three groups (and the cast) for a final dénouement (a "Happy Hour") in the dilapidated brick dining room added to the rear of Linden during its boarding house iteration. In this play however, unlike *Living Rooms*, all the action was sited in the same heterochrony: the 'present' of 1989. *Full House* was directed by Robin Laurie who also directed TheatreWorks' very first , technically site-specific play: performed in and around a family tent pitched on a number of 'locations'.

'In-tents' experiences (1981 – 1984)

The 'tent show' genre was another form of static location play, and TheatreWorks' first example was aptly (and perhaps optimistically) entitled *The Go Anywhere Show*. It was to be the newly formed company's calling card in their chosen site of operations: Melbourne's vast eastern suburbs. Director, Robin Laurie carries a direct personal link between New and Next waves in Australian theatre practice, having originally been a member of the Australian Performing Group ('Pram Factory' – New Wave) and later a key figure in Circus Oz[143]. Laurie was witness to *les événements de Mai 1968* in Europe, had studied Grotowski and Schechner, and brought back from her travels, (building on her experience of agit-prop), a very physical style of performance: creating larger-than-life characters in the best *Commedia* tradition. This style became especially useful in overcoming problems of audibility that usually attend performance in real places.

Laurie had also worked with John Arden and Margareta D'arcy in the Cartoon Archetypical Slogan Theatre. 'CAST' mounted performances at various demonstrations in the UK where the quality of mobility (also common to many of TheatreWorks' location plays), was fully explored, as agit-prop performance often attached itself to moving demonstrations. Thus the requirement to keep moving was paramount. Laurie recalls an illustrative anecdote:
We had to think about making big images because you were moving all the time. It was a parade after all. You had to move past people, do the piece and then move on and do it all again. It wasn't just display... Once I was dressed as a Vietcong, wearing black pyjamas with white face. At one stage [film director] John Duigan [dressed as a US solider] was pretending to rape me – we were doing push ups on the street – and an old lady came up and beat him with an umbrella. We had to

---

[143] A description and analysis can be found in Geoffrey Milne's *Theatre Australia (Un)Limited Australian Theatre since the 1950s*. Australian Playwrights. Ed. Veronica Kelly. Amsterdam; New York: Rodopi, 2004.

think about space, image and movement, and have a clear sense of what they were seeing. [144]

(photo TheatreWorks Archive)
Figure 10. *The Go Anywhere Show* TheatreWorks (Group Devised) 1981
Back: Peter Finlay, Caz Howard, Suzi Fraser
Front: Tony Kishawi, Robin Laurie, Hannie Rayson

This play involved a homeless middle class family who were pretending to be on a camping holiday in Melbourne's eastern suburbs but who were actually unemployed and therefore technically homeless. Thus the shopping centre, or church hall or school in which the Dickens' tent was pitched and around which the performance took place, was potentially their place of abode for the night. Consequently the site of performance bore an ironic relation to its emplacement reinforcing their (comic) self delusion about their real circumstances. A second version of the play, *The Dick and Dolly Dickens Show* was remounted in 1984 and performed in camping grounds along the Victorian coast during the summer holidays. The play enacted TheatreWorks stated intention to 'disturb' its audiences and because of the dispersed nature of spectatorship in public places (such as shopping centres), the element of containerization in *The Go Anywhere Show* remained a work in progress. The real solution was to come with *The Tram Show* a year later but, as with most traditional theatre, *Go Anywhere* audiences

---

[144] Robin Laurie. Personal Interview TheatreWorks Archive, Fryer Library. 28 Sept. 11.

remained essentially static and separate from the action, looking on from outside a performative circle centered in and around the tent. To this extent their subjectivity was more assumed than fashioned and the relation between play and place less authentic.

The 'empty auditorium': a play in cinema (1984)

A third form of static location play was Peter Sommerfeld's *Dee Jay View* produced in the Universal Cinema in Fitzroy in 1984. In a redaction of Peter Brook's idea of the 'empty space' (i.e. 'stage') the raked Universal's auditorium was cleared of seats so that the drama unfolded in what should have been the audience space; while the audience itself was positioned up on the stage/screen area, looking back. Into this empty auditorium director, Barbara Ciszewska, deployed a pared-back performance style devoid of props. This allowed characters to physically occupy, not only the space of an old cinema (a key location for their cultural formation as teenagers) but also each other – sometimes literally as furniture.

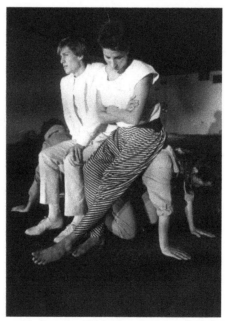

Figure 11. *Dee Jay View* Peter Sommerfeld (1984)
Jeremy Stanford and Suzi Rosedale 'occupy'
Chris Barry and Bernadette Ryan as chairs

At the time (the mid 1980s) TheatreWorks was still theatrically homeless, and so the company remained in the business of finding new places to stage their increasingly, spatially adventurous plays. Thus, while the cinema location for *Dee Jay View* may not be strictly site-specific (in the sense that scenes located other than in a cinema were replicated in the empty audience space – like a more traditional stage play), the location nevertheless did carry a certain resonance for a story set in a Hollywood saturated, 1960s Australia. In this sense the site-specificity of the piece was more thematic than literal, a certain authenticity in spatial relationships was present but varied from scene to scene.

The Pub Show (1985)

A year after *Dee Jay View*, and by way of introducing itself into the St. Kilda community, TheatreWorks produced a play which 'occupied' the Gershwin Room of St. Kilda's iconic Esplanade Hotel. This was Peter Sommerfeld and Dave Swann's *Pub Show* (1985). The core characters comprised a local band called "Eat The Rich" who achieve a success beyond their ability to cope. As the play unfolds 'on stage' the audience get to watch "Eat The Rich" personally implode over the course of playing a bracket of songs for a typical pub-band performance of that era.

(photo Maurice Rinaldi)
Figure 12. *The Pub Show* TheatreWorks 1985
"Eat The Rich" on stage at the Gershwin Room
L-R Leonie Hurry, Jeremy Stanford, Boris Conley, Taya Stratton,
Danny Nash, Caz Howard

For a casual fan of pub bands of that era it was not immediately obvious that a play, as such was actually taking place between (and sometimes during) the songs. Like other location examples, some characters were also salted in among the audience. Here they 'performed' the roles of bouncer, roadie, police officer, and a young groupie who claims to be pregnant to 'Tony' one of the band members. Meanwhile 'Carmen' slyly tries to sell drugs to random members of the audience, breaking through theatre's fourth and fifth walls.

(photo Maurice Rinaldi)

Figure 13. *The Pub Show* Boris Conley ('Trevor Murphy') back to camera
and Paul Davies ('Dug') patrolling the performative domain.

The bouncer and the singing policeman, both *commedia* 'comicos' or 'zannis' and played by the same actor (myself), quite literally 'police' the portal between the heterotopia of the alleged 'rock concert' going on in the Gershwin Room, and ordinary customers and staff in other parts of the hotel, or even in some cases, intruders (literally gate-crashers) from outside the hotel altogether. In this sense *The Pub Show*, unusually for the house sub-genre, managed to construct a sixth wall interface with an outside reality. And in this way the integrity of the mock rock performance is maintained as a counter-site to its ambient physical emplacement (other bars and rooms in the Esplanade Hotel and its immediate surrounds).

The Boat Show (1983)

(photo Ivan Johnston)
Figure14. *Breaking Up In Balwyn* (Paul Davies 1983).
An uninvited passenger waits to board the MV Yarra Princess.

The Boat Show was chronologically the third example of a TheatreWorks' location theatre play but it had a more artificial quality than its trambulating predecessor and was in much less immediate contact with its external world. A river bank is not as accessible to a party boat as a city street is to a passing tram, and therefore what became known as the *Boat Show,* while still presenting a mobile stage, was much less permeable and therefore offered less sixth wall opportunities. Consequently, entrances and exits had to be more carefully stage managed. Examples include the incursion of the ex-husband disguised as a 'gorilla-gram' (Figure 14) and the return of the Greek 'frenchmaid' after interval by means of a commandeered rubber dingy. However, part of the problem of *Breaking Up In Balwyn* derives from the play being, in a sense, too "closed in on itself": an island both aesthetically and spatially. It was simply a too hermetically sealed from its external reality. The play was staged as a divorce celebration, a kind of inverted wedding reception, set aboard a party boat hired for the occasion. Here the audience's subjectivity was framed by their being the invited friends and family of Samantha and Nigel – the gay divorcee and her new boyfriend.

(photo Ivan Johnston)

Figure 15. Enter 'Samantha' (Hannie Rayson) the gay divorcee.
Nigel: "She took the honey out of honeymoon
and spread it on a toast to the bride"

The Boat Show applied similar site-specific strategies to the *Tram* in engaging the senses of touch, taste and smell with which to fashion the audience's subjectivity and aid their immersion in the play's events. This involved serving drinks and 'divorce cake', in addition to showing home movies and exploring haptic space by mixing characters and 'guests' in an anti-bridal waltz.

(photo Ivan Johnston)
Figure 16. Feeling the Actors.
An audience member joins in the anti-bridal waltz with 'Nigel' (Peter Finlay).

The Tram Show (1982-1994)

(image *The Age* 4 Mar. 1982)
Figure 17. *Storming Mont Albert By Tram* (Paul Davies 1982).

Of all TheatreWorks location plays of the 1980s, the *Tram Show* proved to be its most enduring and popular. The quantum leap in forming audience subjectivities here was to make them complicit in the action as fellow passengers on a tram. It provided a secure but permeable *container* plus it moved through a constantly changing landscape ensuring that mobility and sixth wall engagements went with the territory (literally). An audience's subjective experience of the play could also be shaped by a random, outside gaze looking back in – with the added advantage of being in on the joke.

(images TheatreWorks Archive)

Figure 18. *Storming Mont Albert By Tram.* Various scenes on and off the tram.

Trams and busses were not only ideal theatrical containers they automatically implicated their audiences as passengers who were able to follow the action as it happened all around them and as it frequently left vehicle to engage with the space of the street outside; where they could even become aware of their own witnessing via the mirror effect of a tram's window at night (the seventh wall effect).

Additionally, the proximal relations of cast and audience allowed a range of senses to be engaged. To give just two key examples of this 'affective effect'.

Figure 19. The 'Blood' moment in *Storming St. Kilda* 1988.
Ticket inspector Morris Stanley (Johnnie Walker) stares horrified at
what he thinks is the 'derro's' blood. While onlookers erupt with laughter.

Figure 19 shows the moment in the story where the ticket inspector has accidentally stabbed the 'derro' character in an inept tussle over a plastic knife (originally brought on by the punk character 'Terry' – another zanni). As the 'derro' slumps the inspector turns to confront the audience with hands smeared in a thick red fluid. The fact that the audience can already *smell* that it is tomato sauce amplifies their enjoyment of his confusion and distress. They know this is only a piece of theatre and so fake blood is to be expected. However, in a twist on the 'generic credibility' of fake bleeding as identified by Lucy Nevitt,[145] this *really* is *meant to be* tomato sauce – since it stems from the derro's meat pie (put under his coat to keep it warm and accidentally mashed up in there by Morris in their struggle over the plastic knife). As a result, with sauce all over his hands, the 'stage character' Morris acts perfectly within what is generically credible for a theatre performance and 'mistakes' the sauce for blood. The audience experience of this moment comes from the collision of, and disjunction between, all these sensory perceptions. Like an alternating current that creates electricity, complex, sensually rich, information exchanges are taking place as fiction resonates with(in) reality. This is what gave *The Tram Show* and many of Melbourne's location plays their special appeal. But the authenticity of the spatial relationships is what underpins their success.

---

[145] Nevitt, Lucy. "Popular Entertainments and the Spectacle of Bleeding." *Popular Entertainment Studies* 1.2 (2010): 78-92.

Another sense available to the site-specific practitioner is that of touch: haptic space.

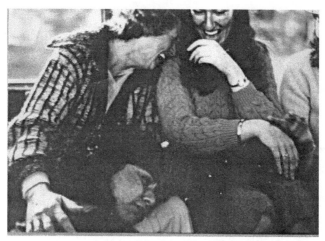

(image TheatreWorks Archive)
Figure 20. Breaking through theatre's fourth and fifth walls.
'Alice' (Mary Sitarenos) collapses into the lap of a passenger
on news of her sacking.
"I remember faces up close…whole families hysterically laughing."[146]

Figure 20 depicts another moment in *Mont Albert* just after the ticket inspector has sacked 'Alice' the conductress, for "gross dereliction of duty" – specifically, for failing to sell a ticket to the punk character. In her grief at losing her job, Alice literally throws herself sobbing loudly, onto the nearest passenger and in this case the passenger involved responds with what looks like sympathy, tempered by shock and amused disbelief that this could actually be happening. In fact, the audience member mirrors Alice's surrendering gesture by turning her own cheek onto the 'passenger' next to her, extending the hug. In this example therefore, the architecture of the inter-personal correspondence between performer and spectator, and between spectators themselves, has shifted some distance from that which is normally available in a theatre that privileges vision. However, haptic relations are also overlaid with cultural tendencies, provisions and taboos, and so are consequently fraught with risk and trespass, requiring careful management.

Nevertheless, the elision of personal space in the confined circumstances of a crowded tram, involving both body contact and body odour, can not only reinforce the *authority* of the invented heterotopia but also fashion an audience's subjective experience of it. This palette of sensual inter-connections, including the

---

[146] Mary Sitarenos, personal interview TheatreWorks Archive, 3 Mar. 2010

pheromone effect, a type of 'sixth sense' or "intra-special, chemical secretions"[147]. By these means the senses can also operate as signifiers of character and social status, not to mention bodily habits and tendencies. Such an order of intimacy is only available when audience and actors share the same 'stage' and that stage 'bleeds' at all points into its own 'auditorium'.

But the authenticating markers of *The Tram Show* didn't just relate to the vehicle's architecture, quotidian route, or a strict observance of public transport protocols and behavior. There were also geographic markers. During the *Tram* and *Bus* collision mentioned above, the *Tram Show's* narrative, couldn't proceed until of course, the tram itself did since it hinged on characters arriving and leaving as distributed along the route,

(Tram Production Documents. TheatreWorks Archive)
Figure 21 Text and the City: working production map showing character entrances and exits for *Storming St. Kilda By Tram* (1988).
Green line shows tram route.

---

[147] 'pheromone'. Shorter Oxford.

Here diegetic and literal spaces where interdependent in such a way that the (spatial) progression of The Tram Show resonated with the city through which it moved at a certain demographic level. For example, wealthy Samantha Hart-Byrne (who's never been on public transport before) alights in middle-class Balwyn, while Cathy Waterman, the escort girl, arrives as the tram reaches a seedier part of town.

Location Theatre Today

By the early 1990s, as Julian Meyrick indicates, Melbourne's inclination towards site-specific practice continued to colonise an increasing variety of real places. A look at the situation today shows that the locus of site-specific practice has shifted (back?) to Europe and in particular to the UK, where both the recently formed National Theatres of Scotland and Wales have a distinct site-specific agenda.

Towards a Sitegheist ?
Prominent Site-Specific Theatre companies 1980 - 2012
From a growing list and in no particular order (additions welcome):
United Kingdom
National Theatre of Wales, **National Theatre of Scotland**, Brith Gof (Wales), Wrights and Sites, **London Bubble,** Out of the Blue (Dance), Red Earth, Gridlron (Edinburgh), **Forced Entertainment (Sheffield).** Shunt, **The Whalley Range Allstars,** Dream Think Speak, **Poor Boy (Scotland),** STATION HOUSE OPERA (LONDON), ART ANGEL, Welfare State, International (Cumbria), Cotton Grass (Peak District), Storm (Coventry), **Blast Theory (integrating web technology)** IOU, **Impossible Theatre, Creation Theatre Company (Oxford),** Test Department, Hide and Seek, Theatre Absolute, Frantic Assembly, Punchdrunk, Wildworks, Poorboy, DREAMTHINKSPEAK, Lone Twin, Kneehigh (Cornwall) Moving Being, Walk the Plank, PICKLE HERRING THEATRE, **Pentabus Theatre,** Theatre Nomad, THE LION'S PART (LONDON), The Olimpias, **Emergency Exit Arts,** Sirens Crossing (Dance), **Boilerhouse,** Cerberus, **The Common Players,** Horse+ Bamboo, **Kunstwerk-Blend,** Riptide, Rotozaza, Foster and Heighes, in situ, Invisible Circus, **Slung Low,** Wilson+Wilson, Scarabeus Theatre, Coco Loco

Figure 22. UK Site-specific companies 1980-2012

It should be emphasized that not all of these groups are exclusively site-specific, and again, this is still very much a work in progress, but there can be little doubt the epicenter of the S-I-T-E-geist in theatre practice has now shifted to the UK and Europe as Figure 22 shows.

However, alternative theatre in Melbourne theatre continues to provide some fertile examples of experimentation with the site-specific form, indeed, some of it still supported by TheatreWorks in a remarkable demonstration of longevity for such a small (and therefore always financially vulnerable) company.

Nicola Gunn has embraced participatory theatre in a new show that invites viewers into the world of a community centre.   PICTURE: JOE ARMAC

(photo Joe Armano *The Age* [17 Sept. 2012]: 20)
Figure 23 *Hullo My Name Is*...(2012) Nicola Gunn far right
at TheatreWorks Parish Hall

Hullo My Name Is, written and performed by Nicola Gunn, serves as a recent example. Here upon arrival, audience members are given their own name tag as a ticket of entry (reading "Hullo My Name Is...") and invested with the role of someone attending a Community Centre (which is what the TheatreWorks space, as Parish Hall, essentially remains).

At one point, armed with a megaphone, Gunn leads her audience out of the building into the random reality of Acland Street where she reflects out loud to all and sundry on the angst of being an artist, going down on one knee on the footpath in front of an empty pedestal (an item of street furniture) to embellish her point. Back at the 'community centre' (Parish Hall) she singles out and then lies on top of an audience member, engaging haptic space to the maximum (and pushing any personal or cultural sensitivities to the limit) by deploying what she calls the 'body blanket' manoeuvre. Then Gunn hands out art materials for a life drawing class and peeling off a dressing gown poses for us clad only in her radio microphone – all the while continuing a monologue that relates an unfolding story of desire and the search for identity (for a 'Name' with to contest and challenge the forces of anonymity).

I can readily accept that this might not be everybody's idea of a great night out in the theatre. But I was amused, intrigued, and a little bit shocked (at the body blanket manoeuvre – perhaps more relieved that it wasn't me). My name was 'Paul" and I knew I didn't have to take part in any of this unless I really wanted to, and in any case, I readily enough found myself holding hands with complete strangers while we all stood with eyes closed in a big circle. But I'm from Byron Bay and am pretty balanced about haptic my relations generally.

In the best traditions of the site-specific genre, *Hullo My Name Is...* is a play about personal isolation that nevertheless creates overt personal connections not only between Gunn and her audience (at times quite intimately so), but also *within* the audience themselves, again crashing through theatre's fifth wall. As in earlier Theatre Works' plays I became part of 'a community of the audience',[148] something not available to the individual spectator at a sight-specific event – whether screen based or live. *Hullo My Name Is...* won the 2012 Melbourne Fringe Award for best "Experimental Performance."

In summary, the point about all the plays under discussion are :

* They provide new ways of presenting & experiencing dramatic stories.

* They do this by fashioning various and subtle new subjectivities for their audiences (compared to more traditional theatrical presentations).

* The organizing principles are: containerization, authenticity (of space and place), complicity (of audience and actors) in the occupation of that place, and mobility (of stage or audience or both).

* Given the interface of fictional and non-fictional elements they also carry elements of risk requiring careful management.

* The quest for authenticity can take architectural, behavioral, demographic, historical forms. This not a call for adherence to a strict set of resemblances but more about implementing a kind of harmonic (spatial) resonance between space of play and place of performance. Such a resonance allows a fuller immersion for an audience in the dramatic story being told.

* The often proximal nature of the experience also allows the deployment of a range of senses beyond sight and hearing: the 'affect effect'.

---

[148] A fuller discussion of this can be found in Paul Davies, "Transiting through the Cultures of Suburbia: How TheatreWorks Discovered the Community of an Audience." *Australasian Drama Studies* 60 (April 2012): 138-156.

* They may sometimes also engage with a reality external to the play (via the 'sixth wall').

And therefore,

* They offer ever more inventive ways of occupying space for performative purposes.

* They also use existing spaces and consequently are relatively inexpensive to mount.

* Consequently, most of the investment goes into people and ideas (instead of real estate).

* Perhaps most importantly, they restore a certain Benjaminian aura[149] to the practice of live theatre and the business of popular entertainment generally, in an age where the vision-centred/screen-dominated, digital revolution produces only virtual audiences for cyber spaces – the very antithesis of the social spaces under discussion here.[150]

Thus if the 1980s could be bracketed at the beginning by the assassination of John Lennon in the streets of New York (definitively ending the dream of the 1960s), and bracketed at the end by the fall of the Berlin Wall (marking the inauguration of the 'New World Order' [sic]) then the decade may well be read as a kind of liminal moment between the end of the dream and the beginning of the nightmare: a kind of drowsy wakefulness in which things actually got done and alternative theatre practice became possible at a professional level across a wide spectrum of companies and activities. We might hesitate to call Melbourne's body of location plays a 'revolution' in theatre practice – it clearly built upon a number of prior inclinations and tendencies – but if only in the cross-fertilization of ideas and people it certainly constituted an important movement, a sub-branch as it were of

---

[149] See Walter Benjamin's "The Work of Art in The Age of Mechanical Reproduction" in *Illuminations: Essays and Reflections*. Ed. and Trans. Harry Zohn. New York: Shocken Books, 1968: 217-252.
[150] Although digital inter-connectivity has already been co-opted as a means of gathering in live audiences for performances. The United Kingdom's Blast Theory company is internationally recognized for this kind of work. Other ways of fashioning audience engagement involve incorporating various strategies for playing games with audiences, including ways of 'crowd-sourcing' the narrative (i.e. where audiences help make up the story). Elements of 'cos play' and flash mobs can also be involved.

the Australian 'Second' or 'Next Wave' theatre. In any case, if the 'art of theatre' (to borrow Appia's phrase) is to find new expressivities, if it is going to be more than just a bunch of voyeurs beholding a mob of exhibitionists, I would argue that it needs to continue to embrace the site-specific model and further explore, as Shakespeare predicted, the almost infinite number of ways in which dramatic fiction *can* be playfully mounted in real places, proving once again Jacques' point in *As You Like It,* that "All the world's a stage."[151]

---

[151] *As You Like It* (Act II Scene vii: 139-142).

LIKE RIDING A BICYCLE...

Achieving balance through mobility
in site-specific performance.

A comparative study of NORPA's *Railway Wonderland* (2015)
and GST's *Sir Don v The Ratpack* (2009)
Australasian Drama Studies # 69 October 2016

Abstract:

According to Peter Brook's famous dictum, it requires more than just an empty space, an actor and someone watching to constitute an 'act of theatre' (*The Empty Space* 1). The actor must also *walk across* the space. Setting aside questions of why he is walking or where (the narrative factor), it is *motion* in theatre practice that remains the connecting spark. And that for site-specific theatre especially, it is mobility - either of audience, performers or stage - that 'ignites' into being the dramatic space in which events may occur.

De Certeau also finds that space is "composed of intersections of mobile elements" and is "in a sense actuated by the ensemble of movements within it". Space is "like a word when it is spoken" (*Everyday Life* 117). Lefebvre, taking his cue from the astrophysics of Fred Hoyle, similarly argues that space may be created "by the energy deployed within it" (*Production of Space* 13).

This article examines two recent productions in real places where the performance space is created and maintained by the movement of actors and/or audience through it. I argue that both Gorilla Street Theatre's *Sir Don v The Ratpack* (November 2009) enacted outside BHP Billiton's annual general meeting, and NORPA's *Railway Wonderland* (November 2015) sited on the platform of Lismore's now disused railway station, institute different practices of mobility which not only facilitate the intrusion of space into place, but also enhance an audience's complicity in the occupation that invariably follows; both vital to the site-specific agenda.

As with riding a bicycle, balance becomes feasible through forward movement. Opposites are reconciled, suspension of disbelief (between place and space) suspended, arrest avoided (mostly), progression of story achieved. Through these strategies, and by these means, the practice of site-specific performance continues to thrive outside dedicated theatre buildings and does so in ways that *move* the 'art of theatre' (Appia) into literally *new territory*.

Richard Sera's assertion that "to move the work is to destroy the work" (qtd Kwon, *One Place After Another* 73) may well apply to site-specific sculpture (one need only look to the peripatetic travails of Ron Robertson Swann's (in)famous *Vault* aka *The Yellow Peril*). However, drawing on my study of TheatreWorks plays in trams, boats and houses (*Really Moving Drama,* 2013)[152] I would argue that quite the

---

[52] Available as a free download at
http://espace.library.uq.edu.au/view/UQ:313649

reverse applies to site-specific performance - where, *not* to move the work, risks potential failure.

(photo Suzi Rosedale)
Figure 1.
The author demonstrating an experimental
'railcycle' with its unique magnetic wheels designed to
reopen the currently disused Casino-Murwillumbah line to local pedal traffic.

As anyone who has made the attempt can attest, remaining upright and unsupported on a stationary bicycle is virtually impossible (skilled circus performers excepted). However, as soon as motion forward is achieved, and peddling begins, a process of equilibrium occurs in which the tendency to fall sideways, suddenly - even mysteriously - evaporates. The phenomenon is in fact a confluence of dynamic, mathematical and gravitational factors designed to keep the centre of gravity of rider and vehicle over the bike's tyres.[153]

This article proposes that the process of staging site-specific theatre involves a similar and equally critical balancing act: between the *place* of performance and the *space* of the production, between the location and the text, the geographical and the metaphorical, "the host and the ghost",[154] the reality - and the fiction

---

[153] For a fuller explanation of this phenomenon see: https://en.wikipedia.org/wiki/Bicycle_and_motorcycle_dynamics (Viewed 15 April 2016).

[154] Pearson, Mike, and Michael Shanks. *Theatre/Archaeology* (London: Routledge, 2001) 23.
"The 'ghost' and 'host'; that 'which is of the site...and that which is brought to the site."

brought into it. I argue that in both cases (cycling and theatre) balance can be achieved through motion (of either time or space).

In *Really Moving Drama*[155] I proposed that these new relationships (text and location, space and place, reality and fiction) required an altogether new order of suspended disbelief. As a result, the more *authentically* a site-specific play inhabited its chosen location, the more successful (or otherwise) the enterprise and the immersion of space of text into place of performance tended to be. This 'creative occupation' could involve many different kinds of resonances, including: architectural, cultural, literary, and historical elements. One outcome was to *move* the practice of theatre into literally new territory and to engage audiences in ways that extended beyond mere sight and hearing: to potentially bring into play all the senses[156] (particularly in the more 'immersive' examples).

Here I extend that argument by proposing that one way of achieving and maintaining an authentic resonance (balance) between space and place is through mobility: either of time, stage, actors, audience - or all four. To invoke Peter Brook's famous dictum, a moment of theatre can occur simply by virtue of an "actor *moving* across an empty stage with someone watching".[157] This implies another, equally vital binary: between the *actor* performing and the *spectator* watching. Setting aside the question of *why* the actor is walking and where she is going (the narrative element), in Brook's analysis it is, above all, *movement across* the stage that draws in the two key components (viewer and actor), linking both to a coherent theatrical event.

In considering recent productions by Northern Rivers' companies (Lismore's NORPA and Mullumbimby's GST) this article seeks to show how these key relationships of space-place, audience-performer, reality-fiction were managed and maintained through the introduction of the element of transportation (movement) either in time and/or space.

NORPA (Northern Rivers Performing Arts) is a medium sized, professional, regional company which operates very much according to the classical community mould; defined by Geoffrey Milne (echoing Abraham Lincoln) as

---

[155] The Author, *Really Moving Drama* (PhD dissertation University of Queensland, 2013). Available online at http://espace.library.uq.edu.au/view/UQ:313649. Viewed 14 March 2016.

[156] These may include sight, touch, taste, smell, sound, proprioception (or kinaesthesia), pain, balance, thirst, hunger, time, direction (magnetoception) and synaesthesia ('seeing' sounds as colours).

[157] Brook, Peter. *The Empty Space* (Ringwood, Victoria: Pelican, 1968) 1.

"theatre by the people, of the people, for the people"[158]. NORPA basically runs the Lismore City Hall as a venue for all kinds of visiting entertainments (including theatre, dance, comedy and music). In addition the company creates original work of its own - productions that are sourced from, and reflect back on their local community. Under founding Artistic Director, Lyndon Terrancini (who has since gone on to mounting Australian Opera productions on and around Sydney Harbour), the company established its site-specific credentials right from its inauguration in the early 1990s with such large scale al fresco events as *The Cars That Ate Paris* (which included cars doing 'wheelies' on the streets outside the City Hall) and *Flood*, a processional event involving hundreds of local people parading through the centre of town. NORPA's current Artistic Director, Julian Louis, arrived in 2007 with similar interests, having previously staged an event involving 30 double decker busses and a circus performance in Circular Quay.

His recent collaboration with Janus Balodis on *Railway Wonderland* (November 2015) was described by the ABC's Michael Cathcart as "one of the great plays of the year" and Cathcart acknowledged NORPA's indelible regional fundamentals by observing that "only these people could tell this story in this way"[159] *Railway Wonderland* takes place entirely in and around Lismore's now disused Railway Station, with the audience sitting on a temporary scaffolding structure built over the railway line itself - effectively providing them with the point of view of passengers on a (disembodied) train.

---

[158] This was a portmanteau definition proposed by Geoffrey Milne, in a personal interview with the author for *Really Moving Drama* (22 Feb. 2010). The full interview is available online at the TheatreWorks Archive: http://espace.library.uq.edu.au/view/UQ:306259 (Viewed 18 April 2016)

[159] Available on line at:
http://mpegmedia.abc.net.au/rn/podcast/2015/10/bay_20151028_1045.mp3 (19 minutes). (Monitored 16 March 2016).

photo Evan Malcolm

Figure 2.
Audience seating for *Railway Wonderland*

Thus, while the audience remains static, the action of the play itself takes place both on the platform (extending out beyond the audience emplacement to either end of the station complex) as well as inside a bus waiting room, visible to the audience through a large glass wall (Figure 3). It is an emphatic reminder that Lismore station, no longer needed for trains, has instead been repurposed as a bus terminal.

photo K Holmes

Figure 3.
Lismore station with the bus terminal visible
through the platform's glass windows.

These two principal loci (platform and terminal) became the means by which a certain chronological mobility was achieved in the play - linking the two main narrative threads: a contemporary story about passengers waiting for a bus (on the other side of the glass) and historical re-enactments in the life journey of Ana (Katia Molino), a 'proxy bride' brought from Italy to Australia in the early 1950s in order to marry a local farmer, whom she had never previously met. Incidents from Ana's past which might credibly have taken place on the platform (arriving in Lismore the first time, fare-welling her son off the Vietnam war in the 1960s, imagining encounters there with her husband etc.) are neatly juxtaposed and interwoven with the various backstories of the contemporary bus travelers located inside the old station building proper. In this way the present is in effect *framed* by the past.

photo K Holmes

Figure 4.
Past tense. Ana "imagines" meeting her husband for the first time.

A spectator's gaze is drawn alternately from the platform/past through into the terminal/present and beyond that through a second glass wall to South Lismore's random traffic flow going about its regular, nightly business: fiction framing fiction framing reality (see Figure 5).

Here the fluctuating mobility both of time and place 'balances' an audience's reception of the play by allowing for an almost seamless segueing from one to the other: place and space, fiction and reality, past and present. This mobility of gaze and fluidity of chronological and spatial emplacement is further enhanced by having actors playing characters from both time periods, moving (with a quick change of costume), from past to present and back again - 'going with the flow'. The combined dramatic and theatrical effects, when mixed with historical film projection, live music, a local choir and sometimes sub-titles in the manner of a silent movie - further enhancing the overall melodramatic effect - were quite mesmerizing in *Railway Wonderland*. This reworking of indicative local stories gathered from a community outreach project)[160] and presented in a real site, redolent with its own history, was undoubtedly a major contributor to the play's sold-out success and its ability to attract audiences from outside Lismore itself.[161]

Director, Julian Louis makes it clear:

The building of the audience opposite the platform is a really neat fit. Suddenly you're reminded you're in a real space. When we elongated that perspective and widened that sense of realness, real place, that was very exciting. [It was the] same with hearing busses and cars; seeing the traffic through the waiting room [added] another layer again. There's a real world out there.[162]

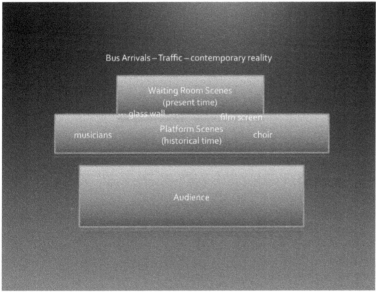

Figure 5.
Diagram of audience and stage relationships in *Railway Wonderland.*

---

[160] A call went out for local stories relating to the Lismore Station to be submitted to NORPA which were curated and read out at the Bryon Writer's Festival in 2009. An earlier production of the play (with a different cast) was based on these stories and given a dramatic treatment through a collaboration between Julian Louis and playwright Janus Balodis. This earlier version was staged by NORPA for a week only in 2012 to an enthusiastic reception.

[161] According to NORPA's own research about 60% of its audience came from postcodes outside Lismore.

[162] Personal interview with the author 21 March 2016.

This spatial arrangement draws an audience's attention into a fluid and constant transitioning between periods, stories, and spaces. As if riding a visual bicycle, their gaze was able to readily travel from the exterior of the platform to the interior of the terminal, from the larger, historical canvas to the inward looking, internalized, selfie-obsessed present. There is no need to suspend any disbelief that this might not now be a bus terminal or that it was once a working railway station. The place begins to speak for itself. There is even a third narrative strand linking would-be lovers in an even earlier time frame: the 1940s. These characters, including the woman's husband, enact a *commedia*-styled take-off of David's Lean's 1945 feature *Brief Encounter* in which two strangers fall in love while making regular trips on the same commuter train. This story of strangers and travelers and the consequences that flow from such a potentially incendiary liaison, playfully counter-point Ana's personal narrative from bespoke bride to fully entrenched local: a story that reflects and celebrates the extensive Italian community found in Lismore and its surrounds today. *Brief Encounter* was based on Noel Coward's 1936 play *Still Lives* - the title itself could be read perhaps as an ironic oxymoron for the idea of an adulterous couple caught up in a constant process of transiting from place to place, from home to fraught liaison.

photo NORPA Archive

Figure 6.
Strangers waiting for a train.
Husband and would-be lover on location at Lismore Station.

For Julian Louis, 'movement' - specifically the choreographing of characters' actions in *Railway Wonderland* was a key initiating element in the design of the production.

The whole show started with movement. I worked with four performers to start with. The four from the waiting room [bus terminal] scenes are the original devising characters. So we started with character and movement. It was about exploring the waiting room as a place of mundanity and melodrama. Boredom and heightened experiences. A place of transition. It was like physical clowning. It is observational and subtle.[163]

photo K Holmes

Figure 7.
Strangers waiting for a bus. The terminal scenes.
"A place of mundanity and melodrama. Boredom and heightened experiences."

---

[163] Personal interview with the author 21 March 2016.

At this point in the play's development there were two separate narrative streams in play.

Julian Louis continues:

I grappled with how this was going to transition to a big site for six months. I thought I might just focus this [the waiting room scenes] into a studio piece and make that work as an extended dance sequence. The railway station was always going to be part of it, but I wanted initially just to follow this movement sequence. Then I realized with the glass wall (Figure 8) the stylized movement could go on inside (to complement the platform scenes). But we needed something to counter that and it would have to be a connection to the audience. And that's where the idea of the Italian migrant story came from. Here I wanted a character singing. To bring in music so we could merge the dance with the melodrama of the song.[164]

photo K Holmes

Figure 8.
Ana framed by the Vox Caldera choir singing through a glass wall.

In *Railway Wonderland* the transitioning of the audience gaze from past to present to real time beyond, echoes Foucault's meditation on the unique, mobile elements available in any rail journey:

[A] train is an extraordinary bundle of relations because it is something through which one goes, it is also something by means of which one can go from one point to another, and then it is also something that goes by.[165]

---

[164] Personal interview with the author 21 March 2016.

[165] Foucault, Michel. "Of Other Spaces." Trans. Jay Miskowiec. *Diacritics* 16 Spring (1986): 23-24.

Michel De Certeau makes a similar point, with a slightly different inflection equating transport to narrative function.

In modern Athens, the vehicles of mass transit are called *metaphori*... Stories could also take this noble name: every day, they traverse and organize places; they select and line them together; they make sentences and itineraries out of them. They are spatial trajectories. In this respect narrative structures have the status of spatial syntaxes.[66]

Foucault and De Certeau imbue items of public transport with a kind of spatially charged narrative potential. As befitting its community ethos, NORPA's *Railway Wonderland* enacts its own unique 'spatial syntax' by embracing and celebrating a public resource that had been taken away from its local community through the agency of a cost-cutting state government. This is the larger story at work here. The ordering of scenes in the play and their deployment across the key places of performance combine to convey a meaning that connects and relates part of a town's common history through one of its most iconic, public buildings - and one which is intrinsically bound up with movement as transport. While 'Station' implies 'stationary' it functions as a place designed specifically to facilitate movement - of goods and people.

Against much local protest (which still continues) the Casino-Murwillumbah rail line was closed down after the last train left Lismore Station in 2004. It had been opened with much pomp and ceremony 110 years earlier in 1894 when it was used extensively to move freight: including cattle, timber, sugar cane, general goods and cream - causing most commuter journeys to be quite slow affairs. Yet a constant political battle has been waged since 2004 to keep the rail corridor in public hands; including a proposal to convert the line to a rail-trail for walkers and cyclists. Others simply want the trains (or at least a light rail) to be restored. Depending on the (constantly deteriorating) condition of the track railcycles may still have their place.

---

[66] De Certeau, Michel. *The Practice of Everyday Life*. Trans. Steve Rendall. Berkley (U California P, 1988) 115.

Figure 9.
Train to nowhere.
Lismore Station, March 2016.

NORPA is one of Australia's most successful and theatrically articulate regional companies. Their entrepreneurship of the Lismore City Hall and their signature, locally-devised productions (often evolving from NORPA's 'Generator Programme') have given the company a significant local profile and well deserved (if often perilous) government funding. It is a testament to the company's endurance and underlying strength that it has been operating now for more than 20 years and continues to manage a full time, professional slate of productions with more site-specific productions on the drawing board, including one set in the historic Eureka Hall (*Dreamland* November 2016).

On the other hand, Mullumbimby's *Gorilla Street Theatre* (GST) received no government funding, was specifically formed with the intention of producing a single performance, and consequently existed for only a few weeks in November 2009. A number of Byron Shire actors and activists were drawn together by Oscar nominated director David Bradbury (another local) to produce an item of filmable public protest outside BHP Billiton's annual general meeting in Brisbane on November 26 that year.[167]

---

[167] An 8 minute version of what was originally a 20 minute total performance is available on You Tube at: http://www.youtube.com/watch?v=cDD1q_sjor0 (Viewed 16 April 2016)

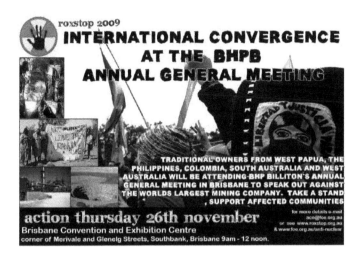

Figure 10.
Poster advertising the "International Convergence" on 26 Nov. 2009.
This larger demonstration provided the framework in which
GST's agit-prop performance took place.
(image Roxstop Collective)

Created out of mines in remote Broken Hill, and now owned by shareholders across the globe, what used to be called "The Big Australian," is currently the largest mining conglomerate in the world. Aware of a forthcoming "International Convergence" (Figure 10). Bradbury,[168] along with a number of people active in the environmental movement, were keen to promote their concerns about the impacts of BHP Billiton's imminent expansion of uranium mining at Roxby Downs. GST 's plan was to re-invoke the idea of political street theatre - where mobility of performance became necessary not only to keep up with the associated procession/demonstration, but was also often necessary simply to avoid arrest. Political street theatre was above all shaped by the underlying fundamentals of mobility (flight or fight).

Again, the chosen location for the performance of *Sir Don v The Ratpack* (outside BHP's Annual General Meeting at the Brisbane Convention Centre) was a necessarily static *place.*

---

[8] David Bradbury was nominated for an Oscar for his highly acclaimed documentary *Frontline* – the story of Australian war cameraman, Neil Davis.

25

Figure 11.
The Brisbane Convention Centre: public space as neo-classic amphitheatre.
Main entrance up the stairs to the right.
(Photo Paul Davies)

GST's solution was to create a "spatial trajectory" by constituting a mock, door-stop press conference complete with cameras and journalists and characters playing the chairman of BHP, 'Sir' Don Argus and his minder/body guard (the 'ghost' of environment minister Peter Garrett). In this way, while the *temporal* element remained constant (since the press conference unfolds in an uneditable live sequence), the *spatial* element was constantly moving as per any 'real' door-stop press conference. Whereas, in *Railway Wonderland* space remained static and time constantly shifted, in *Sir Don* time remained fixed (real time) while the performance space unfolded in a process of constant motion.

Figure 12.
The performance 'circle' begins to form.
Members of GST's 'Ratpack' confront 'Sir Don'
upon his arrival at the bottom of the stairs.
A white elephant of the 'real' demonstration can be seen in the background.
(Photo Paul Davies)

The convention of the door-stop press conference constitutes an improvised contest between a random assemblage of 'paparazzi' with their notebooks and digital recorders on the one side, and the person they are seeking answers from on the other – the latter sometimes flanked by minders, security, police, barristers in eighteenth century costumes etc. Here was political street theatre instituting the "spatial syntax" of an instantly recognizable trope. The familiarity of the door-top press conference allowed GST's street theatre piece to undertake "a dialogue with its place of performance," since producing a press conference outside the Annual General Meeting of a large company, perfectly admits and authenticates the insertion of space (of performance) into this particular place (of production).

GST's intention was to claim and maintain performance space by keeping the press conference as *mobile* as possible. As De Certeau points out, a space exists when one takes into consideration vectors of direction, velocity, and time variables." It is like "a word when it is spoken, that is caught in the ambiguity of an actualization"[169]. Mobility would also allow the GST troupe to raise the

---

[69] De Certeau, Michel. *The Practice of Everyday Life*. Trans. Steve Rendall (Berkley: U California P, 1988)
17.

relevant issues (as journalists) and to move all over the Convention Centre's steps in any direction dictated by the central interviewee: the actor (Mike Russo) playing 'Sir Don'. Or more realistically, to move in any direction dictated by the police who were naturally expected to halt this item of protest in its tracks. However, so 'authentic' was GST's performance that even the police seemed to accept its (dubious) legitimacy.

Like Lefebvre and de Certeau, Mike Pearson and Michael Shanks agree that "events create spaces"[170]. The 'democratic circle' is something they observe forming around any public brawl. This circle (with its echoes of Souriau's sphere)[171] is key to understanding the mechanics of contested spaces, with the proviso that, in the mobile press conference example, there is generally a single combatant on one side answering/avoiding questions, and any number of media players (opponents) on the other, throwing the questions (punches) out. Thus the 'audience' for this fight is, in a very direct sense, also deeply implicated as one of the combatants - setting aside the potential audience witnessing these events via the subsequent media broadcasts, as well any members of the public who might happen to have been going past at the time (see Figure 16 below).

In most examples of this familiar engagement, the common assumption is that the journalists are seeking the truth (or some further complication of the public narrative: a denial, exposure, or trip-up etc.); while the targeted subject aims to subvert the truth or at best avoid making an embarrassing public mistake. Whether correct or not, the basic combative nature of the press conference trope gives it its performative potential. This 'authentic setting,' therefore, allowed GST to shape a piece of latter-day street theatre around the kinds of questions people wanted to ask BHP Billiton's chief executive, but were rarely able to do so. This would (hopefully) draw attention, on a 'public stage' as it were, to the environmental consequences normally glossed over by both the company, and an often compliant or disinterested media.[172]

Over a number of rehearsals, the environmental impact of BHP's activities world-wide was analysed and potential questions workshopped as the genesis of a 'text' for the performance. The issues to be dealt with could be organised thematically under headings like: Toxic Dust, Yellowcake, Water Pollution, Global Warming,

---

[170] Pearson, Mike, and Michael Shanks. *Theatre/Archaeology* (London: Routledge, 2001) 21.

[171] Souriau, Etienne. 'The Cube and the Sphere' *Educational Theatre Journal* 4.1 (March 1952): 11-18.

[172] As Queensland's disgraced former premier, Sir Joh Bejlke-Peterson famously boasted, attending a press conference for him was like "feeding the chooks," a not-so-covert reference perhaps to its acknowledged disinformative function.

Legal Issues, Effects on Indigenous Populations, Industrial Relations, Health and Safety, Nuclear Proliferation etc.[173]

It was resolved that each 'journalist' would draw up a set of questions relating to one of these themes and feel free to fire them at the hapless 'Sir Don' in random order, much like real journalists would do in the circumstances (since most media organizations often have not-so-hidden agendas anyway). Thus, as a rudimentary script developed, characters within the 'Ratpack' were designated as the 'Personal journo' (Don Argus, the real chair of BHP, was about to retire), the 'Yellowcake journo', the 'Legal journo', the 'Water journo', 'Indigenous Affairs journo', and so on. Meanwhile, 'Sir Don', in the time-honoured tradition of such events would give a set of standardised, fairly meaningless, bland and ineffectual replies and literally dodge the questions as he worked his way up towards the entrance to the Convention Centre – while maintaining the illusion that he was in fact the chairman of this vast multi-national en route to its AGM. Such a tactic allowed Mike Russo and Scott Davis (playing 'Sir Don' and his 'minder') to lead the impromptu 'press conference' wherever they liked, or felt able to go. In this way, even if it couldn't break through into the foyer of the AGM itself, Mullumbimby's GST still plotted to get its message across to any interested small investors arriving for the meeting and perhaps even draw in the 'real' media and score points in the even greater contest for 'space' on the evening news.

If Lefebvre's application of Fred Hoyle's astrophysical theory is correct and social space can be "generated by the energy deployed within it",[174] then the space of the moving press conference is 'vectored' into being by the focus that multiple cameras and other recorders have when they are all pointed towards the same object/person.

---

[73] It is sadly, hardly surprising that BHP Billiton's share price crashed again ecently on news of another devastating toxic spill at one of its Brazilian mines.

[74] Lefebvre, Henri. *La Production De L' Espace.* Trans. Donald Nicholson-Smith Oxford: Blackwell, 1991) 13.

Figure 13.
Dramatic energy creating Space
Mapping the performative geography of *Sir Don v. The Ratpack.*
(diagram Paul Davies

Figure 13. shows how performance space is created in *Sir Don* using cameras and microphones which focus the outer edges of the circle towards the centre (not unlike a kind of two-dimensional magnifying glass). In this way the arena of the press conference, with 'Sir Don' marking its gravitational centre point (its 'black hole'), is given precedence over other spaces (such as the real demonstration nearby, and the AGM inside the Convention Centre). However, the journey of *Sir Don v The Ratpack* as a piece of agit-prop, is precisely to move from the realm of the demonstration *into* the ordered space of the AGM, illustrating Foucault's point about the permeability of heterotopia, and the liberative possibilities of simultaneity and juxtaposition that are negotiated within them.

Another way of expressing this is to say that if theatrical space can be generated by the energy deployed within it, then that energy itself originates with the interaction of polar opposites (points of alternate ordering: opposing combatants). Again the 'balance equation' comes into play as the motion forward of stage, audience and performers begins. To return to the metaphor of physics, electrical energy is created by an interchange between positive and negative terminals (direct current) or spinning magnets (alternating current). The polar opposites involved in a meta/physical confrontation, such as GST's 'press conference' are the combatants themselves (Ratpack and CEO). In the adversarial stance taken lies the 'charge' that is required to 'detonate' performative heterotopia[175] into

---

[175] I take the term 'heterotopia' from Foucault's definition in his iconic lecture 'Of Other Spaces' Trans. Jay Miskowiec. *Diacritics* 16 (Spring 1986): 22-27. And also from Kevin Hetherington's subsequent refinement in *The Badlands of Modernity: Heterotopia and Social Ordering* (London: Routledge, 1997).

)eing. Once in motion, such spaces allow different subjectivities to be formed as)articipants with inevitably varying and various points of view are drawn in to the iction. All fights, whether staged or impromptu (matrixed or non-matrixed),[176] are ilso a kind of performance, with narrative through lines, moments of tension,)hysical engagement, and sweaty endings. Even military parlance, language of the iltimate combatants, speaks of a "*theatre* of operations."

*earson and Shanks outline how the performative heterotopia of a typical street ight is formed, and how the resulting subjectivities, based on a circle (Souriau's phere) are innately democratic.

\s a fight breaks out the crowd parts, steps back, withdraws to give the action pace. Instantly they take up the best position for watching, a circle. It's iemocratic, everyone is equidistant from the centre, no privileged viewpoints. 'here may be a struggle to see better but the circle can expand to accommodate iose who rush to see what's happening. Or it thickens. A proto-playing area is reated, with an inside and outside, constantly redefined by the activity of the ombatants, who remain three dimensional...The size and ambiance of the space re conditioning factors. Then just as quickly the incident ends, the space is iundated by the crowd and there are no clues what to watch.[177]

ind so, just as any fight is a form of theatre, most theatre is premised upon some ind of struggle or contest, protagonist and antagonist. After fifteen seconds of pening credits on the YouTube video [178] the contest embedded in *Sir Don v. The atpack* 'breaks out' at the eighteen second mark by the 'Personal Journo' with ie line "There he is!" pointing towards 'Sir Don' and his minder who are just rriving on foot, initiating a convergence of competing 'journalists' towards him. 'his aligns with Dwight Steward's advice for prospective agit-prop practitioners) "[h]ave an elastic beginning for your script, allowing time for a crowd to ather"[179]. Clearly, the GST budget did not stretch to the provision of a limousine)r 'Sir Don's' arrival, and any less a vehicle might have undermined the all nportant element of *authenticity*. Consequently, this opening line was designed) draw attention to 'Sir Don's' arrival on foot and act as the trigger point for

---

[6] See Carlson, Marvin. "David Levine's *Bauerntheater*: The Return of the latrix." *The Drama Review* 52.3 (2008): n. page.

[7] *Theatre/Archaeology* 21.

[8] This opening sequence was not generated by GST directly. Instead it includes)otage of the evacuation of a nearby office building – part of a fire-drill – that just appened to occur immediately after the live performance of *Sir Don* a few blocks vay. The whole incident was captured by GST's various film crews as they were :turning to their cars and incorporated into the You Tube upload.

[9] Steward, Dwight. *Stage Left* (Dover, DE: Tanager, 1970) 24.

other 'journos', who at this moment just happened to be milling around nearby in small, discrete groups.

Figure 14.
The circle intensifies around 'Sir Don'.
The 'ghost of Peter Garrett' (Federal Minister for the Environment at the time)
stands to the left of 'Sir Don' with sunglasses, briefcase and earphone.
(photo Paul Davies)

All of which allowed the GST actors to remain initially indistinct and effectively separate from the larger demonstration which was kept well behind police lines in the background (see Figures 12, 14). Indeed they were also discretely separate from members of the real media who were also present outside the AGM and felt they needed to be part of the general *Sir Don* mêlée once it was instituted - presumably in case they missed out on something.

If GST's performance of *Sir Don* had originated from within this larger, real demonstration, it is doubtful that it would ever have made it even to the intended starting point at the bottom of the Convention Centre's steps: a place that was also monitored by police officers from a covert position nearby. The point here is that the 'heterotopia' of BHP's actual AGM still had to be porous enough (have systems of opening and closing) for the 'real' media and attending investors to get in. Yet the police were marking out a clear Cartesian boundary in order to contain the International Convergence and its large (literal) white elephant off to one side (Figure 14). In this sense, the heterotopia of the GST performance was able to carve out its own spatial niche, a liminal performative heterotopia as it were, separate from the spaces of the other, larger and less invisible events (AGM and demonstration) occurring within the same general, public area.

The effect of the opening line delivered by the 'Personal Journo' is to 'identify' (invest with a fictional authority) the character playing 'Sir Don' and thereby draw the rest of the GST 'Ratpack' into play as the constructed space of the press conference starts to gather shape out of the 'energy' of the oppositional performances brought into being on the footpath. Interestingly, everybody present seemed to understand and accept the role of Sir Don's minder immediately: the 'Ghost of Peter Garrett'. This included the police and other security personnel, none of whom questioned the legitimacy of this character's silent and slightly intimidating presence: a composite of sunglasses, mysterious briefcase and small earphone presumably connecting him to a larger, over-arching panoptic gaze: the world of a higher surveillance scrutinizing and recording everything.

As the mock 'press conference' makes its way up the steps it starts to draw in players outside the immediate GST troupe, including BHP officials, glimpsed in a somewhat flummoxed state in the background (and no doubt wondering who this important person is). Indeed, at the 30-40 second mark a man in a light coloured coat, apparently connected to BHP and obviously concerned that one of his VIPs has been unintentionally accosted by the press contingent, seems to be voluntarily attaching himself to 'Sir Don's' security detail.

At one minute thirty seconds into the video other participants in the demonstration, 'real demonstrators', apparently also ignorant of the nature of the constructed 'performance' occurring, are similarly drawn into the mock press conference, including an indigenous activist immediately behind 'Sir Don'.[180] After questions about the water supply for Roxby Downs (one minute forty seconds), questionable practices involving the military in West Papua working on behalf of BHP (two minutes thirty seconds), carbon neutrality (three minutes), BHP's toxic legacy (three minutes thirty seconds) and nuclear proliferation, the subject turns to yellow cake, a refined form of uranium ore. By now the circle encasing 'Sir Don' has grown considerably and forms an unbroken loop around him. At this point, 'Sir Don' makes a weak joke about how he "wouldn't mind some yellow cake with his morning tea" since he's "feeling a bit peckish" and draws a suitably disgusted response from some of these people. This includes a young anti-nuclear campaigner above and behind 'Sir Don' who seems to be having all her worst fears about the rapacious irresponsibility of big mining companies and their evil directors fully confirmed. (see Figure 15).

[180] Indeed, as soon as the circle of the press conference began forming on the footpath there were loud boos and hisses directed at 'Sir Don' *and* GST's Ratpack. Clearly, from the point of view of the 'real demonstration', both Media pack and Company representatives were perceived to embody two halves of the same problem.

Figure 15.
The circle follows 'Sir Don' (backwards) up the staircase.
A 'real' demonstrator behind 'Sir Don' is shocked
by his remarks about yellow cake.
(Photo Paul Davies

And so, as this roiling intercalation of heterotopia (mock press conference, real demonstration, real AGM) moves vaguely in the direction of the doors of the AGM, like Pearson and Shanks' circle round a fight, the physical form of the Ratpack expands and contracts, elongates into an ellipse at one point, then spreads lengthways up the steps as journalists and onlookers jockey for a better view or greater access to questioning. Such a trajectory takes advantage of the verticality of the steps (facilitating sightlines) while the roving group always stays focused on 'Sir Don', the spatial bedrock of the performance.

Figure 16.
'Real' people outside the GST troupe become involved in the interrogation,
while 'mum and dad' shareholders (small investors) look on from above.
(Photo Paul Davies)

Figure 16 shows how, by this point in GST's mobile production, the collision of all three social spaces is complete: demonstration, annual general meeting and site specific performance.

By the five minute twenty second mark 'Sir Don' (no doubt surprised that he has managed to get this far), calls to his minder and together they step blithely, if somewhat nervously, through the police line guarding the front doors and on into the heterotopia of the official AGM: the inner foyer of the Convention Centre. At this point most of the 'real demonstrators' have backed off assuming, not unreasonably, that their entrance would now be categorically blocked - which it was by a very non-porous police line. However, the constructed space of GST's mock press conference remained so readily recognizable (but invisible as a performance), that having gone through this crucial portal, it was now able to superimpose itself (collide) into its opposed place of ordering: the AGM itself (Figure 17). At which point the momentum of GST's performance seemed unstoppable and was clearly approaching a moment of truth in which the 'game' would well and truly be up!

Figure 17.
Inside BHP's AGM.
Heterotopias collide as the circle reduces down again to a few key players inside
the AGM.
(photo Paul Davies)

However, by now, even the ranks of the 'Ratpack' are thinning, although a determined few maintain their hot pursuit of 'Sir Don', their subjective anxieties (as performers) about getting this far unimpeded, are reflected in the nervous question framed by the 'Radiation/Health' Journo at five minutes, forty seconds.

Questions about the health of BHP workers continue as the press conference hovers under signs welcoming investors into the meeting and trumpeting the company's many achievements. Clearly GST's artificially constructed heterotopia had transgressed about as far as it could into the space of the AGM and matters reach a climax as the questions turn to 'Sir Don's' own health. This was the designated trigger question to end the performance. At six minutes thirty seconds, as he struggles to answer, 'Sir Don' appears to suffer some kind of breathing difficulty, and asking for water, soon collapses to the ground, causing another layer of confusion (seven minutes) as real doctors start discussing the need to call an ambulance. This cohort included prominent anti-nuclear activist, Dr. Helen Caldicott, also an investor/protestor who just happened to be standing nearby, waiting to go into the AGM and make her own points about company policy. (Figure 18).

GST's original idea here had been that, having been confronted by the heinous crimes of his global corporation, by the Ratpack's relentless questioning, 'Sir Don' would undergo a road to Damascus moment, admit his wrong doing and then collapse a broken man. But by now circumstances were starting to spin out of control.

Figure 18.
Finally 'Sir Don' collapses as AGM and performance space collide.
(photo Paul Davies)

¹igure 18 shows doctor-investors, unaware of the general pretence, coming to Sir)on's aid, probably fearing a heart attack, while other shareholders idly look on, ⁻r appear to ignore the 'emergency' altogether. The YouTube video record ends at ₁is point but the 'Happening' itself came to an oddly anti-climactic dénouement ɔme moments later as 'Sir Don' miraculously recovers, gets to his feet, and ₁lmly walks back out of the building - fortunately before any emergency services ɔuld be engaged. Although one police officer was heard to remark sternly to Sir)on's minder that "they shouldn't try anything like that again."[181] Pearson and ₁anks predict that the spectatorship gathered around a fight can just as ₁fortlessly fade away once the action has concluded – as happened here. "The ₁cident ends, the space is inundated by the crowd and there are no clues what to ₁atch"[182]

₁ truth, nobody in GST imagined their ruse would work so convincingly that 'Sir ɔn' and what was left of the combined Ratpack would be able to simply walk ₁st a vigilant police line and enter the foyer of a building where security would ₂ paramount. This other 'audience' (from the space of the corporate meeting), ₁ith its own protocols of behaviour and rights of passage (ownership of shares ₂quired for entry) was nevertheless inevitably drawn into GST's invasion of their ₁ace, however peripheral. The invasion itself had been facilitated by a process of ɔnstant physical motion, authenticating the Ratpack's pretence and demonstrating ₁eir ability to balance opposing forces. The 'unknowing' audience pouring into ₂ e AGM in the background, contained a constellation of small investors, fund

---

¹ As recounted to the author by the actor playing the 'Ghost of Peter Garret'.

managers, corporate staff, media, police and security personnel and more than enough doctors, as it turned out, to handle any medical emergency. There was clearly risk involved at this point in the form of potentially (and irresponsibly) engaging real emergency services to deal with a fake problem. There was also the risk of arrests. Which fortunately also didn't happen.

But risk is always present when fictional elements are inserted into real locations and distinct social formations, but again, I would argue that *balance-through-mobility* is the key factor mitigating against bad outcomes. In GST's case, Dwight Steward's warning about having a definitive conclusion to one's street theatre performance also clearly applies[183]. The collision of created spaces (mock press conference into AGM) becomes fraught as a result of the intervention of real people (doctors in fact) confronting, from their point of view, a real (medical) problem.

What *Sir Don* does demonstrate is the relative ease with which performative heterotopia can be created and how viewers' subjectivities are fashioned and played with once this is convincingly (authentically) in place. It also demonstrates how Foucault's notion of the permeability of heterotopia can be deployed to great effect, melding the spaces of demonstration, mock press conference and official AGM. In such an interplay all these spaces connect with and ultimately challenge each other.

Above all, mobility remained the key organising element in *Sir Don*. The constant moving about of journalists and interviewee, the hankering, restless deployment of cameras and microphones, the urgency of the questions (time is money), all mimicked what happens in a real door-stop press conference. These temporary media events are expected to move.

Finally, both productions offer competing demonstrations of Souriau's declension of theatre space into either the cube or the sphere.

Railway Wonderland in its transitioning from platform to bus terminal and with its audience and performance spaces in rectangular mode (Figure 5) readily meets Souriau's definition of 'the cube' in theatre space.

The cube has a sharply defined form and precise limits; limits that are invariable until a change of place and of setting presents us with another cube, cut out elsewhere in the universe with which we are concerned. In the second place...the little cube is open on the spectator's side. It faces him. It exerts a dynamic force in a horizontal place pointing like an arrow into the hall... And finally, its third trait: its predetermined, confining architecture.[184]

---

[183] *Stage Left* 24.

[184] "The Cube and the Sphere." 13.

On the other hand *Sir Don v The Ratpack* just as readily encapsulates Souriau's idea of the sphere.

No stage, no hall, no limits. Instead of cutting out a predetermined fragment in the world that is going to be set up, one seeks out its dynamic center, its beating heart, the spot where the action is emotionally at its keenest and most exalted. This center is permitted to irradiate its force freely and without limits…
The actors who incarnate this heart, this *punctum saliens*, dynamic center of the universe of the work are officiating priests, magicians whose power extends outward indefinitely into open space.[185]

Whether priests or not, the actors participating in both these plays created a kind of magic that often chimes with site-specific performance.

More than anything else it was the *motion* of the two plays through their chosen places of production that ensured their viability as performances. In *Sir Don* spatial mobility of stage, actors and audience becomes paramount - given the constraints of its real time scenario and the presence of a potentially hostile police line expecting transgression. Movement was also vitally necessary to maintain the press conference illusion: a busy CEO being harassed by the press on his way to work.

In the case of *Railway Wonderland* the 'stationary' nature of a railway 'station' was overcome by locating scenes in areas which framed each other: treating the audience gaze to a pleasurable journey from past to present and back again. Here any notion of a 'real time' unfolding of events was neither necessary or useful. Consequently, the element of mobility in the performance was extended into a collision of different time periods; with equal and stunning effect, a veritable 'wonderland' indeed.

---

[185] "The Cube and the Sphere." 13.

OTHER BOOKS BY PAUL MICHAEL DAVIES

**Storming Mont Albert by
Tram** – one man's attempt to
get home (1982)
https://www.amazon.com/Storming-Mont-Albert-Tram-
Attempt/dp/0648599868
ISBN 9780648599869

Breaking Up In Balwyn – a toast to money, marriage and
divorce (1983)
https://www.bookdepository.com/Breaking-Up-Balwyn-Paul-
Michael-Davies/9781727112566
ISBN 2370000622402
9780648599807

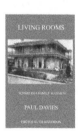

Living Rooms – scenes in a family mansion (1986)
https://www.bookdepository.com/Living-Rooms-Paul-Michael-
Davies/9780648599814
ISBN 9780648599814

Last Train To St. Kilda ? – a heavy rail story (1987)
https://www.bookdepository.com/Last-Train-St-Kilda-Paul-
Michael-Davies/9780648599821
ISBN 9780648599821

On Shifting Sandshoes - an in tents experience (1988)
https://www.bookdepository.com/On-Shifting-Sandshoes-Paul-
Michael-Davies/9780648599845
ISBN 9780648599845

Storming St. Kilda by Tram – another man's attempt to get home (1988)
https://www.booktopia.com.au/storming-st-kilda-by-tram-paul-michael-davies/book/9780648599876.html
ISBN 97806485998 76

Full House/No Vacancies – last night at the Linga Longa (1989)
https://www.bookdepository.com/Full-House-No-Vacancies-Paul-Michael-Davies/9780648599852
ISBN 9780648599852

Storming Glenelg by Tram- one woman's attempt to get home (1992/1994)
https://www.amazon.com.au/Storming-Glenelg-Tram-Womans-Attempt/dp/1976439108
ISBN 9781976439100

33 Postcards From Heaven Ustraylia – gateway to the Rainbow Coast (2005)
https://www.amazon.com/33-Postcards-Heaven-Mono-correspondance/dp/1533585032
ISBN 9780646436265

Really Moving Drama – taking theatre for a ride (2013)
https://www.amazon.com.au/Really-Moving-Drama-Taking-Theatre/dp/1534866752
ISBN 9781534866751

Smoke In Mirrors – screenwriters admit to make-believe (2020)
https://www.angusrobertson.com.au/books/smoke-in-mirrors-paul-davies/p/9780648599883?gclid=EAIaIQobChMI2tS5ldOm6wIVUX8rCh26AwQBEAQYBCABEgLKxfD_BwE

Paul Davies is an award winning screenwriter, editor and playwright who wrote for a number of television series from *Homicide* (1974-5), *The Box* (1975-76) and *The Sullivans* (1976-78) to *Skyways* (1979), *Rafferty's Rules* (1985), *Blue Heelers* (1997), *Pacific Drive* (1996), *Stingers* (1998-2003), *Headland* (2005) and *Something in the Air* (1999-2001). He also helped spark the site-specific performance revolution in Melbourne in the 1980s with TheatreWorks' production of his first play *Storming Mont Albert By Tram* (1982). What became known as *The Tram Show* played over a dozen years to packed trams in Melbourne and Adelaide, generating around a million dollars at the box office and trambulating a total distance that would have taken the production halfway around the world. Its success lead to an outbreak of 'location theatre' in Melbourne throughout the 1980s including the plays: *Breaking Up In Balwyn* (1983, on a riverboat), *Living Rooms* (1986, in an historic mansion) and *Full House/No Vacancies* (1989, in a boarding house). These works became the subject of his book *Really Moving Drama* (University of Queensland, 2013). Both *The Tram Show* and another play, *On Shifting Sandshoes* (1988) were awarded AWGIES, as was *Return of The Prodigal* (2000) an episode of *Something In The Air*. He has written two feature films *Neil Lynn* (with David Baker in 1984) and the Greater Union Award nominated *Exits* (1980). He has taught English Literature and Screenwriting at Southern Cross and James Cook Universities, and conducted writing workshops and script consultancies for Screenworks Northern Rivers, and QPIX in Brisbane. His novel, *33 Postcards From Heaven* was published by Gondwana Press in 2005, and numerous articles, reviews, stories and interviews have been published in *Metro, Cinema Papers, Cantrill's Filmnotes, Australasian Drama Studies, Community Theatre In Australia, The Macquarie Companion to the Australian Media* and *Theatre Research International* (Cambridge University).

(73955)

Lightning Source UK Ltd.
Milton Keynes UK
UKHW020633121120
373270UK00010B/542